Inside the Monster
by José Martí

"It is my duty—inasmuch as I realize it and have the spirit to fulfill it—to prevent, by the independence of Cuba, the United States from spreading over the West Indies and falling, with that added weight, upon other lands of our America. All I have done up to now, and shall do hereafter, is to that end. . . . I have lived inside the monster and know its entrails—and my weapon is only the slingshot of David."

Letter from José Martí to Manuel Mercado,
May 18, 1895

Inside the Monster by José Martí

Writings on the United States and American Imperialism

Translated by Elinor Randall
With additional translations by
Luis A. Baralt, Juan de Onis,
and Roslyn Held Foner

Edited, with an Introduction
and Notes, by Philip S. Foner

Monthly Review Press
New York and London

Copyright © 1975 by Philip S. Foner
All Rights Reserved

Library of Congress Cataloging in Publication Data
Martí, José, 1853–1895.
  Inside the monster.
    1. United States—Politics and government—1865–1900—Collected
works. 2. United States—Foreign relations—1865–1898—Collected
works. 3. United States—Social conditions—1865–1898—Collected
works. I. Foner, Philip Sheldon, 1910–   ed. II. Title.
E661.M29213 1975   320.9'73'08   74-21475
ISBN 0-85345-359-4

"Jesse James, the Great Bandit," "New York Under the Snow," and
"Prize Fight" are reprinted with the permission of Farrar, Straus, and
Giroux, Inc., from *The America of José Martí*, translated by Juan de
Onís, copyright © 1954 by Noonday Press, Inc. "The Great 'Buffalo
Bill,' " "Dedication of the Statue of Liberty," "Coney Island," "The
Chinese in the United States," "Mob Violence in New Orleans," and
"The Labor Problem in the United States" are reprinted with the per-
mission of Southern Illinois University Press from *Martí on the U.S.A.*,
translated by Luis A. Baralt, copyright © 1966 by Southern Illinois
University Press.

First Printing

Monthly Review Press
62 West 14th Street, New York, N.Y. 10011
21 Theobalds Road, London WC1X 8SL

Manufactured in the United States of America

Contents

IV
North American Politics

V
Negroes, Indians, and Other Minorities

VI
Capital and Labor

VII
The Menace of United States Imperialism

Preface

Because his life was cut short at the age of forty-two, José Martí never wrote the volumes he planned on many subjects. Moreover, with the exception of some poetry, he never reached the point of writing a book. The pattern of his thought must therefore be culled from speeches, newspaper and magazine articles, letters, and the preliminary notes for books never written. This constitutes an enormous body of writing. Indeed, Martí's writings, collected and edited by Gonzalo de Quesada y Miranda, fill seventy volumes. Even this edition is incomplete since there still remains uncollected material scattered in South American newspapers. But in these seventy volumes there is abundant evidence of Martí's broad culture and his remarkable talents as a political thinker and organizer; evidence, in short, that has caused him to be regarded as one of the great figures in the history of Latin America.

Unfortunately, the bulk of Martí's writings has not been available in English. There have been only two collections—*The America of José Martí,* edited and translated by Juan de Onís, and *Martí on the U.S.A.,* edited and translated by Luis A. Baralt. Both contain selections from Martí's series of studies of North American life and, in the case of the first collection, some of his writings on Latin America, a few selections from his writings about Cuba, and the diary of his last days. Neither collection, however valuable, includes

Martí's articles on capital and labor in the United States nor those in which he dealt with the rising menace of U.S. imperialism. The translation of Martí's writings on the struggle for Cuban independence, a key aspect of his literary output, and of his literary, educational, and cultural articles as well as his poetry and writings for children, is long overdue.

The project being undertaken here, of which this is the first volume, will make available in English (primarily in translations by Elinor Randall) in three volumes a considerable number of Martí's writings hitherto unavailable in that language. While these three volumes will not constitute the complete Martí, they will give English-reading audiences their first opportunity to become acquainted with the wide scope of his thought. Of José Martí it can truly be said what he himself wrote in a note on Wendell Phillips, the famous American orator and reformer: "An orator shines for what he speaks, but he endures for what he does. If his words are not upheld by his deeds, he will collapse even before he dies, for he has been standing on columns of smoke." What makes Martí's words especially significant is that his life fulfilled the promise in them, and that, as the recent revolutionary history of Cuba fully demonstrates, he stood on much more than "columns of smoke."

Writing in the *Journal of Inter-American Studies* of April 1963, Richard B. Gray observed of Martí's writings on the United States: " . . . if his work were as well known as that of Baron Alexis de Tocqueville's *Democracy in America,* and Lord Bryce's *American Commonwealth,* his significance to the United States would place him above these other writers. For with consummate skill and sensitivity, Martí probed the depths of social, economic and political change in the United States in the last two decades of the nineteenth century, and evaluated its strengths and weaknesses with rare understanding." The writings of Martí included in the present volume substantiate this judgment, as do other of his writings on the United States, such as his brilliant essays on Emerson and Whitman to be included in the third volume. In the present volume, too, one will clearly discern the reasons that led Martí to refer to the United States as the "Other America," in contradistinction to' Latin America—"Our America."

Martí's writings are here reproduced in translation with no substantive change whatever, although misspellings have been corrected when it is clear that they were typographical mistakes. Where Martí was in error in evaluating an historical event, this has been pointed out in the notes, all of which have been furnished by the editor.

The third volume will contain an index for all three volumes.

I wish to thank Southern Illinois University Press for permission to include the following translations by Luis A. Baralt from *Martí on the U.S.A.:* "The Great 'Buffalo Bill,'" "Dedication of the Statue of Liberty," "Coney Island" (I), "The Chinese in the United States," "Mob Violence in New Orleans," and "The Labor Problem in the United States." I wish also to thank Farrar, Straus & Giroux, Inc., for permission to include the following translations by Juan de Onís from *The America of José Martí:* "Jesse James, the Great Bandit," "New York Under the Snow," and "Prize Fight." I wish, too, to thank my wife, Roslyn Held Foner, for translating "The Memorial Meeting in Honor of Karl Marx" and "The First Voting of Women in Kansas." All the other translations of Martí in this volume are by Elinor Randall.

Philip S. Foner

Lincoln University, Pennsylvania
September 1974

Translator's Note

I think it was Cervantes who compared a translation with the wrong side of a tapestry. Some tapestries look rather fine from the wrong side, others ragged and unfinished and bristling with knots and loose threads. At times, in a translation, this is the fault of the translator, at other times many factors are to blame. In attempting to put Martí into English I have tried to enter his century, his background, the tremendous oppression experienced by his country, the attitude of the United States in those days, and Martí's continuously outraged sense of justice. Here is a man deservedly held in the deepest admiration by Spanish speakers the world over, and known by only a smattering of speakers of English. The challenge of disclosing him and his monumental struggle to an enlarged public—especially now—acted as a constant spur when the going got rough, as it often did. A friend once said that if a book review omits mention of the translation, the translator can consider his work successful. In other words, if the translation does not obtrude, all is well. One should feel he is reading the original, not a translation. This is a big order and seldom possible to achieve.

Martí's *Obras Completas* (Complete Works) consist of over two dozen fat volumes of closely written pages. He was killed at the age of forty-two in the cause he spent the greater part of his short life fighting for, and since he was so extremely active one wonders when he found time to take up a pen. His

13

style varies from brief, pithy, and at times incomplete sentences to page-long, highly intricate ones, and it is these last
named which have presented the greatest difficulties. I have
broken them up when possible, but there were times when
their full meaning, or when the sweep and continuity of some
particular thought, would have been lost or diminished by so
doing. Another stumbling block was encountering words not
found in any dictionary, including that of *Americanismos.*

At this point I would like to thank Robert Conlee for his
assistance in the area of the United States Civil War. The
work of Juan de Onís furnished tremendously helpful guide-
lines in a few of the selections, and I am immensely grateful
to him. I have tried to steer clear of present-day colloquial-
isms in order not to stray too far from the style of the late
nineteenth century, Martí's in particular. A few, however,
may have slipped in. Some of the translating had to be almost
literal, some quite free, in attempting to transmit the writer's
thought throughout. As every translator well knows, each
time he or she goes over a section of the work, more changes
appear to be needed. So the final draft is never final. But
there comes a point of diminishing returns, and do we have
an endless amount of time?

Elinor Randall

Albuquerque, New Mexico

Introduction
by Philip S. Foner

During the years 1810–1825 Spain's colonies in the New World revolted and achieved independence. Only Cuba and Puerto Rico remained of what was once the great Spanish empire of the West Indies, Central and South America. Of these two, Cuba was by far the more important to Spain. Following the destruction of the sugar economy of St. Domingue (later to become Haiti), Cuba gradually emerged as the world's largest producer of sugar. By 1838 it was the prize of Spain's reduced overseas empire. Its contribution to the Spanish treasury alone made it an important possession for the perpetually bankrupt Spanish monarchy.

As the sugar economy expanded, slaves poured into Cuba from Africa. Between 1762 and 1838, 391,024 Negroes were brought to the island, and despite the acceptance by Spain in 1817 of a British-inspired agreement to end the slave trade, the flow of slaves from Africa not only continued but increased. Slaves were imported illegally in greater numbers after 1817 than when the trade was legal.

Cuban white society was mainly made up of Creoles, born in the New World, and Peninsulares who were born in Spain. The political affairs of the island were dominated by the Peninsulares, who occupied nearly all of the positions in the colonial bureaucracy. The Peninsulares also dominated the commercial life of the island. The Creoles, on the other hand,

15

were principally landowners—cattleraisers and tobacco, coffee, and sugar planters—and the professional people.

An inevitable conflict developed between these two white groups and increased in intensity in the nineteenth century. While the Peninsulares were fanatically pro-Spain, as might be expected from the political and economic advantages Spanish policies afforded them, the Creoles resented the restrictions imposed upon their political aspirations and upon their freedom to trade under Spanish mercantilist policies. While Cuba was emerging as the world's largest producer of sugar, the colony was still functioning under Spain's backward and chaotic colonial policies, and a leading characteristic of the island's political life was the notorious corruption of the Spanish officials. Inevitably, the ideas of the Creoles ran counter to Spanish colonial policy. Furthermore, as travel brought them into contact with conditions in other countries, particularly those in the nearby United States, the Creoles increasingly resented the corrupt, inefficient, and frequently repressive Spanish colonial rule in Cuba.

Some Creoles believed that only through independence could Cuba achieve a modern political and economic form of society. Even during the Latin American independence struggles, there were Cubans who favored joining the revolutions against Spain and ridding the island of domination by the mother country. In 1825, to assist these revolutionists, Mexico and Venezuela planned an expedition to Cuba to aid in the independence struggle. But the United States, fearing an independent Cuba would lead to the end of slavery with repercussions in the Southern states, let it be known through Secretary of State Henry Clay that it would block any move to liberate Cuba from Spain. Another factor influencing this decision was the belief of the American government that in due time, under the operation of the law of political economy, Cuba would fall into the lap of her North American neighbor. The United States was not only becoming a major market for Cuban sugar, but despite Spanish restrictions, an important source of its manufactured goods.

Hence, as John Quincy Adams put it, as long as Cuba remained part of Spain, in time it would, like a ripe apple, fall into the lap of the United States.[1]

Independence movements arose and fell after the 1820s in Cuba. The struggle for liberation from Spain was retarded by the simple fact that the Negro population grew enormously with the rise of the sugar economy. In 1842 the official census reported a population of 1,007,624 inhabitants: 448,291 white, 152,838 free colored, and 436,495 Negro slaves. The danger of slave insurrection increased with the growth of the black population, and Cuban planters increasingly looked upon the Spanish government, and particularly the Spanish military power on the island, as the major safeguard against rebellious slaves.

To be sure, the value of Spanish protection of person and property in a slave society clashed with the restrictions imposed upon the island by Spanish imperial policies. The Cuban planters demanded the right to buy goods from countries other than Spain and to sell in a market larger than that offered by the mother country. But as long as slavery was the key to Cuba's prosperity and protection against the slaves was embodied in Spanish power, the Creoles swallowed their distaste for the repressive features of Spanish rule and turned a deaf ear to appeals for liberation of the island from the mother country.

However, both Peninsulares and Creoles were opposed to any attempts from Spain, egged on by England, to alter or abolish slavery, the key to the prosperity of Cuba. Consequently it is not surprising that when Spain appeared to be veering toward supporting abolition of slavery, thus seemingly abandoning its role as protector of white Cubans against blacks, schemes of annexation to the United States, where slavery flourished, emerged. But as the fears that Spain would interfere with slavery subsided, annexationist sentiment in Cuba lost its main appeal. Annexationism continued, but the main initiative now came from the predominantly pro-slavery groups in the United States who saw in the annexation of Cuba a vast area for the expansion of the Cotton Kingdom and the acquisition of increased political power in the national government. In the end, Spain's refusal to sell the island to the United States and the opposition of anti-slavery expansionist forces in the North either to purchase or capture of Cuba through filibustering expeditions, doomed the annexationist movement in the United States. With the outbreak of the Civil War in 1861, annexation, for the time being, was dead.[2]

In 1865, Spain, suffering from internal dissension and political and economic difficulties, and fearing the rise of independence movements in Cuba, adopted a policy of conciliation toward its colonial possession. A royal decree of November 25, 1865, established a Colonial Reform Commission to discuss proposals for reforms in the island. Despite conservative opposition in Madrid, the Spanish colonies in the Antilles elected twenty commissioners, sixteen of whom came from Cuba, and the remaining four from Puerto Rico.

The election of commissioners in Cuba and the debates in Madrid created a wave of excitement in the island and fostered the hope that at last the long-awaited reform of Cuban political and economic life was on the way. The complete failure of the Reform Commission led to bitter protests in the island, but Spain paid no attention. Indeed, in early 1867, the Spanish government, without consulting the colonies, imposed a new tax on the island ranging from 6 to 12 percent on real estate, incomes, and all types of business. The new tax, moreover, was on top of the enormous customs duties about which the Cubans had continuously complained. Coming at a time of economic depression in the island, the new tax stimulated a tremendous increase in political discontent and brought to a focus longstanding grievances. This was particularly true in the eastern or Oriente section of the island where the smaller planters felt the burden of Spanish repression most sharply. Meeting in Masonic lodges and other political clubs, the rebellious forces planned a revolutionary uprising to liberate the island from Spain.

The revolutionary upheaval came on October 19, 1868, with the flaming "Grito de Yara" (Cry of Yara), and initiated the First War for Independence, which lasted ten years.

The *mambises*, as the rebel forces of white and Negro Cubans were called, ill-armed and half starving, many armed only with machetes, roamed over the mountains and plains of Oriente, and steadily proved that the belief that the revolt could be easily crushed was an illusion. The Cuban struggle for independence was seriously hampered by a failure to confront squarely the problem of the role of the Negroes and of slavery, by strife and petty jealousies among the leaders, a chronic shortage of supplies and ammunition, the reluctance of the troops of one area to fight in another region, and the inability to win major support for the revolution among the wealthy sugar planters in the west (Occidente), who stood firm with Spain. It was further hampered by the fact that while Spain was able to obtain the most modern rifles from the United States, the attempts of the rebels to win recognition from the North American democracy so as to be able to purchase arms and supplies, were unsuccessful. The United States still hoped that Spain would offer to sell the island, and even when several Latin American countries proposed that Spain be pressured to grant the Cubans independence with compensation to be provided by these countries and the United States, Hamilton Fish, Secretary of State, bluntly rejected the proposal.

Despite these tremendous handicaps, the rebels were able to defy the Spaniards for ten years. The Cubans had a number of outstanding leaders, especially Máximo Gómez, the Dominican leader of the Cuban Liberating Army, Antonio Maceo, the Negro independence fighter, who proved to be the most successful and most determined military leader during the war, Ignacio Agramonte and Calixto García. Gómez, a genius at guerrilla warfare, made the Cubans masters of this technique of fighting. Maceo, a free Negro, whose entire family joined the revolution from the beginning, repeatedly defeated the Spaniards in engagements, and rose rapidly to be Brigadier-General of the Liberating Army, and Chief of the Second Division of the First Corps. Although he was compelled to combat racist opposition, the "Bronze Titan," as Maceo was called, continued to fight the Spaniards with undiminished zeal, inspire his men, and lead the rebel forces through the difficult and bitter struggle against Spain. Maceo won renown throughout Cuba because he refused to sign the Pact of Zanjón ending the war in 1878. His "Protest of Baraguá" was a great manifesto of opposition to surrender without achievement of the main goals of the revolution— independence and abolition of slavery—and made his name a household word in Cuba and gained him international renown.[3]

In reality the Pact of Zanjón was nothing but a truce. The First War of Independence had opened an abyss between the Spanish metropolis and its Cuban colony that could never again be closed. Revolutionary activity did not cease after 1878, and it received an added impetus with the abolition of slavery in Cuba. As long as the rich sugar planters of the west depended upon Spain for protection against their slaves, they had clung to their alliance with the mother country. But after slavery was abolished in 1880, the Spanish alliance lost its attraction. The economic advantages of independence, espe- cially free and unlimited trade with the United States, held more interest. In the revolutionary movement leading to the Second War for Independence in 1895, one among many stands out: José Julián Martí y Pérez, "the Apostle," a great poet and writer and a genius at political organization.

Martí was born on January 28, 1853, in a humble two- story house on Paula Street in Havana. His father, Mariano Martí y Navarro, the son of a poor ropemaker in Valencia, Spain, had come to Havana as a sergeant in the Spanish army, married a girl from Spain, Leonor Pérez y Cabrera, and decided to remain in Cuba, hoping to find a better life for himself there. He obtained a transfer to the police force and served as a night watchman in Havana and other cities.

Although his father's meager resources limited his interest in his son's education, the boy's godfather agreed to pay for his studies at the Municipal School for Boys in Havana. At the age of thirteen, he entered the Colegio de San Pablo. Its director was Rafael María de Mendive, a revolutionary poet and journalist, who had dedicated himself to "furthering the advancement and improvement of the society" in which he lived. Martí continued his studies under Mendive until his teacher was imprisoned, allegedly for attending a political rally at a local theater. A visit to his imprisoned teacher left an indelible imprint on the young boy's mind.

When the "Grito de Yara" echoed across Cuba, Martí was only fifteen, too young to join the *mambises* on the battlefield. But he did write a long epic poem entitled "Abdala," glorifying the revolution and the fighters for independence, which was published in Mendive's journal, *La Patria Libre* (The Free Homeland). It was not long before Mendive was exiled, and Martí himself arrested and condemned to hard labor. The cause of his arrest was a letter he and his best friend, Fermín Valdés Domínguez, had written accusing a fellow student of being an apostate for having marched in a parade with the Spaniards. The authorities found the letter, and on October 21, 1869, the two boys were arrested and confined in the Havana city jail. Four and a half months later, on March 4, 1870, the two were tried by a court-martial. Martí's friend was given six months; he himself, insisting throughout the trial that he alone was responsible for the letter, received the harsh sentence of six years at hard labor in the government quarries.

Though still a boy, Martí spent six months in backbreaking stonecutting, which left him a physical wreck, half blind and with a hernia caused by a blow from a chain which troubled him the rest of his life. Thanks to army friends of his father, Martí spent only six months in the quarry, and was then transferred temporarily to a prison on the Isle of Pines. He was finally pardoned in January 1871, but to keep him from further seditious activities, the authorities deported him to

Spain. Still half blind from the work in the sun and suffering from the hernia, he wrote to his great teacher, Mendive: "I have suffered much, but I am convinced that I have learned how to suffer. If I have had strength for it all and if I possess the qualities that make me a man, I owe it to you alone. From you I have acquired whatever virtue and kindness there is in me."[4]

On January 15, 1871, Martí left for Spain, and from that day until April 11, 1895, when he landed with an expedition to head the Second War for Independence, he was to visit the island of his birth on only two brief occasions.

Martí completed his academic education at the universities of Madrid and Zaragoza. He read the classics, frequented literary salons, and went regularly to the theater. Yet while he continued his studies, he devoted much of his time in Spain to political agitation. Immediately after arriving in Madrid in January 1871, he published a scathing denunciation of Spanish treatment of political prisoners in Cuba, *El Presidio Político en Cuba* (Political Imprisonment in Cuba). Written at the age of eighteen, it revealed Martí to be a writer of distinction and it had an important impact on liberal circles in Spain. On the first anniversary of the execution of student demonstrators, shot on the streets of Havana on November 27, 1871, Martí published a poetic ode to the martyred students, *El 27 de Noviembre de 1871.* At the end, Martí emphasized that "there is a limit to weeping over the graves," and he called upon all Cubans to swear "an oath of infinite love of country . . . over their bodies."[5] The publication was reported to have had an electric effect on Spanish public opinion.

After he arrived in Spain in 1871, Martí had looked forward to the day when Spain would become a Republic. Then, perhaps, Cuba might live harmoniously and peacefully with Spain. But the news of the killing of the students wrought a complete change in his outlook. The bloody incident destroyed forever all desire on his part for anything less than complete independence for Cuba, and he made a vow to devote his life to this cause. Still, he believed that a Spanish Republic might result in the withdrawal of the army from Cuba and the granting of independence to the island. In February 1873 occurred the event Martí and all other Cuban exiles had been waiting for. Early in the year an artillery corps of Vitoria mutinied. When the Cortes dissolved the corps, the government fell apart and the king, Amadeo, abdicated. The Cortes met on February 11 in joint session, ushered the king out of Spain, and proclaimed the Republic immediately thereafter.

Martí was in the press box at the Cortes on that historic February 11. But his joy was diminished when he heard a Republican deputy, in hailing the newborn Republic, salute the unity of Spain and Spanish Cuba. Four days later, Martí sent an extensive essay, the second of his great political tracts, entitled *La Republica Española y la Revolución Cubana* (The Spanish Republic and the Cuban Revolution), to Don Estanislao Figueras, the head of the Republican movement. How, he asked, "can Spain deny Cuba the right to be free, which is the same right she used to achieve her own freedom? How can she deny this right to Cuba without denying it for herself? How can Spain settle the fate of a people by imposing on them a way of life in which their complete, free, and obvious wish does not enter at all? . . . A Republic that did these things would be a Republic of ignominy."[6]

Martí's essay was published in pamphlet form. But the Republic paid no attention to it whatsoever. By March 1873 it was clear that the new Republican regime in Madrid was as intent as the old monarchical one upon exterminating the Cuban patriots. After the Republic fell in January 1874, and a year later, when Cánovas, the conservative statesman, reestablished the monarchy under Alfonso XII, it was clear as never before that the Cuban question would only be settled by force of arms. Even the most optimistic of Cubans living in Madrid understood now what Martí had been saying for months: that nothing could be expected from Spain, and that

Cuba's future would be decided only by the Liberating Army.

Martí's sentence of confinement to Spain was finally lifted in January 1875. He had graduated from his university studies and had passed examinations for the degree of Doctor of Philosophy and Humanities with outstanding grades. Since he had been exiled, he was unable to return to Cuba legally, especially during the period of war. In order to be closer to home and to join his parents, he settled in Mexico, after short stopovers in Paris and London. He spent almost two years in Mexico, earning his livelihood as a journalist, and achieving local prestige as a lecturer and orator. His play, *Amor con Amor se Paga* (Love Is Repaid by Love), written for the Spanish actress Concha Padilla, was successfully presented in Mexico City, and he soon gained a reputation as a member of the literary salon of "Rosario de la Acuna," which spread throughout much of Latin America, and together with his writings, made him a figure of importance on the continent.

Martí participated in debates at the Hidalgo Lyceum, represented the workers of Chihuahua at a workers' congress, published "Bulletins" in *Revista Universal,* a magazine dealing with national affairs, and in his newspaper articles and forum discussions devoted special attention to the plight of the Indian in Mexican society. ("Until the Indian is allowed to go forward, America will not begin to advance," Martí emphasized.) He also pleaded eloquently for the Cuban cause and raised funds for the revolutionary movement on the island. Nevertheless, being a foreigner, he refused to participate in Mexican party politics.

When Porfirio Díaz entered Mexico City and began the long reign of dictatorship, Martí decided to leave. Feeling that perhaps his presence might revive the fighting spirit of his countrymen, exhausted by nine years of war, Martí returned to Cuba in January 1877, landing in Havana under an assumed name—he used his second name, Julián, and his mother's maiden name, Pérez. He spent a month at home without being identified. But his precarious position made it virtually impossible for him to work, and he soon saw, too, that the cause of Cuban independence was lost for the time being. He therefore returned to Mexico and then went to Guatemala. There, thanks to a distinguished Cuban, José María Izaguirre (a former teacher in Bayamo, forced into exile), who had been appointed Director of the Normal School by liberal-minded President Justo Rufino Barrios, Martí found employment as professor of history and literature. In addition to teaching, he lectured, founded cultural clubs, helped edit the *Revista de la Universidad,* and wrote articles on the new civil code. Also while in Guatemala he wrote the play *Drama Indio,* and *La Niña de Guatemala,* one of his most famous poems. The former, unfortunately unfinished, was a strong indictment of the country's bigoted, backward clergy. The latter was written after the death of María Granados, the daughter of General Miguel García Granados, a former president of Guatemala and a friend of Martí, who reportedly died of tuberculosis, but who, according to Martí, actually perished of love for him. Thus he wrote in his poem:

> Like burning bronze
> Was her forehead
> At my farewell kiss; the forehead
> Which I have loved most of all
> In my life.

> . . . .

> They say she died of cold;
> I know she died of love.

During this period Martí met Carmen Zayas Bazán, a beautiful daughter of a wealthy Cuban exile, whom he married on December 20, 1877. They lived in Mexico and Guatemala until the Ten Years War ended in 1878. A general amnesty was then declared by Spain, and the young couple was finally able to return and settle in Cuba. Their return was hastened by a grave injustice done to Izaguirre by President Barrios which prompted Martí to resign his teaching position. When Martí and his young bride, expecting a child, returned to Cuba, they found things little better than before. The key provision of the Pact of Zanjón ending the Ten Years War, promising Cuba the same political concessions as Puerto Rico then enjoyed, proved to be a hoax. Puerto Rico, it was revealed, was still legally in a state of siege, and she actually enjoyed no other political right than representation in the Cortes. Supported by the most reactionary elements in Cuba and by statesmen in Spain who considered all Cubans except the most reactionary groups in the island as disloyal, the government in Madrid continued to undermine the hopes that had surged with the capitulation at Zanjón. Even those who shunned a renewal of armed hostilities were forced to concede that it was obviously impossible to force Spain to listen in this critical moment to the plea for justice for Cuba. But beyond this they refused to go.

There were others, however, who raised the need for beginning again the task of liberating the island from the Spanish yoke. In conversations with associates in Havana, Martí immediately began to advance the position that Cuba must continue the struggle to obtain its independence, and to that end there was only one path to follow—armed revolt. In these discussions, he was soon supported by Juan Gualberto Gómez, the distinguished Negro revolutionist who had returned from Paris where he had assisted Francisco Vicente Aguilera in mobilizing support among the Cuban exiles for the Ten Years War. Martí and Gómez met in the law office of Don Nicolás Azcárte, and despite Azcárte's warning that they were pursuing a dangerous course, they formed a close friendship, united by the common desire to liberate their country. Together the Negro and white revolutionaries worked for independence: Gómez through political articles in *La Libertad,* a daily paper newly founded by Adolfo Márquez Sterling, and Martí in private conversations and public addresses. In one speech, Martí openly referred to Cuba as "Our Nation," and in another, on April 19, 1879, at a banquet in honor of Márquez Sterling, he stated his willingness to support only those who would agree to work energetically for a radical solution to all of Cuba's problems. He made it clear that he believed independence, not autonomy under Spain, was the solution. Rights, he declared, were "to be taken, not requested; seized, not begged for." Ramón Blanco, the Spanish Captain General present, remarked after hearing Martí's revolutionary address, "That Martí is a madman—but a dangerous madman."[7]

On August 26, 1879, the revolt erupted in Cuba. This brief struggle, known as "La Guerra Chiquita" (The Little War), erupted in Santiago de Cuba, and was led by Generals Calixto García, José Maceo, brother of Antonio Emilio Núñez, Serafín Sánchez, and Francisco Carillo. These rebel leaders, Negro and white, were followed by hundreds of former *mambises.*

Alarmed by the growth of the revolutionary movement, the Spanish government retaliated by making wholesale arrests of all persons suspected of sympathy with the rebellion. In Havana the arrests were so great in number that the revolutionary movement was crushed. Inevitably Martí's turn came. Captain General Blanco, who had called Martí "a dangerous madman," urged his immediate imprisonment. But under pressure from Martí's friends, he promised him that he would not be brought to trial if he declared in the newspapers his adherence to Spain. "Tell the General that Martí is not the kind of man that can be bought," Martí replied.[8] The result was deportation once again to Spain.

On September 25, 1879, José Martí was deported under "surveillance" to Spain. During his brief stay in Cuba, he had become a father: his young bride had given birth to José Martí Zayas Bazán, to whom Martí was later to dedicate one of his loveliest collections of poetry, *Ismaelillo.* But by the time he left Cuba, his marriage was failing, for Carmen disapproved of his political involvements, and her husband was not one to allow domestic concerns to stand in the way of his revolutionary activities.

Escaping from his Spanish prison, Martí made his way to Paris, and then settled briefly in New York. Here he served as subdelegate of the Revolutionary Committee in charge of the war in Cuba. (Juan Gualberto Gómez was the delegate.) Soon came the shattering news of the surrender of Calixto García and the almost total deterioration of the Little War. By September 1880 there was only the valiant young Emilio Núñez left fighting. All the other chieftains had surrendered. Finally, his camp at Los Egidos completely surrounded by a concentration of Spanish troops, Núñez agreed to negotiation, on condition that General Blanco would allow him to request the necessary authority to do so from the Revolutionary Committee in New York. The answer came twenty days later in the form of an official authorization signed by three officials of the Revolutionary Committee, one of whom was Martí. With the authorization came a letter from Martí in which he advised Núñez, "as a revolutionist, a man who admires your energy, and as an affectionate friend, not to remain futilely on the battlefield to which those whom you are defending are powerless to send aid." It was now necessary to concede defeat, and draw the obvious lessons from it so that the future struggle, an inevitable one, would be successful.[9]

With Núñez's surrender, the Little War was over. Captain General Blanco publicly proclaimed "the nefarious separatist flag again subdued." The New York Revolutionary Committee disbanded.

Appointed a professor in Caracas, Martí left on March 21, 1881, for Venezuela, where he vowed to "arouse the world" to the Cuban cause. In addition to teaching he edited *Revista Venezolana,* the first issue of which came off the press on July 1, 1881. But his stay in Caracas was cut short by a dispute with the dictator-president, Guzman Blanco, and he left Venezuela on July 28 for New York.

Except for short trips to Mexico, Central America, Santo Domingo, and Jamaica, always in the interest of Cuban independence, Martí lived in the United States during the last fourteen years of his life. Most of these years were spent in New York or on visits to other cities, especially those like Tampa and Key West, Florida, in which there was an important colony of Cuban exiles, and most of his time was devoted to organizing for the second and final war for the independence of Cuba.

In 1881, Martí was twenty-eight. He was slightly built and of medium height, with a high forehead and penetrating eyes, slender and frail. His hands were artistically long and narrow, delicately shaped and always moving. He habitually dressed in black suits and a black silk bow tie. His clothes were never new because he led a very meager existence writing for his living in New York, but they were always scrupulously cleaned and neatly pressed. Martí was constantly on the go and seemed to possess boundless energy. He wrote for leading newspapers in Latin America and for the *New York Sun;* he translated books into Spanish; he edited *Patria,* the organ of the Cuban Revolutionary Party, and *La Edad de Oro* (The Golden Age), a magazine for Latin American youngsters; he wrote poetry, essays, articles, plays, and children's stories; he served as consul for Uruguay and Argentina. And all the time he spoke at countless meetings, many sponsored by the Cuban tobacco workers, and poured out a stream of pamphlets, articles, and essays for the Cuban revolutionary cause.

Martí's writings in preparation for the Second War for Independence will be found in another volume. In the pages below will be found the articles in which this enormously talented man who, in addition to his legal studies, had studied philosophy, Greek and Greek authors, Hebrew, geography, and Spanish history, and had come to know Latin America intimately, conveyed to Latin Americans a picture of the United States.

Shortly after his return to New York from Caracas, Martí began to contribute regularly to Caracas' *La Opinión* and his reputation as a writer soon caused the editors of the Buenos Aires *La Nación,* the leading newspaper in Latin America, to invite him to contribute articles on the United States. Invitations for similar articles also came from *El Partido Liberal* of Mexico, *La Opinión Pública* of Montevideo, and others. He accepted eagerly, not only to buttress his precarious finances but also because of the opportunity he now had to reach a vast public. No one had previously had such a chance to interpret the United States to so many people in Latin America and through *La América* and *El Latino,* published in the United States, to Latin Americans in this country.

Martí's steady stream of excellent articles, in superb Spanish, were read all over South America and "made the United States known as it was never known before."[10] His newsletters covered every aspect of American life. There were descriptions of Coney Island in summer, commencement in a girls' school, agricultural exhibitions, the opening of the Brooklyn Bridge, the installation of the Statue of Liberty, the memorial meeting to honor Karl Marx, Christmas and New Year's in New York, the publication of new books, murder cases and trials, the Negro and Chinese questions, the plight of the Indians, trade union and political conventions, women's suffrage, election campaigns, labor strikes, conditions of European immigrants. He introduced to Spanish America, in deft portraiture, such writers and thinkers as Emerson, Whitman, Whittier, Longfellow, Mark Twain, Louisa May Alcott, George Bancroft, Washington Irving; such social reformers as Wendell Phillips, Henry Ward Beecher, Peter Cooper, Henry George, and Father Edward McGlynn; and such political figures as Grant, Garfield, Blaine, Tilden, Cleveland, Benjamin Harrison, and many others. Many of these biographical essays are among his masterpieces: Emerson, whom he deeply admired because of his complete independence of mind; Whitman, whom he regarded as a "natural" poet belonging to no school, in contrast to "puny poets," and an exponent of "the poetry of liberty"; Wendell Phillips, of whom he wrote, "The whole Universe took the form of a Negro slave in his eye," and "He was implacable and fiery, as are all tender men who love justice"; Peter Cooper, of whom he said, "He puts in practice the human Gospel," and "He saw himself as the administrator of his wealth and not as its owner"; Mark Twain, whose *A Connecticut Yankee in King Arthur's Court* he described as a "fight, cowboy style, with a lasso and gun" against oppression and poverty.

Over the years Martí produced a series of intelligent critiques of American politics, education, and culture. These are not mere journalistic impressions, but are rich in analysis. Martí showed that he was not only a competent, articulate synthesizer of descriptive details, but adept at understanding the changes taking place in American society in the decade and a half between 1880 and 1895—the stratification of economic classes, the alienation of American workers, and the transformation of competitive into monopoly capitalism and its impact on American expansionism—and the danger this held out for Latin America.

When Martí arrived in the United States in 1880, he was immediately attracted, even dazzled, by its democratic institutions, its creative power, and the opportunity it provided for every kind of individual initiative. To one coming from Cuba, Spain, and some of the Latin American republics, with their feudal societies, social castes, clerical hierarchies, and artificial inequalities, the North American democracy seemed indeed a Promised Land. In "Impresiones de América" (Impressions of America) published in *The Hour,* he exulted: "At last I am in a country where everyone seems to be his own master. Here, one can be proud of the species. Everybody works. Everybody reads." And again: "I feel obligated to this country, where the unprotected always find a friend. A kind hand is always outstretched to those looking for honest work. Here, a good idea always finds welcoming, soft, and fertile ground. One must be intelligent, that is all. Do something useful, and you will have everything you want. Doors are shut for those who are dull and lazy; life is secure for those who obey the law of work." In one of his letters from New York, dated October 29, 1881, to the newspaper *La Opinión Nacional,* he wrote:

> These amazing people were born of the union of America with work, married in Good Faith in the home of Liberty. A hundred years ago these cities were villages; these bays, empty beaches, and the whole country, the domain of an arrogant and idle lord who ruled his sons like vassals and wrote his laws with the tip of his whip and sealed them with the heel of his heavy boots. The people fought, suffered cold, and overcame hunger. And after a long and painful courtship, they at last won Glory.[11]

Little by little, however, the bitter reality of many aspects of life in the United States cleared away the mist from his eyes. Martí had arrived in the midst of a radical transformation in economic and social life, and he was quick to realize that his concept of the United States as a land where social distinctions were being obliterated and where the poor had equal opportunities with the rich to enjoy the fruits of democracy was in need of revision.

The 1880s were characterized by the rapid growth of American industry, accompanied by a tremendous concentration of capital and the appearance of giant corporations. With the rise of industrial trusts, like the Standard Oil Company, and huge banking houses such as J. P. Morgan & Co., monopoly became the dominant feature of American capitalism. The age of the small manufacturer, the age of free competitive enterprise, was passing. It was being replaced by what was widely called in the eighties "The New Feudalism." Said President Grover Cleveland in a message to Congress on December 3, 1888: "As we view the achievements of aggregated capital, we discover the existence of trusts, combinations, and monopolies, while the citizen is struggling far in the rear or is trampled to death beneath an iron heel. Corporations, which should be carefully restrained creatures of the law and the servants of the people, are fast becoming the people's masters."

"There are too many millionaires and too many paupers," declared the *Hartford Courant* in 1883. All of America was a land of contrast, of poverty amidst enormous wealth. At one end of the scale was magnificence unstinted. The "robber barons" who made up the new plutocracy vied with each other in "conspicuous waste." At the other end of the scale, the workers, earning between 50 cents and one dollar for a working day of ten to twelve hours, lived in gnawing poverty, lacking the bare necessities of life.

The masters of capital, of banking, industry, and commerce, were also masters of political life. The pernicious influence of big business in all branches of government—executive, legislative, and judicial—had already been noted by Mark Twain in *The Gilded Age,* which he published (in collaboration with Charles Dudley Warner) in 1873. But in the 1880s it reached such scandalous proportions that scarcely a week passed without some public disclosure of advantageous and lawless concessions granted to corporations, passed into law by bribed legislators, signed by corrupt executives, and approved by judges who were subservient tools of the corporate interests.

The 1880s were also years of great workers' struggles. In cities and towns, the armies of labor organized and gave expression to the pent-up bitterness of years of exploitation in a series of strikes that shook the nation to its foundations. Never before had the United States witnessed labor struggles of such vigor and scope.[12]

Martí observed and reported these radical changes. His reports reflected a new view of the United States. As early as 1882 he wrote:

We are at the height of a struggle between capitalists and workers. The first can count on bank credit, funds expected from their debtors, payment of bills on fixed dates, and knowing where they stand at the end of the year. For the workers there is the daily reckoning, the urgent needs that cannot be postponed, the wife and child who eat in the evening what the poor husband worked for in the morning. And the comfortable capitalist compels the poor worker to work at a ruinous wage.[13]

A year later, he described the poverty of the working class districts of New York:

... in the infected slums where one can see thin and filthy hands appearing above the roofs of tenements, like the ragged flags of some tremendous army on the march; in the damp streets where men and women crowd together and mill about, with neither air nor space, much as beneath the surface of roots the ugly and deformed worms, in which vegetal life is being transformed, are lazily unrolling; there in the dark and rambling buildings where people in the dregs of poverty live in stinking cells filled with dank and impure air; there, like young corn in a plague of locusts, the children of the poor are dying by the hundreds in the plague of summer; there, as ogres do to children in story books, the *cholera infantum* sucks the children's lives away. A boa constrictor would leave the children of the poor in no worse condition than the New York summer leaves them—withered, wasted, cadaverous, all skin and bones. Their little eyes resemble caverns, their heads are bald like the heads of old men, their hands are bunches of dry twigs. They drag themselves about like worms, exhale in groans. And I say that it is a national crime, and that abolishing this unnecessary misery is an obligation of the state! [14]

Appalled by the unscrupulous amassing of riches and the political corruption he saw all about him, Martí wrote fiery dispatches condemning the "cult of wealth." In his letter to *La Nación,* April 8, 1888, he wrote: "In the United States, virtue is everywhere being discarded as not being remunerative; the most ample liberty, the freest press, the most prosperous business, the most varied and fertile nature are not enough to save republics that do not encourage sentiment, nor find a condition worthy of higher esteem than wealth." As he saw it, the power of big business had succeeded in corrupting "the courts, the legislatures, the church, and the press, and has succeeded in twenty-five years of partnership in creating in the freest democracy of the world the most unjust and shameful of oligarchies." Speaking for all "honest Cubans," he wrote eloquently in a letter to the *New York Evening Post:*

> They admire this nation, the greatest ever built by liberty, but they dislike the evil conditions that, like worms in the heart, have begun in this mighty republic their work of destruction. They have made of the heroes of this country their own heroes, and look to the success of the American commonwealth as the crowning glory of mankind; but they cannot honestly believe that exclusive individualism, reverence for wealth, and the protracted exultation of a terrible victory are preparing the United States to be the typical nation of liberty, where no opinion is to be based on greed, and no triumph or acquisition reached against charity and justice. We love the country of Lincoln as much as we fear the country of Cutting.[15]

In his brilliant essay on General Grant, during which he reviewed the entire sweep of American history between 1860 and 1865 and vividly portrayed the military developments of the Civil War, Martí observed: "It goes without saying that the president does not use funds from the national treasury for the benefit of his family or friends, or shape the nation to his liking, or numb the spirit of the laws by neglect or misapplication. He must govern with integrity, apply the laws his people give him, without taking for himself or for his friends and relatives what the nation entrusts him for safekeeping. Government is obedience." His chief criticism of Grant as President was "his deplorable inability to recognize the gentle dignity of modesty and the greater influence exerted, even in practical matters, by those who in true republics do not use the trust placed in them to set themselves above those republics." These observations surely have a contemporary ring! So too does Martí's comment, in the piece dealing with "Political Corruption," on the alliance between big businessmen and politicians: "They worship power for its own sake, as the only law they respect, and look upon themselves as its high priests and as having an innate right to grab all power within their reach."

Martí did not share the widespread belief that granting women the right to vote would greatly assist in removing corruption from American politics—indeed, in his article "The First Voting of Women in Kansas," he displays a male chauvinist attitude by identifying political maneuverings and wheeling and dealing as reflections of womanlike characteristics—but he did express his conviction that the working class, including working-class women (black as well as white), would cleanse the Augean stables of American politics.

As a whole, the women of the United States did not please Martí. He was disturbed by the sight of a "young lady, physically and mentally stronger than the young man who courts her," and questioned more than once why the women in the United States should look so masculine. Their virile existence deprived them of the calm beauty and the exquisite sensitiveness that made of women, in his view, superior beings. He had a painful suspicion that wealth was their only unit of measure, and felt that many were "too richly dressed to be happy."

Three American women whom Martí did respect greatly were Clara Barton, Harriet Beecher Stowe, and Helen Hunt Jackson. When Johnstown, Pennsylvania, was destroyed by flood on May 31, 1889, Clara Barton took her place among the eight thousand men who cleared away the ruins. With a red cross on her arm and a white apron over her gray dress, she was there with her doctors and aides, to die if necessary. "Lively, eloquent, ugly yet very beautiful," was Martí's estimate of her.

Mrs. Stowe, whose *Uncle Tom's Cabin* was "a tear that speaks," had opened up hearts to compassion for the Negro, whom no one helped to liberate more than she. And another woman, Helen Hunt Jackson, had worked tenderly and wisely, year after year, to alleviate the misfortune of the Indians. With a strong mind and a loving heart, she had written her charming novel, *Ramona,* one of the five books Martí translated into Spanish. (The others were *Called Back* by Hugh Conway; *Logic* by W. Stanley Jevons; *Roman Antiquities* by A. S. Wilkins; and *Greek Antiquities,* by J. P. Mahaffy.)

Although, as we shall see in the third volume of the present collection, Martí strongly favored education for women equal to that offered to men, he still believed that a woman's main duty was to provide a home for her husband and children. His cure for drunkenness was not legislation to outlaw the sale of liquor but an amiable wife: "A cultured, attractive woman is the only efficacious enemy of alcohol. A friendly home is the safest rival of the beer parlor."

In "The Chinese in the United States," Marti carried this concept to such an extreme that it contained elements of a racist stereotype. (A somewhat similar insensitivity is expressed in Martí's use of the word "savage" in his generally sympathetic discussion of the North American Indian.) Apart from ignoring the conditions that led to Chinese emigration—attributing to a national type behavioral characteristics related to their socioeconomic situation—he blamed their plight in this country partly on the fact that they had arrived here without wives. (He ignored, of course, that the Chinese had no choice in this matter since only males were recruited as cheap labor in the construction of the transcontinental railroads.) "A married man," Martí wrote, "induces respect. The man who resists helping another life, displeases. Woman is man's nobility." One might conclude from this that the Chinese were themselves to blame for the fact that they were ostracized by white Americans.[16]

Although Martí noted the conflict between labor and capital in American society and reported extensively on it during the period 1883-1886, he did not voice any belief in the existence of truly antagonistic social classes. For a time he wrote that it was not so much the exploitation of capitalists but the protectionist system, established by the government, that was responsible for the wretched conditions of the workers. Moreover, if there was a conflict of classes, then both capital and labor were alike to blame, and none more so than the socialists and anarchists who stood for stirring up class antagonisms rather than let the social process evolve "naturally." Thus while he honored Karl Marx, in a dispatch of March 1883, "for the way he puts himself at the side of the weak ones," and wrote of him as the "titanic interpreter of the anger of the European worker," a "man ridden with the anguish to do good," he felt that Marx "went too fast," and that his followers were too much in favor of violence. He himself found the principles and teachings of Henry George more to his liking, since they could bring about social change by the simple process of the single tax and land reform, without requiring a revolutionary change.[17]

Martí wrote sympathetically of the fact that members of the Knights of Labor were forced into strikes by "the insolence and contempt of organized capital, from its illegitimate combinations, from the system of unequal distribution of profits that keeps the worker in his perpetual state of destitution." But he also wrote that when these same workers went out on strike, they acted illegally to break the law and by their use of violence, justified the swift retribution brought down on their heads by the courts. In truth, Martí at this stage believed that it was possible for the American worker to gain his demands without a revolutionary struggle, and he blamed the foreign-born, immigrant worker for introducing into the American labor scene ideas and practices which might have been suitable in the decadent, backward society of Europe, but which were out of place in the young, developing society of the United States. Martí at first condemned the Chicago anarchists on trial for the Haymarket bomb tragedy for failing to understand that the United States was not Europe, and that there was no need for revolutionary violence in American social conflicts. He made it clear that he wanted the workers "to find an outlet for indignation . . . but without seeing it explode and cause fright."[18]

Martí never became a socialist, but his article "The Schism

of the Catholics in New York," published in *El Partido Liberal* (Mexico City) and *La Nación* (Buenos Aires) on April 14, 1887, and especially the article "A Terrible Drama: The Funeral of the Haymarket Martyrs," published in the same Buenos Aires paper on January 1, 1888, indicate that he was shedding many of his earlier conceptions about capital and labor in the United States. Martí voices his admiration for the rebellious Father McGlynn and his contempt for the ecclesiastical hierarchy for disciplining the priest because he supported the political aspirations of the working class, and he takes special pains to defend not only the priest's right to stand beside the poor, but his duty to work along these lines in behalf of the exploited sections of society. With this article, moreover, Martí discards the view that both capital and labor are to blame for the turbulent social conflict and comes down fully and unequivocally on the side of the workers against the callous capitalists. Moreover, he understands now, as he did not before, that it is the political and press spokesmen for the capitalist class who are fundamentally responsible for much of the violence in the relationship between capital and labor. Thus he writes scornfully: " 'Look to the law for righting your wrongs!' said the political parties to the workers for censuring them for their attempts at violence or anarchy, but as soon as the workers organized themselves into a party to look to the law for help, they were called anarchists and revolutionarics." Then in "A Terrible Drama" he abandons his earlier hostility to the radicals, including the socialists and anarchists, and while he does not embrace the socialist cause and its ideology, he shows an understanding of the need for a revolutionary party to defend the proletariat's interests. The article makes abundantly clear Martí's respect for the courage of the condemned Chicago anarchists and their devotion to their principles, his sympathy for the proletarian cause as well as his understanding of the role of the state, and especially the courts, in defending the interests of the business power over the interests of the working class.[19]

As he witnessed the transformation in the United States

during the 1880s, Martí was aware that it posed a real danger to Latin America. In the prologue to his *Versos Sencillos* (Simple Verses), he describes his anguish at the thought of the Latin American people being dominated by the United States. He remembers having written those verses in

> That anguished winter in which, through ignorance, or through fear, or through courtesy, the Spanish-American peoples gathered in Washington, under the fearsome eagle. Which one of us has forgotten the coat of arms, that coat of arms where the eagle of Monterey and of Chapultepec, the eagle of López and of Walker grasped in its claws all the flags of America? And the agony in which I lived until I could ascertain the caution and liveliness of our peoples; and the horror and shame in which I was held by the legitimate fear that we Cubans might, with parricidal hands and for the sole benefit of a new master in disguise, aid in the preposterous plan of drawing Cuba away from the homeland that claims her and in her finds completion—from the Spanish-American homeland. . . .[20]

That "anguished winter" which Martí mentions was in the year 1889, when James G. Blaine was Secretary of State and the real leader of the new Republican administration under President Benjamin Harrison. Even before he took office, reports began to appear in the press that Blaine favored the acquisition of Cuba to secure the United States a valuable source of sugar and a strategic outpost for defense. Hailing the stand of the Secretary of State, the expansionist elements looked forward to the extension of American economic and political influence abroad. "That day is not distant," Senator Randall Gibson prophesied, "when the dominion of the United States will be extended . . . to every part of the American continent—British America, Mexico, Cuba, Central America, and the islands on our coast."[21]

That "anguished winter" was also the winter when the first Pan-American Conference was held in Washington. All the republics of Latin America except Santo Domingo sent delegates in response to a call issued by Secretary of State Blaine. Blaine spoke of the need "to cement interests" among all nations in the Western Hemisphere, to "bring about peace," to "cultivate friendly commercial ties with all American countries," and to improve communications. But the expansionist press in the United States, praising Blaine's action in calling the conference, talked frankly of the real reasons for the gathering. Editorials headed "Manifest Destiny," "Ships to South America," "Now It Is Our Gulf," "Reciprocity, the First Step to American Penetration" appeared daily. "Americans," said the *New York Tribune*, "are obliged to reconquer their commercial supremacy . . . and to exercise a direct and general influence in the affairs of the American continent." Other papers predicted the conference would lead to the establishment of an American protectorate over the republics of Latin America.[22]

As Uruguay's consul in the United States, Martí was in close contact with the delegates to the conference. He had followed Blaine's career with great care and written about him many times in his dispatches to the Latin American press. At first his comments were full of praise for Blaine, especially for his role as Secretary of State in 1881 in helping to settle frontier disputes in Latin American countries, and Martí called him "a friend of South America." But by 1884, his opinion of Blaine had changed considerably, largely because of the Secretary of State's part in the Peru–Chile dispute over claims on guano territory. Blaine was accused of trying to incite war between Chile and Peru in order to further his pecuniary interests. A congressional investigation cleared him of this charge, but censured him for the "obvious impropriety" of his actions in pushing claims against Chile and Peru. Martí saw Blaine's conduct as that of a man who "does not feel shame to use strength when he has it," and who believed that "now is the occasion for the United States to stretch its hand, and set it down wherever it reaches." By the mid-1880s Blaine had come to represent for Martí all the evil and corruption in American politics, a man who was "purchasable, who true to his character, buys and sells in the market of men," a man who sought "under the pretext of treaties of commerce and peace, the wealth [from other nations] of which the economic eras of the Republican Party had begun to deprive the [North American] nation."[23]

Martí saw clearly the danger to the economic and political independence of Latin America in Blaine's "covered game and . . . secret intention" to use the Pan-American Conference to expand U.S. economic and political domination south of the border. He knew, too, that a number of Latin Americans at the conference failed to see this danger, and what was more important, that several Cubans were ready to raise the question of Cuban independence at the gathering in the hope of obtaining the direct assistance of the United States. This Martí unalterably opposed. "I don't want the principle established of putting our fortunes into a body where, because of its influence as a major country, the United States is to exercise the principal party," he wrote to his friend Gonzalo de Quesada. The participation of the United States in Cuba's struggle for independence was fraught with danger: "Once the United States is in Cuba, who will get her out?" The only road for Cuba to follow was to win independence on her own and hold firmly to her sovereignty during and after the revolution. This was the only way to achieve "the reality of independence."[24]

In a two-part article, "The Washington Pan-American Congress," published in *La Nación,* December 19 and 20, 1889, Martí ripped aside the mask of Blaine's supposedly benevolent purpose in calling the gathering, and exposed it as American imperialism. He favored, he pointed out, Pan-Americanism, but not a Pan-Americanism such as Blaine's, which was shaped by the specific objective of extending the commercial opportunities of the United States in the hemisphere, not a false and obsequious Pan-Americanism which would serve as a mask for U.S. imperialist policy. But this was precisely what the conference was seeking to achieve.

The idea of reciprocity, proposed by Blaine, appeared on the surface to be a liberal trade policy, but when one examined it closely, it became clear that it was a device for the United States to dump surplus products on the Latin American market, and dominate that market for North American economic interests. All this would be the prelude to political control of Latin America.[25]

Martí foresaw clearly that the underdeveloped countries of Latin America, so fortunately endowed with raw materials and natural resources, would remain poor if they allowed their wealth to be siphoned off to the United States, and permitted the North American juggernaut to set terms of trade that favored it at the expense of its weaker neighbors. Would these countries remain disorganized and easily manipulated by the United States, under whose control would pass exploitation of Latin America's natural resources? In short, would they allow themselves to be wantonly exploited by the United States hiding behind seemingly liberal proposals? He concluded his article with the warning that the Pan-American Congress would demonstrate if the countries which defended the independence of Spanish America would make the necessary steps to resist

> attempts at domination by a nation reared in the hope of ruling the continent. Present-day events are proof of these attempts at dominance, and this at a time when the eagerness for markets on the part of its inflated industries, the opportunity to impose the predicted protectorate upon both the distant nations and the weak ones nearby, the material strength needed for the assault, and the ambitions of a bold and rapacious politician, are described as reaching a peak.

Martí's article helped to alert the Latin American nations and was largely responsible for the failure of the conference to agree to any of Blaine's major proposals. As Martí recalled in 1894:

> American industries had drifted along, discounting the future, on the assumption that when the domestic market would be replete

it would be ever so easy to empty the excessive production into
the weakened republics of the American continent: such was the
purpose, and no other, of those comedy reciprocity treaties, and
that was the unlawful end, timely diverted, of that stilted fabric,
the Pan-American Congress. The plan failed, because there was no
lack of forethought in the Spanish republics, nor of clear-eyed
sentinels.[26]

Modesty no doubt kept him from mentioning that he himself
had been the foremost of the "clear-eyed sentinels."

In 1891 Martí again warned the Latin American nations of
U.S. imperialist aims. The occasion was the International
Monetary Congress, called by Secretary of State Blaine,
which met in Washington, D.C., from January 7 to April 3,
1891. As the largest silver producer in the world, the United
States sought to persuade the Latin American republics to
adopt bimetallism and the equalization of gold and silver.
This would help it in getting all other nations to adopt the
same policy. The greatest part of the world's silver supply
was produced in the Americas, most of it in the United
States, and in the 1890s the market was glutted with the
precious metal. Blaine hoped to find in the International
Monetary Congress the proper remedy.[27]

However, Martí, who was appointed Uruguay's delegate to
the Congress, wrote a magnificent study of the origin and
purpose of the conference, which proved that the great
majority of the Latin American countries, lacking silver, had
little to gain from the proposed plan. Once again he warned
that economic domination would lead to political domination. In one of his most famous observations, he wrote:
"Whoever says economic union says political union. The
nation that buys, commands. The nation that sells, serves.
Commerce must be balanced to assure freedom. The nation
eager to die sells to a single nation, and the one eager to save
itself sells to more than one. A country's excessive influence
over the commerce of another becomes political influence."[28]

Martí's warning, delivered as a speech at the March 30 session, had its effect. His report was unanimously accepted, and he is given credit for having "thwarted the designs of the Department of State."[29] Its effort, acting for American silver interests, to impose a currency program on the Latin American nations was turned back.

Martí's prominent role in the activities of the conference led the Spanish ambassador in Washington to complain to his superiors in Madrid that it was an incongruous situation for a Cuban revolutionary to be holding the position of consul in New York for another country. When news of this reached Martí he resigned from the positions of consul for Argentina, Paraguay, and Uruguay in New York in October 1891, and devoted himself entirely to the Cuban revolutionary movement.[30]

The years Martí spent in the United States alerted him to the danger facing Spanish America. "What is apparent," he wrote in 1889, "is that the nature of the North American government is gradually changing its fundamental reality. Under the traditional labels of Republican and Democrat, with no innovation other than the contingent circumstances of place and character, the republic is becoming plutocratic and imperialistic." American imperialism, he was convinced, was about to launch an offensive to engulf Latin America, and would begin by swallowing Cuba.[31]

In the next volume we will see how Martí worked indefatigably to prevent the swallowing of Cuba by the North American giant while organizing to achieve its independence from Spain. For as he wrote on a notepad on the eve of his death: "Cuba must be free—from Spain and from the United States."[32]

Notes

1. Philip S. Foner, *History of Cuba and Its Relations with the United States*, Vol. I (New York, 1962), pp. 124-69.
2. Ibid., Vol. II (New York, 1963), pp. 9-115.
3. Ibid., pp. 162-275.
4. Jorge Mañach, *Martí: Apostle of Freedom*, trans. Coley Taylor, introduction by Gabriella Mistral (New York, 1959), p. 76.
5. José Martí, *Obras Completas* (La Habana, 1946), Vol. I, pp. 34-41. Of the various collected works of Martí, this, the "Lex" edition, is the most convenient. The most complete, however, is "Editorial Trópico," published in Havana between 1936 and 1949.
6. Ibid., p. 49.
7. Félix Lizaso, *José Martí: Martyr of Cuban Independence*, trans. Esther E. Shuler (Albuquerque, New Mexico, 1953), pp. 135-38.
8. Mañach, op. cit., p. 162.
9. Martí, op. cit., pp. 70-72; Foner, op. cit., Vol. II, pp. 278-88.
10. Sturgis E. Leavitt, in preface to Manuel Pedro González, *José Martí: Epic Chronicler of the United States in the Eighties* (Chapel Hill, North Carolina, 1953), p. viii.
11. Martí, op. cit., Vol. I, p. 1341.
12. Philip S. Foner, *History of the Labor Movement in the United States*, Vol. II (New York, 1955), pp. 3-14; Eliot Jones, *The Trust Problem in the United States* (New York, 1921), pp. 20-22; *Hartford Courant*, reprinted in *John Swinton's Paper*, December 30, 1883; Charles E. Spahr, *An Essay on the Present Distribution of Wealth in the United States* (New York, 1896), p. 114.
13. José Martí, "Knights of Labor Strike," *La Nación* (Buenos Aires), January 27, 1884. The entire article appears below.
14. José Martí, "Coney Island," *La Nación* (Buenos Aires), October 21, 1883. The entire article appears below as the second of the "Two Views of Coney Island."
15. José Martí, "A Vindication of Cuba," *New York Evening Post*, March 25, 1889. The entire letter appears below, under the heading "Cuba and the United States."

Francis Cutting was one of the leaders of the American Annexationist League. This is one of the most frequently quoted sentences of Martí dealing with the United States.

When Martí was twelve years old, Abraham Lincoln was assassinated, and he joined in the mourning. "For two men I trembled and wept on learning of their death," he wrote later. One was Don José de la Juz y Caballero and the other, Abraham Lincoln. (See Emeterio S. Santonvenia, *Lincoln in Martí: A Cuban View of Abraham Lincoln* [Chapel Hill, North Carolina, 1953], p. 4.)

16. Martí, *Obras Completas* (La Habana: Editorial Trópico, 1936-1949), vol. XXXVII, p. 199, LV, p. 128; Martí *Obras Completas,* vol. I, p. 1646. The article, "The Chinese in the United States," appears below, pp. 231-234.

17. José Martí, "Memorial Meeting in Honor of Karl Marx," *La Nación* (Buenos Aires), May 13 and 16, 1883, and "Henry George and Land Monopoly," ibid., August 15, 1886. Both articles appear below.

18. José Martí, "Knights of Labor Strike," "An Epidemic of Strikes," and "The Labor Problem in the United States," *La Nación,* January 27, 1884, May 9, June 4, 1886. The three articles appear below. See also "El Proceso de los Siete Anarquistas de Chicago" (The Trial of the Seven Anarchists in Chicago), *Obras Completas,* Vol. I, pp. 1736-41.

19. José Martí, "The Schism of the Catholics in New York," *El Partido Liberal* (Mexico), *La Nación* (Buenos Aires), April 14, 1887, and "A Terrible Drama: The Funeral of the Haymarket Martyrs," *La Nación* (Buenos Aires), January 1, 1888. Both articles are complete below. For a discussion of Martí's changing views on capital and labor, see Martínez Bello, *Ideas Sociales y Económicas de José Martí* (La Habana, 1962); Carlos Rafael Rodríguez, *José Martí and Cuban Liberation* (New York, 1953); and Juan Marinello, "El Pensamiento de Martí y Nuestra Revolución," *Cuba Socialista,* January 1962, pp. 16-37.

20. Selections from *Versos Sencillos* will appear in the third volume of this collection.

21. *Congressional Record,* 50th Congress, 1st Session, p. 7653.

22. Richard Carlyle Winchester, "James G. Blaine and the Ideology of American Expansionism," unpublished Ph.D. thesis, University of Rochester, 1966, pp. 66-78; David S. Muzzey, *James G. Blaine: A Political Idol of Other Days* (New York, 1934), p. 207; *New York Tribune,* October 1, 1889; *New York Herald,* October 8, 1889.

23. Martí, *Obras Completas* (La Habana, 1941), Vol. XXXI, pp. 36-37; *Obras Completas* (La Habana, 1946), Vol. I, pp. 306, 1417, 1875.

24. Ibid., Vol. I, pp. 390-92. The complete letter, "Cuba Must Be Free of the United States As Well As of Spain," will appear in the second volume.

25. The complete two-part article appears below.

26. José Martí, "To Cuba," *Patria,* January 27, 1984. The article will appear in the second volume of this collection.

27. Winchester, op. cit., pp. 83-84.

28. José Martí, "The Monetary Congress of the American Republics," *La Revista Illustrada* (New York), May 1891. The article appears below.

29. Manuel Pedro González, *José Martí, Epic Chronicler of the United States in the Eighties* (Chapel Hill, N. Carolina, 1953), p. 56.

30. Herminio Portell-Vilá, *Martí, diplomático* (La Habana, 1934), pp. 18-19.

31. Martí, *Obras Completas,* Vol. XXXVII, p. 56.

32. Emilio Roig de Leuchsenring, *Martí Anti-Imperialist* (La Habana, 1967), p. 5.

I

Prologue

The Truth About the United States

In our America it is vital to know the truth about the United States. We should not exaggerate its faults purposely, out of a desire to deny it all virtue, nor should these faults be concealed or proclaimed as virtues. There are no races; there are only the various modifications of man in details of form and habits, according to the conditions of climate and history in which he lives, which do not alter the identical and the essential. Superficial men who have not explored human problems very thoroughly, or who cannot see from the heights of impartiality how all nations are boiling in the same stew pot, and how one finds in the structure and fabric of them all the same permanent duel between constructive unselfishness and iniquitous hate, are prone to amuse themselves by finding substantial variety between the egotistical Saxon and the egotistical Latin, the generous Saxon and the generous Latin, the Saxon bureaucrat and the Latin bureaucrat. Both Latins and Saxons are equally capable of having virtues and defects; what does vary is the peculiar outcome of the different historical groups. In a nation of English, Dutch, and Germans of similar background, no matter what their disagreements, perhaps fatal, brought upon them by the original separations between nobility and the common man who founded that nation together, and by the inevitable (and in the human species innate) hostility of greed and vanity brought about by aristocracies confronted with the law and

self-denial revealed to them, one cannot explain the confusion of political customs and the melting pot of nations in
which the conquistadors' needs permitted the native population to live. With parricidal blindness the privileged class
spawned by the Europeans is still barring the way to those
frightened and diverse peoples. A nation of strapping young
men from the North, bred over the centuries to the sea and
the snow and the virility aided by the perpetual defense of
local freedom, cannot be like a tropical isle, docile and smiling, where the famished outgrowth of a backward and war-
minded European people, descendants of a coarse and uncultured tribe, divided by hatred for an accommodating submission to rebellious virtue, work under contract for a government that practices political piracy. And also working under
contract are those simple but vigorous Africans, either vilified
or rancorous, who from a frightful slavery and a sublime war
have entered into citizenship with those who bought and sold
them, and who, thanks to the dead of that sublime war,
today greet as equals the ones who used to make them dance
to the lash. Concerning the differences between Latins and
Saxons, and the only way that comparisons can be drawn,
one must study the conditions they may have shared. It is a
fact that in those Southern states of the American Union
where there were Negro slaves, those Negroes were predominantly as arrogant, shiftless, helpless, and merciless as the
sons of Cuba would be under conditions of slavery. It is
supinely ignorant and slightly infantile and blameworthy to
refer to the United States and to the real or apparent con-
quests of one or more of its territories as one total nation,
equally free and definitively conquered. Such a United States
is a fraud and a delusion. Between the shanties of Dakota and
the virile and barbaric nation in process of growth there, and
the cities of the East—sprawling, privileged, well-bred, sensual, and unjust—lies an entire world. From the stone houses
and the majestic freedom north of Schenectady, to the
dismal resort on stilts south of St. Petersburg, lies another
entire world. The clean and concerned people of the North

are worlds apart from the choleric, poverty-stricken, broken, bitter, lackluster, loafing Southern shopkeepers sitting on their cracker barrels. What the honest man should observe is precisely that it was not only impossible to fuse the elements of diverse tendency and origin out of which the United States was created, within a period of three centuries of life in common or of one century of political awareness, but that compulsory social intercourse exacerbates and accentuates their principal differences and turns the unnatural federation into a harsh state of violent conquest. It is a quality of lesser people and of incompetent and gnawing envy, this pricking holes in manifest greatness and plainly denying it for some defect or other, or this going to great lengths of prediction, like someone brushing a speck of dust off the sun. But it is a matter of certification rather than of prophecy for anyone who observes how in the United States the reasons for unity are weakening, not solidifying; how the various localities are dividing and irritating national politics, not uniting with it; how democracy is being corrupted and diminished, not strengthened and saved from the hatred and wretchedness of monarchies. Hatred and misery are posing a threat and being reborn, and the man who keeps this to himself instead of speaking out is not complying with his duty. He is not complying with his duty as a man, the obligation of knowing the truth and spreading it; nor with his duty as a good American who sees the continent's peace and glory secure only in the frank and free development of its various native entities. As a son of our America he is not fulfilling his obligations to prevent the peoples of Spanish blood from falling under the counsel of the smirking toga and the skittish interest, whether through ignorance or disillusionment or impatience, in the immoral and enervating servitude of a damaged and alien civilization. In our America it is imperative to know the truth about the United States.

Wrongs must be abhorred, whether or not they are ours. The good must not be hated merely because it is not ours. But it is worthless and irrational and cowardly for inefficient

or inferior people to aspire to reach the stability of a foreign
nation by roads other than those which brought security and
order to the envied nation, through individual effort and the
adaptation of human freedom to the forms required by the
particular constitution of that nation. With some people, an
excessive love for the North is the unwise but easily explained expression of such a lively and vehement desire for
progress that they are blind to the fact that ideas, like trees,
must come from deep roots and compatible soil in order to
develop a firm footing and prosper, and that a newborn babe
is not given the wisdom and maturity of age merely because
one glues on its smooth face a mustache and a pair of side-
burns. Monsters are created that way, not nations. They have
to live of themselves, and sweat through the heat. With other
people, their Yankeemania is the innocent result of an occasional little leap of pleasure, much as a man judges the inner
spirit of a home, and the souls who pray or die therein, by
the smiles and luxury in the front parlor, or by the champagne and carnations on the banquet table. One must suffer,
starve, work, love, and study, even in vain, but with one's
own individual courage and freedom. One must keep watch
with the poor, weep with the destitute, abhor the brutality of
wealth, live in both mansion and tenement, in the school's
reception hall and in its vestibule, in the gilt and jasper
theater box and in the cold, bare wings. In this way a man
can form opinions, with glimmers of reason, about the au-
thoritarian and envious republic and the growing materialism
of the United States. With other posthumous weaklings of
Second Empire literary dandyism, or the false skeptics under
whose mask of indifference there generally beats a heart of
gold, the fashion is to scorn the indigenous, and more so.
They cannot imagine greater elegance than to drink to the
foreigner's breeches and ideas, and to strut over the globe,
proud as the pompom tail of the fondled lap dog. With still
others it is like a subtle aristocracy which, publicly showing a
preference for the fairskinned as a natural and proper thing
to do, tries to conceal its own humble halfbreed origins, un-

aware that when one man brands another as a bastard, it is always a sign of his own illegitimacy. There is no more certain announcement of a woman's sins that when she shows contempt for sinners. It matters not whether the reason is impatience for freedom or the fear of it, moral sloth or a laughable aristocracy, political idealism or a recently acquired ingenuity—it is surely appropriate, and even urgent, to put before our America the entire American truth, about the Saxon as well as the Latin, so that too much faith in foreign virtue will not weaken us in our formative years with an unmotivated and baneful distrust of what is ours. In a single war, the War of Secession, more concerned with whether the North or the South would predominate in the Republic than with abolishing slavery, the United States lost more men per capita than were lost in the same amount of time by all the Spanish republics of America put together,[1] and its sons had been living under republicanism for three centuries in a country whose elements were less hostile than in any other. More men were lost in the United States Civil War than in Mexico to victorious Chile in the naturally slow process of putting upon the surface of the New World, with nothing but the enterprise of popular instinct and the rhetorical apostolate of a glorious minority, the remote peoples of widespread nuclei and contrary races, where the rule of Spain had left all the rage and hypocrisy of theocracy, and all the indolence and suspicions of a prolonged servitude. From the standpoint of justice and a legitimate social science it should be recognized that, in relation to the ready compliance of the one and the obstacles of the other, the North American character has gone downhill since the winning of independence, and is today less human and virile; whereas the Spanish American character today is in all ways superior, in spite of its confusion and fatigue, to what it was when it began to emerge from the disorganized mass of grasping clergy, unskilled ideol-

1. Confederate dead during the Civil War have been estimated at 258,000; Union dead at 360,000.

ogists, and ignorant or savage Indians. And to aid in the understanding of political reality in America, and to accompany or correct with the calm force of fact the ill-advised praise (pernicious when carried to extremes) of the North American character and political life, *Patria*[2] is inaugurating, with today's issue, a permanent section devoted to "Notes on the United States." In it we will print articles faithfully translated from the country's earliest newspapers, without editorial comment or changes. We will print no accounts of events revealing the crimes or accidental faults, possible in all nations, where none but the wretched spirit finds sustenance and contentment, but rather those structural qualities which, for their constancy and authority, demonstrate two useful truths to our America: the crude, uneven, and decadent character of the United States, and the continuous existence there of all the violence, discord, immorality, and disorder blamed upon the peoples of Spanish America.

Patria (New York), March 23, 1894

2. *Patria* (Fatherland) was founded by José Martí in New York on March 4, 1892, to spread the propaganda of the Cuban Revolutionary Party and was generally recognized as its official organ. It was edited by Sotero Figueroa, a Puerto Rican Negro.

II
North American Personalities

Wendell Phillips

Many trifling occurrences in the gay city and many congressional squabbles filling newspapers and conversations these days seek in vain expression through my pen. In vain do events weigh upon our memory (where we would rather they were not): a bandit's wife showing off, in a circus before cigarette-smoking and yelling children, the weapon with which her husband had taken so many lives; a murderer who exhibits himself on tour, the friend who killed her husband for a few dollars, and who now reenacts the scene of the

1. Wendell Phillips (1811-1884), one of the greatest of the Abolitionists, a peerless orator who used his great power of speech and pen in behalf of a wide variety of causes, including women's rights, penal and labor reform, and temperance, as well as antislavery.

Besides, this article, Martí published an appreciation of Wendell Phillips in the March 1884 number of La América. Again in a letter to Bartolomi Mitre y Vedia, December 19, 1882, he referred to Phillips as the "great humanitarian orator."

Martí was pleased to learn that George William Curtis (1824-1892), essayist, editor, and noted orator, agreed with his estimate of Phillips. Curtis, he reported to La América, had written him: "I am happy to note that your appreciation of the great orator and mine do not differ in the least." Martí had been a bit concerned lest his evaluation of Phillips did not coincide with the opinion of "his own compatriots. But now we see with satisfaction there is a point-by-point coincidence. . . ."

For Martí's appreciation of Phillips in La América and the comments on Curtis, see Obras Completas (La Habana, 1946), Vol. I, pp. 1078-83.

murder for the approving pleasure of Western crowds, with the same gun and dressed in the same clothes.[2] In vain we hear the din of political or private disputes that sound the way a blade of tin would sound against an angel's sword. Wendell Phillips is dead! That illustrious mouthpiece of the poor; that magnanimous, shining knight of justice and eloquence; that famous orator who faced selfish mobs and made them follow him or, when they shrieked like barbarians, knew how to throttle them; that indefatigable abolitionist of whom John Bright[3] said he had no equal, either among Americans or Britishers, for the pureness of his heart, the majesty of his speech, or the serenity of his character—speaks no more! There is no need to wail over his death, a simple, ordinary event which comes as a reward for leading a clear life, to be awaited calmly and received tenderly. Great men, even those who have found their real greatness within themselves, and have cultivated it and used it to the benefit of others, are but vehicles of great forces. They come and go in waves. Their piercing pains, their resplendent martyrdoms, their clusters of sonorous and flaming words, their toilsome merits are, in the presence of eternity, like the white foam that breaks into a mist against the rocks or shatters, spreads, and sinks silently in the sand.

It was he who raised to his lips the cup of pleasure and then lowered it, smiling, to walk arm in arm with the humble. It was he who soon discovered that life has its plebeians[4]—

2. The references are to the public appearances of Jesse James' widow, and of one of the Ford brothers, the famous outlaw's murderers. See Martí's article on Jesse James below.

3. John Bright (1811-1899), English orator and statesman, leader of the free trade agitation in England which resulted in the repeal of the Corn Laws. Bright was a supporter of the Union and antislavery cause during the Civil War.

4. Martí may have been referring to the fact that Wendell Phillips, almost alone among the Garrisonian Abolitionists, displayed interest in the problem of white wage workers as well as of the black slaves in the antebellum period.

those who love but themselves and bring all the world to their pillows and their mouths, and its nobles—those who are devoured by a craving to do good, who would quench their neighbors' thirst with their own blood, their hunger with their very heart, who fill the lamp of mankind with the oil of their souls. It was he who, when placed by the accumulation of wealth in an exalted position that inebriates and withers as orgies do, saw through the mountain of death, saw within himself, and was aflame with love, love which is always painful, and avoids contagion. It was he who lifted the wretched out of their wretchedness, claiming for himself as the only worthwhile pay the ever-bitter pleasure of having defended them. It was he who among the general perversion of mental and moral powers found in himself a splendid and broadening intelligence which he held up reverently, as the priest does the host. It was he who was absorbed in helping others and disdained the great advantages that nature's benevolent caprice had showered upon him, because they profited only him. He is now a hero, an apostle, before whom every honest man should stop to kiss his death-cold hand.

It was nearly fifty years ago. The crowd was roaring. Channing,[5] a great orator, had called the people of Boston to a meeting to condemn the murderers of worthy Elijah Lovejoy,[6] a brave advocate of the abolition of slavery, who died

5. William Ellery Channing (1780-1842), clergyman, author, leader of American Unitarians and known as the "Apostle of Unitarianism." Channing was the idol of many Abolitionists, and his writings, especially *Negro Slavery* (1835), helped the cause, but he was not fully an Abolitionist himself.

6. Elijah Parish Lovejoy (1802-1838), editor and Abolitionist who became a symbol of free speech and "the martyr Abolitionist." Ordained a Presbyterian minister in 1833, Lovejoy became editor of a Presbyterian Abolitionist paper, and after being hounded out of Missouri, a slave state, by proslavery mobs, had moved up the Mississippi River to Alton, Illinois, a free state, where he hoped that he would be safer. There, however, three presses were destroyed by mobs opposed to his Abolitionist principles, and Lovejoy himself was struck

beside his printing press. Who said there was no poetry in our times? A certain Austin,[7] a bulldog, Governor of the State, called the Negroes beasts and said such things as only owners of men are good at saying. The meeting, made up of owners, cheered frantically in Austin's honor. Someone had risen, pale and serene, to speak. The air was at once full of booing. There was interference, fist shaking, heckling; the hall was like a strange, gnarled trunk putting forth torsos and claws of wild beasts. What a great pleasure it is to face it! Someone was heard saying the young advocate of the slaves was a son of a Mayor of Boston and reluctantly they quieted down. Austin turned pale! The air was no longer filled with boos but with fiery invectives, with frightful ghosts! The portraits of the founding fathers seemed to leave their frames, revengeful, and shake their fists at the defenders of slavery. There was a new, weak attempt at heckling, but great golden words, a golden orb seemed to fill the hall. "Hurrah! hurrah!" People embraced each other, elated. The claws changed to wings. Hurrah! Hurrah! Wendell Phillips had spoken! Oh, word . . . inspired . . . fashioner of wings![8]

The next day Boston and all the North felt like a mother to whom a child had been born. Nations tire of their great men, of seeing them always so high, and in the end lose that loving respect they had for their stature. They also tire of the monotony and drabness of virtue. Yet there is no deeper joy than to feel that from the people's ranks has come, and

---

down and killed by a bullet during the defense of the fourth press. His death, wrote John Quincy Adams (1767-1848), sent a "shock as of an earthquake throughout this continent."

7. James T. Austin (1784-1870), who was attorney-general, not governor of the state of Massachusetts, at the time the meeting was held to protest Lovejoy's slaying in Boston's Faneuil Hall ("cradle of liberty"), December 8, 1837. Strongly anti-Abolitionist, Austin praised the mob which killed Lovejoy and compared them with the patriots of the Boston Tea Party.

8. Martí frequently used the metaphor of the wing to express flight or loftiness.

among them lives, an extraordinary creature. Later they may
bite him, stone him, disfigure him, and abandon him. During
his thirty years of abolitionist propaganda Wendell Phillips
was scoffed at, insulted on the streets, and even accused of
being a villain and a traitor.

But now he is dead. Arms are presented; flags are at half-
mast; there is mourning from all the pulpits; statues are being
chiseled; all heads are bared in the cold and in the snow when
he passes!

It was an irresistible impulse that aligned him with that
propaganda, then demagogic and almost opprobrious, for he
was Harvard's most eloquent student, in possession of a fortune and the greater fortune that comes with being born to
an old, respectable family. Where might he not have sat, this
portly, cultured gentleman, in whom seemed to shine, as in
Motley,[9] that austere gracefulness of the good New England
stock? What public honors, what handsome profits, what a
vast, pleasant reputation, what a comfortable easy life might
have been his by simply following in the footsteps of the
powerful, or by merely not joining those who stood in their
way? Wendell Phillips had loved his eloquence because it issued bravely from his mouth as eloquence always should. He
could see and hear himself modeling with his strong hands a
more just and generous motherland and then lighting with
the light of his eloquence the statue his hands had fashioned.
Alone in his young lawyer's office he would ponder on the
meeting of sharp wits in court as in an eager and dashing
fencing match; and he paced up and down continuously as
though pushed by winged spirits within him. But one day a
mob passed his window pulling the Abolitionist Garrison by a
rope tied around his neck.[10] It was a well-dressed mob. They

9. John Lathrop Motley (1814-1877), American diplomat and historian, Harvard graduate and Wendell Phillips' close boyhood friend.
Martí misspells his name, calling him "Mottey."

10. In 1835 the English Abolitionist George Thompson came to the
United States on a lecture tour. On October 21, the Boston Female

insulted and struck their prey. They laughed at his plight. Then and there Phillips raised his fists to those scoundrels and never lowered them again.

He married Justice. He bartered the ambition of shining by his own natural gifts for the humble glory of sacrificing them for the benefit of others who, while recognizing their glory, would bite the hand that helped them and pay him nothing. He preferred that exquisite satisfaction which lightens and perfumes the soul of those who consecrate themselves to pure justice and to the reconquest of man to the luxury and quiet of Boston life. He found himself alone, alone among fanatics and weaklings, face to face with a human crime and an immense evil, and all his insights and energies concentrated in spite of himself and by mere force of gravity upon the great task, and he acquired, by dint of a powerful imagination, the consistency, impenetrability, and height of a mountain. Thus the earth, when it rises at a given point, leaves vast plains around it. In that formidable thirty-year task, Wendell Phillips was just that: an advancing mountain.

The whole universe assumed in his mind the shape of a Negro slave. If the universe had shown signs of favoring slavery, like the mob that had applauded Austin in Faneuil Hall,

---

Anti-Slavery Society held a meeting, at which a mob of several. thousand persons assembled, expecting to tar-and-feather Thompson. The latter, however, had been warned, and the crowd, searching for a victim, seized William Lloyd Garrison (1805-1879), leader of the Abolitionist forces demanding immediate emancipation and editor of *The Liberator,* dragged him with a rope around his neck through the streets, and would probably have lynched him if Mayor Theodore Lyman had not intervened.

Martí's observation that the mob that attacked Garrison was a "well-dressed mob" is confirmed in Leonard Richards' recent study of anti-abolitionist mobs, which concludes that quite often they were composed of the upper class of commercial and professional men. See *Gentlemen of Property and Standing* (New York, 1970), Chapter 5.

he would have faced the universe, his glance cutting, dazzling, his word precipitous, flaming. In Wendell Phillips this condensation of forces necessary to oppose successfully a grave, extended evil, at the same time deprived him of the minor talents of adjustment, those petty, bitter talents that great souls seldom acquire. This developed in him from his scanty knowledge of real life, a knowledge which is indispensable if one is to hit upon the laws that govern life. Without that knowledge, discovering the laws of life is as impossible as practicing medicine without having laid eyes on a human body.

An exalted love of sacrifice, of human perfection, of purity was innate in Wendell Phillips. From his schooling, in which he excelled, he derived an impetuous inclination toward the extraordinary. His heroic campaign, since he never had to toil for his bread, sprang from intercourse with the superhuman and the supreme, even before his contact with hard, plodding existence had given him that melancholic and healthy tolerance which tempers the soul without impairing its merits, rather affording it the greatest merit of all, which is to exert wholesome influence through those merits.

The contact with the superhuman alone naturally turns the spirit away from merely human solutions. Whoever has the extraordinary within him, apart from the extraordinary that History, Letters, and Arts add, is in no position to legislate in the field of the ordinary. An eagle cannot trot; and such is life's aim: to make an eagle trot!

Thus this man who raised a prophetic voice, no less vibrant, magnificent, or marvelous than those trumpet blasts that destroyed the walls of Jericho, shook the North American people with a vigor that grew with each new difficulty; stirring whatever depth of generosity and sociability their mercantile, individualistic lives and breath of long, infamous abuse left them. He whose every trait was surprising and loving, ignored at times perhaps with an intolerance necessary to the success of his campaign, the merits of those who, guided by a better knowledge of the human and the possible, hoped to put an end to slave traffic by less boastful and less violent means. Wendell Phillips would hear of no peace except on perfect, immediate, and extreme terms. Whoever delayed he called a traitor and branded him on the forehead. Since it seemed, according to Calhoun[11] and his followers and against Charles Sumner[12] and the North, that the Constitution of the United States favored slavery or allowed it, Phillips did not hesitate to call the Constitution criminal. "I fail to see," he said, "how a constitution that is static can fit a country that moves on."[13] And since in order to practice his legal profession he was required to swear loyalty to a constitution he considered iniquitous, he did not swear, thereby closing to himself a career which would have been brilliant. He was not among the prudent, who transform, and are necessary, but among the impatient, no less precious, who shake the judicious and whip the selfish who stand in the way of the judicious. His fiery lash cracked over all their heads!

What should not be, should not be. Any deviation from absolute justice, no matter what conditions of the times or reasons might seem to justify it, seemed to him a crime: the higher the one who deviated was, the greater the crime. So Washington owned slaves? Well, he was "a great slave-

11. John C. Calhoun (1782-1850), states' rights advocate and defender of slavery, leader of Nullification. Calhoun was for many years Senator from South Carolina.

12. Charles Sumner (1811-1874), great foe of slavery and champion of equality for Negroes, leader of the Radical Republicans during and after the Civil War. Sumner was assaulted on the floor of the Senate by Preston Brooks of South Carolina for his antislavery speech, "The Crime Against Kansas," in 1856. During his long convalescence, Massachusetts kept his seat vacant for him.

13. Wendell Phillips was a leading proponent of the Garrisonian concept of a proslavery Constitution. For a summary of Phillips' views on the Constitution, see Irving H. Bartlett, *Wendell Phillips, Brahmin Radical* (Boston, 1961), pp. 119-20.

holder."[14] Henry Clay was "a great sinner."[15] Daniel Webster was "a menagerie of wild beasts and a heretic who had leaned his head on the Delilah lap of slavery."[16] If the villainy of slavery were mentioned in conjunction with anyone dead, he would exhume the culprit, as the bishops did Pope Formuosus,[17] sit him on the bench and sentence him. In these unilateral trials, in a grandiose way, a marvelous person with a worm in his side was no longer a marvel: instead of extracting the worm carefully, he preferred to knock down the marvel with a single blow.

14. Martí is referring to a passage in Phillips' speech, "Surrender of Sims," in which he described how "sixteen or seventeen years ago, Peleg Sprague, standing on this platform [in Faneuil Hall], pointed to this portrait [of Washington], and called him 'that slaveholder.' " (*Speeches, Lectures, and Letters of Wendell Phillips* [Boston, 1863], p. 60.) Sims was a fugitive slave who was returned to his master from Boston.

15. Phillips used that term to describe Henry Clay (1777-1852), Senator from Kentucky and known as the "Great Compromiser," in his speech on "The Philosophy of the Abolition Movement," delivered before the Massachusetts Anti-Slavery Society, Boston, January 27, 1853. See Wendell Phillips, *Speeches, Lectures and Letters* (Boston, 1884), p. 113. For Martí's opinion of Henry Clay, see below, p. 84.

16. Martí is paraphrasing Phillips on Daniel Webster (1782-1852) after he delivered his March 7, 1850, Senate speech defending the Compromise of 1850. Phillips wrote: "See to it, when Nature has provided you a monster like Webster, that you exhibit him—himself a whole menagerie—throughout the country." (Ibid., p. 48.) Again in his lecture on "Public Opinion," in discussing Daniel Webster, Phillips said: "He bowed his vassal head to the temptations of the flesh and lucre. He gave himself up into the lap of the Delilah for slavery, for the mere promise of a nomination. . . ." (Ibid., p. 49.)

17. Pope Formosus (c. 816-896), Pontiff from 891 to 896 whose posthumous trial was unprecedented in papal history. He was disinterred by his successor Stephen VII, and his corpse was submitted to trial for alleged crimes, following which his election as Pope was declared invalid.

There was in him a certain confidence in the purity of his loves, a certain artistic and exquisite finish to his intellectual sacrifice, a certain reliance on the honesty of his purpose, and a certain superior, genuine conception of man against which man himself was not allowed to turn, all of which at times made him harsh in opposing other men, when, in the free exercise of their will, they attacked liberty. Thus the arrogance of his virtue sometimes made the most dedicated champions of justice seem despotic. He conceded to justice unlimited rights, but he also believed that tyranny of virtue was efficacious and natural. Moved by these impulses he would speak in a hollow tone to a public unaccustomed to the absolute, a public which, if it ever declines in the future, be what may its visible magnitude, will decline because of its love for and practice of the concrete.

A people only follows those who set out to lead them and weld them into a unit. A man of virtue will never mold a people into one. They will hold on to him in the hour of danger, or cross the seas to fetch him, but they will give themselves again, with a minimum of compunction, to the man who shares their puerilities and vices.

Wendell Phillips' only hour of triumph was the fleeting moment when political factors brought at last the solution which rationalized virtue had preached through him. But one could easily see his anger and deep sadness at the tumultuous and mechanical life which a majority of his compatriots led. It pained him sorely to see the country's life centered on moneymaking. What he had, he gave. He would turn in wrath against the North: "Cotton is choking you! Machines are not going to save you!"[18] Jingling of money is all one hears; there

18. Martí is quoting from Phillips' lecture, "The Lesson of the Hour," delivered at Brooklyn, New York, November 1, 1859, following John Brown's raid at Harper's Ferry, in which he said: "They breathe that atmosphere; they do not want to sail outside of it; they do not attempt to reason outside of it. Poisoned with printer's ink, or choked with cotton dust, they stare at absolute right, as the dream of mad-

is nothing in the country but squeaking of wheels, market dust, and clinking of dollars. "You have been corrupted by the sordid economy of Franklin's Poor Richard." "Either you uplift your souls or sooner or later you will crumble to earth." [19]

Never did that ardent knight of human dignity, that admirable person consecrated to the highest objectives, purest sufferings, most exquisite satisfactions, that great indefatigable, fluent orator, flatter the masses' passions, not even to insure for his ideas a momentary success. Progress consists in growing and ascending, not in shrinking! Those who court the masses or public passions are as vile as those who search out women to cater to the vices of their cronies and their kings. Such men may be skillful, but they are vile, if not traitors, even if they were born with exceptional gifts, and all the more so if they were so born, for then they are twice traitors: to their motherland and to the spirit of man.

No, court the masses he did not, nor did he ever think a truth and leave it unsaid. His speech was an arsenal or a torrent of clean, sturdy, hard arrows such as those that Norman kings taught their sons to shoot into oak trunks. In his tremendous invectives he used all the resources his language offered, plus his own gift for rounding them out and magnifying them.

He did not discuss: he established. He did not argue: he chastised. He pointed out what was vile, not stopping to prove his claim. His words were serene and lofty like his face; elegant and impassive just as he was. He launched his anathemas surely and quietly. He did not allow himself to be carried away by emotion nor did he try to carry away his pub-

---

men." (James Redpath, *Echoes of Harper's Ferry* [Boston, 1860], p. 45.)

19. The exact equivalents of these quotations do not appear in Phillips' writings and speeches, but he was a frequent critic of the cash-nexus and the corrupting influence of money in American society and politics.

lic: North Americans do not like to hear displays of passions they do not share. Some of Wendell Phillips' paragraphs are like grand sword duels, some others, which he uttered without scarcely changing his tone, sound like great judgments passed from tall black clouds out of the fiery books of the Prophets. The monstrous and the oceanic appeared everywhere in his eloquence. No other North American orator had the grandeur of ideas, the perfect construction, the harmony and roundness of the phrase—the artistry, in fine—in the measure which he had. A Southern colonel once said: "He is like an infernal machine set to music." "He spoke like a gentleman in a parlor." In the subtlest manner, with a mellow voice, he left a piercing dart in the breast of every slavery sympathizer. But when, because of requirements of his art or of his public, an attitude of greater disdain or wrath became necessary, he would display the holy ire which was always stored within him and convert his eloquence from that fine steel blade into a tremendous, rigorous catapult. A lion's claw, in a glove. He was implacable and fierce like all gentle men who love justice.

La Nación (Buenos Aires), March 28, 1884
Dated New York, February 11, 1884

Henry Garnet, Famous Negro Orator

While those friends of American glories were gathered to see that the man deserving of honor would not be given it, some other men, grateful for the good they received from Reverend Henry Garnet, decided to drape in mourning for his death the church that was his, and to recount in solemn ceremony the humility, eloquence, greatness, firmness, and enterprise of the celebrated Negro speaker. On one most solemn day the sun's rays that penetrated the lofty windows of the Capitol in Washington shone upon the ample bronze brow of a proud man whose calm voice was delivering eloquent and magnanimous phrases. He was Henry Garnet, the first Negro to be seated, as a venerable clergyman, among the

1. Martí's article was written in connection with the Memorial Services in Cooper Union, May 10, 1882, for Reverend Henry Highland Garnet. In its report of the event the *New York Times* reported on May 11: "Rarely has so large an audience of representatives of the colored race assembled in the City as that which gathered in Cooper Union last evening to pay tribute to the memory of the late Rev. Dr. Henry Highland Garnet. The seats were all filled before the beginning of the services."

Henry Highland Garnet (1815-1882), the grandson of an African chief, born a slave in Maryland, escaped to the North with his family in 1824. After studying in New York's Free African School and Canaan Academy in New Hampshire (until local farmers destroyed the school), white men sheltered by the dome of that stark Capitol. [2] On another unforgotten day an imposing young man was speaking in a most passionate and cultured manner before the New York Anti-Slavery Society, whose members admired his youthful proficiency, the evangelical quality of his turn of phrase, his faultless speech and the manliness of his kindly attitude. He was Henry Garnet, returned from his difficult college education, who for the first time in public was displaying his oratorical skills. And that wretched chore boy who washed dishes and cutlery, and did odd jobs, and signed on as a cabin boy in a little steamer plying the seas to Cuba? [3] He was Henry Garnet, who showed lazy, proud, and impa-

---

he completed his education at Oneida Institution and became a well-known minister in Troy, New York, and New York City. Famous as a militant Abolitionist and for advocating that slaves rise up and end the institution by violence, Garnet by the 1850s had also become well known as a leader in the African emigration movement and as head of the African Civilization Society.

Although Garnet was a great orator, Martí never wrote a special piece about the greatest of the black orators, Frederick Douglass, whom he referred to as "the slave orator" and "the eloquent mulatto." (*Obras Completas*, [La Habana, 1946], Vol. I, pp. 1637, 1791.)

2. Martí is referring to the fact that on February 12, 1865, in the hall of the House of Representatives, Reverend Garnet preached a sermon commemorating the passage of the Thirteenth Amendment abolishing slavery by Congress. His sermon made him the first Negro to speak in the halls of Congress. For his speech, "Let the Monster Perish," see *The Voice of Black America: Major Speeches of the United States, 1797-1971*, Philip S. Foner, ed. (New York, 1972), pp. 307-16. At the time he delivered the sermon, Garnet was pastor of the Fifteenth Street Presbyterian Church in Washington, D.C.

3. It is strange that Martí does not mention in his summary of Garnet's life that the black orator was a champion of Cuban independence and a chief speaker at the meetings held by Negroes of New York in support of the Cuban Revolution during the Ten Years War. (See *Slavery in Cuba: A Report of the Proceedings of the Meeting held at Cooper Institute, New York City, December 13, 1872* [New York, 1872], pp. 15-17.)

tient men how, from a little Negro cabin boy—son of fugitive slaves who went naked through the snow and suffered hunger and cold in the woods—one could go on to become a pastor of a church, a teacher, a member of a Frankfurt congress,[4] a mediator for free labor in England, a leader of his race, a representative upon foreign soil of a nation of fifty million subjects, an orator upon whose pure, proud brow the serene and grandiose light of the Capitol played as if in fond caresses. Persecuted in the Southern states, the Negroes came to New York and called at Garnet's home as if it were the home of a patriarch; there he prepared them to live in his house and his church, and they listened to him as to a Messiah and obeyed him as if he were Moses. When Garnet was deprived of the use of a leg, and advanced in his use of Latin, it was fame that he brought, wrapped in his fearless antislavery ideas, to Canaan Academy which became a fortress for those ideas, replete with zealous soldiers. And the partisans of slavery collected ninety-five pairs of oxen and yoked them to the Academy and tore it up by the roots, while murderous bullets cut through the air in search of "that audacious Negro with the high forehead."[5] His language was not mutilated or imperfect like that of almost every man of his race in the world, but correctly punctuated and exemplary. His eyes evinced honesty, his lips truth, his whole person respect. He rendered it and inspired it. In a group of men, he seemed to be the leader. He was a clergyman in Washington, and shone as a virtuous and eloquent one. He was also a clergyman in New York, in a church of his own, and every year he made his parishioners more loving and humble. With his right arm he fended off every blow that the unjust Negro directed at the white man who had helped to free him, and with his left

4. Garnet was a delegate to the Congress of the Friends of Peace, held in Frankfurt in 1851.

5. Garnet's brief stay at the Canaan Academy in Canaan, New Hampshire, in 1835 was interrupted when the Academy was destroyed by an infuriated mob of farmers opposed to the education of Negroes.

he deflected from the heads of the Negroes all the blows directed at them by the white men who scorned them without reason because they saw them as victims of the harm they did them. Garnet, who died as Minister in Liberia,[6] was neither ashamed of the wretchedness of his race nor did he share it. He despised hatred. He deeply loved white men and Negroes alike. He died beloved.

La Opinión Nacional (Caracas), March 31, 1882

6. After the Civil War, Garnet was president of Avery College in Pittsburgh and U.S. Minister to Liberia, the black independent state founded by the American Colonization Society in the early 1820s for settlement by free blacks from the United States.

General Grant

1

Grant came from a poor family. As a boy he carted firewood, and was more at home with horses than with books. In military school he excelled in fine horsemanship, later became a captain in the war with Mexico, and either because he overindulged in liquor or kept shady accounts, he was asked to resign from the army. His fortieth birthday found him setting up pins in a bowling alley, tanning hides, and collecting rents. Four years after that he was commander-in-chief of a standing army of 250,000 soldiers fighting for man's freedom. In another four years he was chaotically presiding over his republic.

Then he traveled over the world, received the keys to its finest cities, and the world turned out to welcome him, led by its kings and presidents, after which he fell into the hands of commercial enterprises because of a vulgar desire for wealth. Now he is dead, ennobled by his sufferings. Followed

1. Ulysses Simpson Grant (1822-1885), eighteenth President of the United States. Honored for having helped save the Union, he brought to the presidency an incompetence which led to an administration noted for corruption and poor management even though he himself was personally honest and well-meaning. A remarkable military commander himself, his *Personal Memoirs* (New York, 1885-1886) are rated among the best of all military recollections.

71

by 50,000 soldiers, the generals he defeated in battle accompanied him to his tomb. These are a new breed of men living in radiant times, men who in twenty years have learned how to unabashedly love the man who dashed their hopes, laid waste their domains, and defeated them on the battlefield. These are men who do not mortgage their lives and the peace of their homeland to avenge defeats and settle grievances!

One fights when there is a cause, since Nature put the need for justice into some hearts and into others the need for disregarding and spurning it. Men fight, but once justice has been done, the memories of common contact with death make men worthy of the name forget their hostilities, enter a greater brotherhood, and settle down, ennobled by the national abundance that falls to nations whose sons have proved their mettle. The brave forget, but after the wars are over, it is evident that those who fought less bravely and most unjustly and live in fear of their victory, forget the least. There are nations and men that show a facade of gold, but harbor a cave of restless hobgoblins within. Only petty nations perpetuate their civil grudges. It is a good thing that man-to-man and horse-to-horse struggles make ferocity finally bow to the dictum of reason. After Washington's Federals had won, and like the Confederates at Appomattox after conceding defeat, the soldiers took leave of their generals and returned to the free endeavors that preserve men's strength and majesty, enriched by their new stature and that of their adversaries, without burdening their country with their idle arms by demanding wages, like crass mercenaries, merely for having done their duty.

Ulysses S. Grant was born of poor parents in a spacious but humble wooden hut in an out-of-the-way corner of Ohio; marble buildings and stone mansions were hung with velvet and black crepe as Johnston,[2] whom Grant's lieutenant Sher-

---

2. Joseph Eggleston Johnston (1807-1891), Confederate general who lost to Grant at Vicksburg and, outmaneuvered by Sherman, was relieved of his command. He was then placed in command of the Army of the Tennessee, lost, and had to surrender to Sherman.

man ousted from Atlanta;[3] as Buckner,[4] from whom Grant himself took 17,000 prisoners at Fort Donelson; as Fitzhugh Lee,[5] soldier and nephew of that brilliant and devout man whom Grant alone forced to surrender, followed his casket to the tolling of all the church bells in the land. Mountains culminate in peaks and nations in men. Let us observe the making of a great leader in a modern nation.

The house of his birth was like the cottage of many a poor settler: one story, wooden walls, gabled roof with a chimney at the crossing, front door flanked by two small windows, a board fence, a shrub-filled backyard with woodlands behind it, and a tree at the door. There in the affection of his good wife, Grant's father would rest from his leather-tanning when he was not busy telling about the deeds of his ancestors who were brave and resolute Scotsmen, or skillfully dashing off a newspaper article. Grant was the product of eight generations of American farmers and soldiers. Are the traits of parents purified as they are passed down to the children? Can it be that men are merely embodiments of concentrated and intensified spiritual forces? "Steadfast, steadfast!" read the mottoes of Grant's lineage, blazoned on a smoking mountain and on four flaming hills: "Steadfast, Craig Ellachiel!" One of the bravest English regiments in India bequeathed its courage to Grant. Flaming mountain, regiment, firmness—all are found

3. William Tecumseh Sherman (1820-1891), Union general who served in the Mexican War, fought at Bull Run, and served with Grant at Shiloh (1862) and at the capture of Vicksburg (1863). Placed in command of the Army of the Tennessee, he became noted for his famous march to the sea from Chattanooga to Atlanta, September 2 to December 2, 1864.

4. Simon Bolívar Buckner (1823-1914), Confederate brigadier-general who surrendered to Grant at Fort Donelson (1862), was exchanged, and was made lieutenant-general.

5. Fitzhugh Lee (1835-1905), Confederate cavalry commander who later became Governor of Virginia and Consul-General of the United States to Cuba. He was the nephew of Robert E. Lee and wrote a biography of his uncle.

in Grant and all move forward with him, mauling, crushing, pounding, mowing down.

On the Chickahominy when he had just lost 11,000 men within a quarter of an hour, he ordered the attack renewed without leaving his campchair. At Vicksburg he said to an old lady who had given him some water: "Here I stay till I take Vicksburg, even if it takes me thirty years!" In Chattanooga: "Upward, upward!" up the mountain, into the clouds, over the clouds. To those below it looks like ribbons of flame, the gunfire rattles like drumbeats, the muskets flash, the flag unfurls. Bullets rain down from the crest on the Confederates below; the burning mountain!

As a child he learned little. Books annoyed him as they always would. At the age of two they say he heard a shot without flinching: "More, more!" At eight he was climbing onto every horse in sight. Although his body appeared to be frail, it was actually strong. He was reared like every poor country-born child of his times: school in winter, work in summer.

At twelve he drove the buggy of some ladies on an outing. As they were fording a stream, the terrified ladies noticed that the horses were losing their footing: "Be quiet; I'll get you through safely." And so he did.

He wanted his father to buy him a horse to team up with one he already had, and he would pay for it by carting firewood cut by one of the hired hands. For eight months he carted the firewood. One day there was no sign of the hired hand, so he unhitched the horse, made it drag the logs onto a fallen tree trunk from where he rolled them onto the wagon, and then brought them home. "What happened to the hired hand?" "I don't know and I don't care; I loaded the wagon by myself."

So this son of a plain and loyal mother and an intelligent if unlucky father was growing.

Through the good offices of his congressman, he entered West Point Military Academy at seventeen. He excelled in riding; his studies lagged behind. He was the best rider in his class; but at the end of his courses, out of a class of thirty-nine he placed twenty-fifth. He was given to silence, obedient and polite, and not fond of games: "a good boy." He was rather fond of mathematics, had greater facility in military discipline, tactics, ordnance, and ballistics than in mineralogy, geology, chemistry, engineering, and mechanics. He fell deeply in love, a sign of personality. He married young, a sign of nobility. And with the rank of second lieutenant, he went to the front like all young soldiers.

In the United States of those days, ambitious men and partisans of slavery had joined forces to snatch from Mexico a portion of her territory. American settlers poured into Texas and rose up with it as a state rightfully belonging to the Union of the North in accord with the will of its inhabitants, Mexico objected. The Southern slaveowners who had been fighting since the turn of the century to introduce slavery into the free states, or increase the number of slave states, favored the annexation of Texas on that basis.[6] The presidential candidate Van Buren criticized the proposed annexation on the grounds that it would bring about an unjust war with Mexico; but his opponent Polk, who personified the idea of annexation, was elected.[7] On the pretext of defending their Texan citizens, American troops entered the state and went beyond its southern borders. Arista's forces made a stand against them, thus giving Polk the excuse to consider the war

6. The annexation of Texas was accomplished by joint resolution of Congress in 1845, after failure to achieve senatorial ratification of a treaty in 1844 due to opposition from antislavery forces. Texas entered the Union as the twenty-eighth state and as a slave state.

7. Martin Van Buren (1782-1862), eighth president of the United States (1837-1841), was deprived of nomination as the Democratic candidate for president in 1844 because of his opposition to the immediate annexation of Texas as a slave state. James K. Polk (1795-1849), who received the nomination and went on to be elected, pushed the annexation of Texas and supported the plans for a war with Mexico.

declared.[8] Taylor marched on Mexico and had Grant join him.[9] They made headway,[10] as injustice usually does.[11] Grant fought the beardless cadets who fell smiling side by side on the lava beds of Chapultepec, in the shadow of the last Mexican flag. In one engagement Grant was cited for bravery, and that was as far as he distinguished himself, although he was twenty-five at the time. He served well as a paymaster, and learned how to care for soldiers on campaigns and how to manage their horses and supplies. To maintain

8. On April 25, 1846, after many diplomatic disputes and negotiations, the Mexicans entered the disputed territory between the Nueces and Rio Grande rivers into which General Zachary Taylor had moved his troops in July 1845 even though there was ample evidence that he was encroaching on Mexican territory. Calling this an invasion of American territory, Polk, who had been waiting for the opportunity, requested a declaration of war against Mexico, which Congress passed on May 12, 1846.

9. Zachary Taylor (1784-1850) struck at Mexico right after war was declared. Taylor became president of the United States later.

10. The Mexicans were defeated at the first great battle of the war at Palo Alto on May 8, 1846, and successive Mexican defeats followed at the battles of Resaca de la Palma, Buena Vista, Pueblo, Molina del Rey, Chapultepec, and Mexico City, which was captured on September 14. Santa Anna, the Mexican commander-in-chief and president, resigned the latter office, and on February 13, 1848, the Treaty of Guadalupe-Hidalgo was concluded, terminating hostilities. Under the peace terms, Mexico surrendered about half of its territory to the United States.

11. Martí fails to mention that Grant also viewed the war as an unjust one forced on Mexico by the United States. In his *Personal Memoirs,* he writes that the annexation of Texas was wrong, and "even if the annexation itself could be justified, the manner in which the subsequent war was forced upon Mexico cannot. The fact is, annexationists wanted more territory than they could possibly lay any claim to, as part of the new acquisition. . . . The Southern rebellion was largely the outgrowth of the Mexican War. Nations, like individuals, are punished for their transgressions. We got our punishment in the most sanguinary and expensive war of modern times." (Vol. I, pp. 55-56.)

greatness it is essential to have a knowledge of detail; a driving force must be sustained by experience.

2

When he returned from Mexico where he had become a captain, he seemed not to have performed his duties as soberly as decorum advises. It is common belief that this sad habit of his grew so obvious that, had he not agreed to accede to the resignation requested by his superior officers, he would have faced court-martial. In all fairness, however, it seems unlikely that he pursued such a habit in the dark and bitter years spent in dull occupations until the outbreak of the Civil War, although some of his biographers do attribute certain of his wartime attacks and blunders to the persistence of this habit alone, even in his days of glory. Grant went about from village to farm. He set up a billiard hall in California, but the venture failed. Then he lived on a farm belonging to his wife, where he cut wood, carried it to town, and sold it at a loss. He was not much of a rent collector because his generous nature made him too lenient, and he could not bear the sight of poverty. He found wealth desirable, but he was anything but stingy or a bully by nature, so that when he went about collecting rents while on his wood-selling rounds—strongbodied and deliberate in his walk, his face hidden under the wide drooping brim of a felt hat, wearing a longsleeved shirt and with his breeches tucked into his high boots—the accounts left unpaid outnumbered the ones paid. Yet he always recalled those hard times with pride. "Those were good days, friends," he once said in the White House to one of his former customers, since elected to Congress, who timidly paid Grant a visit after the latter had become president; "those were good days, because I was doing my very best to support my family." And he continued the conversation with his former customer's wife, recalling those cold mornings when he used to carry wood, stack and measure it with his own hands, after which he would go to her husband's office to be paid. He was in such straits, however, that he was forced to accept a position at six hundred dollars a year in Galena where his father and brother had a tannery and leather store. By then Grant was approaching forty.

He was a better listener than a talker. All the townspeople considered him a commonplace kind of a man. He aspired to a position as a surveyor but failed to obtain it. He used to take walks, smoking the while, silent, and never showing impatience. The war had made him deeply envious of those who, through the vagaries of fortune or the influence of powerful friends, acquired prominent positions possibly without the qualifications he felt that he himself possessed. But even a sharp eye could barely notice this envy in those first bursts of confidence of his—rare, to be sure, as confidences should always be—to a military friend whose affection for Grant had almost reached the point of worship. This friend was Sherman, who took care of Grant's interest as if he were his own son, and who was more concerned with Grant's reputation than with his own.

Sherman was tall, eloquent, fiery, restless, inspiring, outspoken, anxious, and formidable; Grant was short, broadshouldered, slow, sober of speech, with an impassive look in his eyes, a man who drank in all he heard but seldom commented upon it. Grant formed his ideas with difficulty, slowly turning over in his mind what he had heard; Sherman spilled his plans and ideas to his silent friend like a shower of sparks. At times Grant would refuse to respond to one of Sherman's entire speeches. He withdrew into himself, and although he was always quick to praise his subordinates with a singular and total generosity, and to spontaneously recognize the part they played in his victories, if he felt their influence he would never show it. And he disliked making use of the ideas of others until, after having considered and revised and knocked them about, he ended by adopting them as his own. His person attained such exaggerated proportions that it took on the highest importance to him and clouded his judgment.

But in those dark days in Galena when he was obscured in the tannery, he gave no evidence of any remarkable qualities whatever, whether because his unfortunate departure from the army and the lack of success in his humble undertakings had left him discouraged and had undermined his self-confidence, or because, consumed by the impatience that is characteristic of strong and extraordinary natures, he was a constant prey to the mute anger arising from the contrast between dull reality and courageous desire. Silence is the virtue of great characters; complaining is their prostitution. Whoever is capable of something and dies before his hour has come, dies in peace, for in some sense he does achieve. And if not, well and good; there is greatness enough in the capacity for greatness.

Grant's was not an amiable disposition, and if he did not actually reject the few signs of affection he inspired, he never sought friendship, even in his darkest hours. He lived and explored within himself. He came from the countryside, ever new and original, and from himself. He had few ingredients of the usual, humanly speaking, and always felt strange and persecuted among people; at times overwhelmed, like a man defeated at every step; at times rebellious, like a man urged on by a higher voice. These reasons and his painful memories of military life, exacerbated by his failure to obtain the post of surveyor, led Grant to shun politics, too complicated even in villages not to inspire fear and a feeling of defeat in simple souls. Yet it was not that he disliked artifice intrinsically; but being martial by nature, he found it easier to attack and capture than to charm and be patient, and he had none of that subtlety and flexibility which in political life spells success. His administrative nature recoiled from the constant and trying servitude which is nearly always the price of political prominence. He might indeed have wished to enter politics, but only as if entering an enemy city: on his own terms. The way politics was going, he did not put it in a very good light at times, but in his country politics was the only form of authority. He affiliated himself with the Democrats because in those days that party stood for states' rights and the rights of individuals, and Grant was always very protective of his own. But in all his forty years he had voted in only one election, and in a republic a man who fails to vote is like a deserter in the army.

An irresistible feeling of friendliness draws rare spirits together. Looking closely, one finds two kinds of men in perpetual conflict: those who spring from Nature strong and genuine, active and solitary, recognized and acclaimed only in times of great crises when they are needed; and men who are cast in conventional molds, who hide their spirit as if it were a sin, who defend and add to the established, who live in comfort and happiness and are useful in the social movement only as a healthy force for resistance in cases where a natural character, drunk on success, swells with conceit and self-affirmation.

Another son of Nature lived in Galena: the lawyer Rawlins,[12] a paragon of virtue, wholly courageous and just. He talked explosively. His thoughts originated within him and left his lips like streaks of lightning. His concise manner of speech had the grandeur of the apostolic word and the supreme eloquence of life itself, compared with which the academic turn of phrase pales like a painted coquette beside a young girl of natural beauty. Rawlins had made his living from charcoal burning until he was twenty-three, that same Rawlins who would later die as Secretary of War. He was self-educated, taught himself law, earned the respect of his associates unaided, grew accustomed to thinking and working

12. John A. Rawlins (1831-1869), lawyer and soldier who became an aide-de-camp to Grant early in the Civil War, rose to high positions in the Union army as Grant rose, and became brigadier-general. Rawlins edited Grant's papers and dispatches during the war, and after Grant was elected president he became Secretary of War for a brief period.

alone. And alone he could think and work fearlessly because he was governed by a single-minded passion for justice. But he had that higher wisdom which, through prolonged suffering, rewards men of true courage, a fortunate quality that in a group of unaffected characters sets the unselfish man apart from the egoist. The egoist has more personality than the unselfish one, at least on the surface, but only in the unselfish one is there true greatness. Rawlins was well endowed with the powers of expression, with intuition, stability, honesty, and judgment. He crushed intrigues as if they were vipers. He could not tolerate an injustice or an affront, even against a turtledove. He wanted truth to triumph, even if his role in the triumph was never discovered. Ever since Grant's leather-selling days, he had been growing closer and closer to this man. He drew inspiration from Rawlins' pleadings; in his good judgment he found a master; Rawlins expressed to perfection and in a finished form the ideas which, in their rudimentary and instinctive form, had taxed Grant's brain. The lawyer and the tanner of hides discussed the quarrel with the South that was descending upon them—the quarrel whose increasing effrontery amazed the people of Galena and of the entire Union.

3

Those were the days of the noblest crusade that men had ever seen. The states in the North were seething from one ocean to the other: "There must be no more slaves!"

From the time that Garrison founded *The Liberator*,[13] there was no peace in the Union. How ideas grow and spread! In 1831 *The Liberator* was an insignificant newspaper, the first mouthpiece for the Abolitionist concept. By 1840 it had

13. *The Liberator,* a weekly antislavery journal advocating immediate emancipation, began publication on January 1, 1831.

set at odds the major parties competing for power, and formed the Liberty Party, composed of Abolitionists who insisted upon the preservation of the Union because slavery stood for "a contract with hell and a pact with death." The 7,000 who voted for the Liberty Party in 1840 grew to 62,500 four years later.[14] In 1848 they numbered 300,000. Joining forces in a formidable organization composed of the Abolitionists of all parties, they now demanded "a free soil for a free country."[15] By 1856 they had 1,341,000 members, and in 1860 they were joined by the President of the Republic, Abraham Lincoln.[16] Where has man seen a higher form of nobility, such generous enthusiasm, such a flaming message, such unselfish leadership, such fruitful and militant courage? Because of the love of adventure and a desire for heaven,

14. The Liberty Party, a minor but important party, was organized in April 1840 with an Abolitionist platform calling for the end of slavery wherever it existed. Although it polled only 7,000 votes in 1840, in the ensuing years it succeeded in splitting the Whig Party. In 1844 the Liberty Party's candidate, James G. Birney (who had also been its 1840 candidate), won 62,300 votes, sufficient to defeat the Whig Party in New York.

Garrisonians did not support the Liberty Party since, under their interpretation of the Constitution as a proslavery document, it was morally indefensible for Abolitionists to vote and hold office.

15. The Free Soil Party, organized in 1848, was not, like the Liberty Party, Abolitionist. It was principally concerned with the status of slavery in the territory obtained from Mexico, opposing the further extension of the institution. Its presidential candidate in the election of 1848 was Martin Van Buren.

16. Abraham Lincoln (1809-1865) was elected sixteenth president of the United States in 1860 on the Republican ticket. While Martí is correct in indicating the links in the antislavery struggle from the formation of the Liberty Party in 1840 to the election of Lincoln two decades later, it should be borne in mind that the Republican Party was not an Abolitionist party, and stood solely for opposition to the further extension of slavery in the territories and not for interference with the institution where it already existed.

other crusaders have fought in times of war; but these American crusaders gave up the security of their homes in a period of peace and prosperity to free the most miserable race on earth. Theirs were the funds that cost them dearly; theirs the all-consuming arguments; theirs the families, the anchor of life, the bond of love in a free and prosperous land. Accustomed to having its way, the South looked angrily upon Northern opposition and, standing above its slaves, defied the common people of the free states.

The North—slow to act, like all the strong, and cautious, like all workers—at first looked fearfully, and always sorrowfully, on the dangers of the rupture the South was provoking. There had been no peace since 1831 when *The Liberator* appeared. The South used every means to persecute Garrison's newspaper; through President Jackson it asked Congress to enforce strict measures against all Abolitionist propaganda.[17]

The South demanded more land for slave breeding; the North, obliged by the Constitution to recognize slavery in states where it was already established, relied upon the Constitution to oppose its introduction into new states.[18] If a territory entered statehood, the South would claim it for itself in order to extend slavery and thus gain a voting advantage over the North in the Senate. And the North, weary of the arrogance and inhumanity of the South, would claim as free the new state, already flooded with Southern marauders

17. Among measures directed against *The Liberator* and other anti-slavery papers (with the consent of President Andrew Jackson, himself a slaveholder) was the termination of mail delivery of these papers to anyone in the South. Thus the Abolitionists were deprived of the freedom of the mails as well as other rights, including the right of petition in Congress.

18. Nothing in the Constitution guaranteed slavery where it already existed, and the Liberty Party actually called for its abolition in the South as well as in the territories which were under the direct jurisdiction of Congress.

challenging Abolitionist settlers for possession of the land
with nocturnal raids and rural forays. When Wilmot asked for
freedom of choice as to whether those states entering the
Union as a result of the Mexican War wanted to be free or
slave,[19] the South rose up in indignation as if a blow had been
struck at its vitals. It countered the energetic stand of the
North, the policies of the Free Soil Party, and the words of
Wendell Phillips with this brazen proposal put forth by Calhoun[20] when the question arose of admitting California as a
free state: legal formalization of an equal balance of power in
Congress between the North and South. Henry Clay's powerful persuasion obtained the famous compromise that postponed the conflict already impending in 1850,[21] by which

19. The Wilmot Proviso, introduced in 1846 by David Wilmot
(1814-1868), congressman from Pennsylvania, did not call for freedom
of choice. It stipulated that neither slavery nor involuntary servitude
should ever exist in any part of the territory that might be acquired
from Mexico as a result of the war then in progress. The House passed
the resolution several times, but it was always defeated in the Senate.

Popular sovereignty, which involved freedom of choice, provided
that people of a territory had the right to decide for themselves
whether they wished the territory to be admitted to the Union as a
slave or free state. It was first formulated by Senator Lewis Cass of
Michigan, but became associated with Senator Stephen A. Douglas of
Illinois, who included this principle in the Compromise of 1850 for the
territories of New Mexico and Utah and especially in the Kansas-
Nebraska Act of 1854.

20. Under the provisions of the Compromise of 1850, California
entered the Union as a free state. John C. Calhoun, senator from South
Carolina, who opposed this settlement, advanced his theory of "concur-
rent majorities" under which a section like the South had the right to
veto an act passed by the majority in Congress.

21. The Compromise of 1850 was Henry Clay's last effort to
appease both the South and the North. Henry Clay (1777-1852),
lawyer and statesman, senator from Kentucky and U.S. Secretary of
State, was most famous as "The Great Compromiser" and "The Great
Pacificator" because of his role in achieving the Missouri Compromise
and the Compromise of 1850.

the South agreed to recognize California and the District of Columbia as free,[22] and the right of New Mexico and Utah to declare themselves free or slave, in exchange for the North's acceptance of Texas as a slave territory, and the return of runaway slaves under a Fugitive Law.[23] The South, so far always the victor, felt safe. The frustrated North thundered in shame against the Fugitive Law. Diplomatic envoys on the side of the South met in Europe to publicize projects to extend slave territory.[24] And in 1856, in opposition to the Republican Party, which came into being with a million and a half votes against the spread of slavery into the free states and territories, the presidency went to Buchanan,[25] one of the three envoys to Europe. The North picked up the gauntlet. The North was now one party and the South another.

What Northerner would return a runaway slave? The legislatures of the free states passed laws to offset the effects of

22. The Compromise of 1850 did not abolish slavery (only the slave trade) in the District of Columbia. Slavery was not abolished in the District until 1862, when it was accomplished by compensating the slaveholders.

23. The Fugitive Slave Act, part of the Compromise of 1850, strengthened enormously the power of the slaveowners to recapture fugitive slaves. The provision relating to Texas dealt with the fixing of its western boundary at the one-hundred-third meridian, and payment to Texas of $10 million for giving up its claims to New Mexico. Texas had already been a slave state since its annexation in 1845.

24. The reference is to the Ostend Manifesto, an unofficial declaration made at Ostend, Belgium, in 1854 by the American ministers to Spain, France, and England, declaring that the possession of Cuba was necessary to the peace of the United States, and that if Spain refused to sell the island, then the United States was "justified by every law, human and divine," in seizing Cuba by force.

25. James Buchanan (1791-1868), fifteenth president of the United States, elected president in 1856 on the Democratic ticket, had been one of the three signers of the Ostend Manifesto, and had helped draw up the infamous document. The other two were Pierre Soulé and John Y. Mason.

the Fugitive Slave Law.[26] The zeal of the martyrs and apostles was intensified again, and the ardor of the enthusiastic
spread among the apathetic. John Brown[27] offered himself in
sacrifice and turned idea into action. From the gallows on
which he died because he went counter to the written law, an
army sprang up and multiplied with tremendous speed, seeking men to lead it and a battleground. When in the new
elections the Republican Party elected Lincoln in a glorious
onslaught, without a single vote from the routed South,[28] the
ominous war was now on every tongue. The South Carolina
legislature called a convention to discuss the right of a state
to secede from the Union, and South Carolina and eleven
other states did secede.[29] Meeting together, they formed the

26. Personal Liberty Laws were enacted by ten Northern state legislatures after passage of the Compromise of 1850 including the new
Fugitive Slave Act. They forbade their officers to aid in the arrest of
fugitive slaves, denied the use of their jails for detaining such fugitives,
and ordered their courts to provide jury trials for all seized blacks.

27. Leading a group of nineteen men that included five Negroes and
his own sons, John Brown (1800-1859) attacked the federal arsenal at
Harper's Ferry, Virginia, October 16, 1859, with the aim of fomenting
a slave rebellion and eventually establishing a Negro republic in the
mountains of Virginia. Brown and his men captured the arsenal, but the
next day a company of U.S. Marines under Colonel Robert E. Lee
assaulted the group, killed ten, and took Brown prisoner. After a hurried trial, the wounded Brown was sentenced to be hanged. Brown's
bravery and dignity during the trial and on the scaffold moved millions
of people to regard him as a hero. Among the Negro people, he was
regarded as a saint.

28. Martí must mean that Lincoln did not win with a single electoral vote from the South. Of his 1,860,000 popular votes, 26,000
came from the entire South, a meager support but certainly more than
"a single vote."

29. Actually eleven, not twelve, states seceded. On February 4,
1861, when the Confederate States of America were formed, seven
states had seceded, and after the firing on Fort Sumter in mid-April
1861, four others followed. Four slave states, Maryland, Kentucky,
Missouri, and Delaware, did not secede.

Confederate States of America and elected Jefferson Davis president.[30] Arsenals, customs, forts, all the government installations and property in the South fell unopposed into the hands of the Confederates, who finally fired on Fort Sumter. A railsplitter was in the White House, a tanner of hides in Galena.

Grant heard the news. "I have been trained to be a soldier at government expense," he said, "and I haven't yet paid my debt in full." In an ardent speech Rawlins broke with his party and upheld the Union in whose defense he enlisted at once. Lincoln had called for 75,000 volunteers and since Grant was the only military man in Galena, he was assigned the task of instructing the Galena company and delivering it to the governor. It is painful to recall how in those days the crestfallen soldier had to go from door to door like a beggar, seeking a command that was denied him everywhere. The man who five years later was to lead four armies to certain victory, could not at first find the humblest post in the military forces of his country. He applied to the Adjutant General and received no answer. Twice he applied for an appointment under McClellan,[31] who knew him; both times he was refused. For lack of instructors they finally made him colonel of a regiment which he trained and organized so well that when he was named brigadier-general, thanks to a state representative who had always been fond of him, nobody who had seen him with his soldiers was surprised. Rawlins, who sel-

30. Jefferson Davis (1808-1880), member of the House of Representatives, who resigned to serve in the Mexican War, later became U.S. Senator from Mississippi and left the Senate when Mississippi seceded. He was chosen president of the Confederacy in 1861 and later elected for six years.

31. George B. McClellan, Union general, was commissioned general-in-chief in 1861 but was removed by Lincoln in November 1862, following the battle of Antietam, because of his longstanding unwillingness to act decisively against the enemy. McClellan was the unsuccessful Democratic candidate for president; he opposed Lincoln's Emancipation Proclamation, but was defeated.

dom made mistakes, was already at his side as his secretary and adjutant "preparing him for victory." Rawlins, the veiled suggestion, the skilled but modest advice, the prudence that restrains, the word that polishes. And then was seen again the power of man to rise to the level of his difficulties.

When war was declared, the United States counted a total of 16,000 men in its armies, and when it ended five years later, Grant had under his command 1,000,561 soldiers on active duty and 2,254,000 in the reserves. Buchanan's secretary of war[32] scattered that 16,000-man army in various parts of the nation so they could not prevent the armed organization of the Confederacy which was racing the North to cover its territory with soldiers. Within a few days the North had raised an army of volunteers. The cities and states organized troops, vying with one another. The government offered each volunteer from one to four hundred dollars, and immediately there were 750,000; soon afterward 450,000 more; then another 300,000. These sudden manifestations of strength seemed even greater at the moment of appearance because of the hesitation and reluctance preceding them. The casual observer usually mistakes this for indifference, when in reality it is only the natural caution used by a marvelously prosperous nation that examines its problems thoroughly before deciding on some new course of action that could endanger the nation. An elephant takes longer to get up from the ground than a deer.

4

In the beginning almost nobody foresaw the magnitude of this tremendous war. One general laughed at another's re-

32. John B. Floyd (1807-1863) was U.S. Secretary of War from 1857 to 1960, when President Buchanan asked him to resign. He served later as brigadier of volunteers in the Confederate army.

quest for 200,000 soldiers to defend a position in the West; but in a later campaign 100,000 Federals died in a single winter between the Rapidan and the James which flow close together and in nearly a parallel course. There were no encounters where the casualties did not run into the thousands. Shiloh, Gettysburg, Antietam, Chattanooga, Wilderness, Chickahominy—which of them did not see at least 2,000 dead?

And when Grant advanced against Lee, powerful and impregnable as a moving mountain, the Federals were dying in a single field of operations from May to June at the rate of 1,000 per day. Columns, forward march! A nation fashioned by men of all nations must remain free for all men! President Lincoln set four million slaves free[33] in a promise to God to "give them their freedom if the Confederates were thrown out of Maryland." And those opposed to granting freedom to four million men must surrender, crushed for all time.

There are no political decoys that can give their cause even a semblance of right. Wars should be seen from the clouds. It is quite just for half a million human beings to have died in order to preserve for humanity the only free home it has in the world. Wavering, contriving, locked in an embrace even to make war, men must appear from up there like those living tubers, swollen with invisible worms, fighting in enormous masses, moving slowly and incessantly to break the roots of trees that may themselves be turning into tubers in a freer

33. This is not accurate. Lincoln never actually set four million slaves free. The Emancipation Proclamation issued by President Lincoln on January 1, 1863, as a military measure, gave freedom only to slaves in those states which were in rebellion against the Union, and did not apply to the border states of Delaware, Kentucky, Maryland, and Missouri, nor to that part of the Confederacy already occupied by Northern troops. The abolition of slavery for all held in bondage did not occur until the ratification of the Thirteenth Amendment later in 1865, by which time Lincoln was dead. However, there is no doubt that Lincoln's Emancipation Proclamation marked the turning point in the war, and led eventually to the total abolition of slavery.

and more animated form of life. Mankind is like a closed fist pushing from the depths of the earth to break free. Where is the man who fails to discern, in the immensity of sorrow in his rudimentary state of being, the joyous glory awaiting him after his painful but purifying passage through the world? What peace must there be to balance such a beginning! It is a moving experience to conceive of such supreme happiness, yet how few men, satisfied with their small projects, are permitted a glimpse of it from their sack of bones!

The war bursts into flame; the South hurls itself against the North; it controls the Southern coast. The Confederate capital is established at Richmond, thirty leagues from Washington, the capital of the Union. It dominates the entire Southeast: the James and the Potomac in the East, the Mississippi in the West, and the ports at the junction of the Ohio, swollen not far upstream by the Tennessee and the Cumberland. Whoever has the rivers has the victory, for rivers are the arteries of war. All the land they drain goes with them. Shutting off the Mississippi to the Federals, the Confederacy cannot have its states hemmed in by the sea on one side and the river on the other, nor can the rebel states of the East be separated from those of the West which it wants to breed slaves. How can rivers furnish water for men such as these?

By securing the mouths of the Ohio, the Tennessee, and the Cumberland, the South is assured of the central states which become the northern and western fronts in the war. Illinois, Missouri, Tennessee, and Kentucky meet at the junction of the Mississippi and Ohio rivers like the spokes of a wheel. Whoever holds the Tennessee has an open waterway to the heart of the rebel state of Alabama. Whoever holds the Cumberland has Tennessee and Kentucky. Galena is in Illinois whose southern boundary is at the mouth of the Ohio. The troops from that sector are commanded by Grant, of Galena! The Confederates move up to that hub to forestall a Federal advance, and to extend northward, with a buffer zone of defense, the territory covering their network of railroads, so necessary for transporting troops and supplies. The

railroad lines of Mississippi, Alabama, Georgia, South Carolina, and Virginia meet at Chattanooga on the Tennessee. So
the Confederates fortify the rivers. They enclose themselves
within a bastion of river and sea.

Their West is covered by the Mississippi; their North by the
Ohio, Tennessee, and Cumberland; their Eastern flank by the
Atlantic; their Southern by the Gulf of Mexico.

Vicksburg defends the Mississippi against the Federals,
Fort Henry the Tennessee, Fort Donelson the Cumberland.
Charleston protects the coast in the East, and New Orleans in
the South. In times of war it is not necessary to occupy all
points, only the principal ones. In the interior the Potomac
and James rivers, their banks crowded with campaign tents,
defend Richmond. From the outset, then, the war will be a
struggle for the rivers; the seaports are less important. The
armies willl take their names from the rivers. Their routes are
already laid out for them. If New Orleans and Charleston
must be taken by sea, Forts Henry and Donelson must be
taken by land to control the Tennessee and go down it to
Alabama. Vicksburg must be taken to occupy the Mississippi
and divide the Confederacy. The Potomac and the James
must be crossed to take Richmond.

Hence the laborious plans, the paralysis of the armies of
the North, the element of surprise, the jealousy between generals. Only the genius is unruffled by the unexpected, for
that is his natural domain. They do not see that this is a war
of size and numbers, and can be won only with size and
numbers. There is one who is aware of it, but so far he holds
his peace; there is one whom an inspired and energetic man
advises. It is not a matter of defeating a scientific, but an
intrepid enemy. Only bravery can defeat bravery. The South
has the upper hand; there is no time to produce a perfect
army. Perfect armies are not improvised. The South attacks
with its brilliant and disordered masses; they must be met, if
possible, with larger numbers. If the North stops for preparation, so will the South; and after intensive preparation both
North and South would be equal. "The first to attack will

win," said Grant at Fort Donelson, as he did throughout the war, with barely enough soldiers to use against the enemy. While the academic generals wander through the environs of the defiant Potomac, their bravery bogged down by scholarly theories, there goes Grant with his highcrowned hat and a cigar between his teeth "to be the first to attack."

Paducah is in Kentucky on the Ohio near its junction with the Tennessee. Cairo is where the Ohio and the Mississippi meet, and is the key to the West. The rebels are already raiding the loyal state of Kentucky. Grant must take the mouth of the Ohio, on the Mississippi, even before attacking Fort Henry to secure the Tennessee and Fort Donelson to secure the Cumberland. He occupies Paducah without violence. "I am not concerned with opinions," he says in his proclamation, "only with armed rebels and with those who aid and conceal them." Grant's good judgment always sensed the utility and lofty purposes of Rawlins' plans, and Rawlins put into beautiful and memorable form the confused inspirations of his chief. Grant approaches Cairo, which has 7,000 men, with only 3,000 still untried and undisciplined federal troops. The enemy comes out to meet him, the day ends in hard fighting, and he appears to have won. During that night of waiting, "my heart was in my mouth." Dawn finds him bound for Cairo, abandoned by the Confederates. "Never again did I hesitate in attacking the enemy."

5

Grant is now in command of the Cairo sector. His horse, wounded at Belmont, has recovered, and "Forts Henry and Donelson are on my mind." The general in charge of the department fails to understand his impatience. Finally Grant descends upon Fort Henry and it surrenders to the advancing fleet. Leaving 2,500 of his men there, since he now commands the mouth of the Tennessee, he marches with the remaining 15,000 against Fort Donelson which lies on a rise between two little streams emptying into the river, and from this high ground its cannon have a long range. The enemy pretends to attack Grant's center, but actually concentrates on the farthest flank of his troops. Grant leaves it there, brings his own troops to the top of a height nearby, and fires from there on the fort which is now at his mercy. Of the commanding officers who one after another abandon it, the fort finally falls from the hands of Buckner, who sues for terms. "Unconditional surrender" is the only kind Grant will accept. "Here I come, over the ramparts!" Fifteen thousand prisoners give themselves up with Buckner, and the Cumberland is Grant's—to Grant the first great victory of the war. He may take an occasional idea from others, and if he thought it good perhaps an entire plan of battle such as General Thomas' plan for Chattanooga[34] or his adjutant Rawlins' for Vicksburg; but the attack itself, the surprise maneuver, the avoidance of disaster, the unusual deployment of his troops, the immediate perception of a momentary advantage are Grant's own procedures, and for them he needed no help from others. Hesitate? The rocks upon which he unleashed the battle may hesitate, but not he. With Grant it was his "insensitivity to danger," not courage. It never occurred to him that he could be defeated. Delayed, yes; but never defeated. The attack shatters the enemy's front lines, but tenacity wins the battle. Where other generals withdraw, Grant stays his ground and wins. Now their hands are around his throat; the dead lie so thick around him that his horse has no place to put its hoofs; they have him backed up against a river. But he

34. General George Henry Thomas (1816-1870), Union general who, in defending his position at Chickamauga when the rest of the army retreated, was given the nickname "the Rock of Chickamauga." He commanded the Army of the Republic with Grant at the Battle of Chattanooga.

concentrates his forces, smokes his cigar, calmly awaits the reinforcements that are sure to arrive, and gathers his men about his cannon. "I will defeat them!" he says, and he does.

So it went at Shiloh, leaving the South astonished at such power of resistance, and the North appalled at such slaughter. Despite the Fort Donelson victory, the general in charge of the department, a straitlaced man, relieves him of his command "because he has returned to his old bad habits," the general said, referring to his drinking. But Rawlins convinces the general of his mistake, and Grant is reinstated. The Confederates do not want Grant, supported by reinforcements, to go down the Tennessee and threaten one of their railroads. At a time when he is away from the camp and his officers off guard, they attack the Union forces who here stand fast, there fall in droves, elsewhere desert. Shiloh was "terrible." But Grant has come in time, and with his calm and courage manages to keep the lines of his Federals unbroken until nightfall. With his remaining troops he fires on the advancing enemy, thus preparing the charge he plans as soon as reinforcements arrive. These appear at an opportune moment, and with their aid he scatters the Confederates. But his victory is shocking. The element of surprise is attributed to an oversight, or to some miscalculation. His chief mistrusts him. In Washington, where he never sought friends, the armchair strategists have little regard for him. Those who suspect his strength attack him. Washington is a hotbed of intrigue throughout the war.

Jealousy can be disguised by patriotism. The incompetent put stumbling blocks in the way of the competent. What do they care about their country? They worry that someone may gain the upper hand over them. Men whose desires overshadow their abilities, or whose ambition outweighs their patriotism, think more of their jobs or status than of saving their country. These factors, together with the jealousies resulting from the war with Mexico, caused Grant to justly resent the appointing of men to high places, a habit that paralyzed the war effort and deprived him of his finest troops. And so this hatred for Washington was building up in him—a hatred composed of fear and scorn that was finally to be toned down by the wisdom and greatness of Lincoln. Yet Grant was not able to forget, or he had no desire to do so, which may explain that *conquistador* manner of his in which his personal wishes mingled with certain crude instincts of honesty. It was not until he came to enjoy too much authority, which his people only slightly begrudged him, that he became so fond of Washington that he turned into the personification of its dangers and vices. But after Shiloh the good offices of the man who commissioned him brigadier restored his command. In those days when Grant felt himself unheeded, and perhaps forever put off the road to victory, his gray eyes would sometimes become misty. Men who concentrate everything in themselves suffer greatly.

He was again at the head of his army, and was not to relinquish his command until at the gates of defeated Richmond where, with his natural magnanimity, he refused to enter as a conquering hero. He led his army. He held the Tennessee. The generals of the Potomac and the James either won or lost, but they did not cross those rivers. Not so with Grant: he crossed them all! Now on to Vicksburg, sentinel of the Mississippi!

It had been a mistake to divide into small units, whose movements were exposed and difficult, an army that must rout an enemy concentrated in formidable positions. The general who concentrates his forces has the distinct advantage of compelling the enemy to give or receive battle on the ground of his choosing. There is a vast difference between fighting where the enemy has been prepared to make a stand, and where he has to go hastily and without warning. Grant has always been in favor of forcing the enemy to give battle. There is no danger in concentrating; the enemy must also concentrate, and not go off on raiding expeditions when its own vital points are threatened.

Grant moves his forces on Vicksburg: his own troops, Sheridan's,[35] and the reinforcements from Washington.

He goes by land, with the enemy cavalry close behind. He moves along the river under the eyes of an anguished nation awaiting the outcome. Vicksburg is surrounded on every side by marshland. Where to engage the enemy in battle? Where to pitch camp so that the tide will not come up to the soldiers' knees? A canal to bypass Vicksburg to the south was impractical.

The North becomes impatient with the delay.

In Washington there is talk of a change in command. "God bless him," Lincoln says to Charles Dana,[36] present editor of the *New York Sun* as he leaves Washington for Vicksburg, traveling through the enemy lines, since there is no other way to go, to see what is happening there. He arrives. He sees being done what should be done. Rawlins proposed running the enemy batteries down river, for there is no alternative. "Madness!" say the other commanders, but the madness must finally be attempted. The army descends the Mississippi under the cannon of Vicksburg and another fort to the south; the troops disembark. Grant attacks Jackson[37] to the east where he routs a strong Confederate force. He throws back the rebel troops when they come out from behind the impregnable ramparts at Vicksburg. The garrison is starving, and surrenders.

35. Philip Henry Sheridan (1831-1888), Union cavalry general, famous for his ride from Winchester to Cedar Creek in 1864 and for leading his Army across the Confederate line of retreat from Appomattox, helping to force Lee's surrender in 1865.

36. Charles Anderson Dana (1819-1897), managing editor of the *New York Tribune* (1847-1862), Assistant Secretary of War (1963-1864), and especially noted as editor and owner of the *New York Sun* (1868-1897).

37. Thomas Jonathan ("Stonewall") Jackson (1824-1863), Confederate general who was known for his outstanding generalship. Jackson was wounded in battle by fire from his own troops on May 2, 1863, and died eight days later.

6

The Mississippi lies open to the Federals with 27,000 enemy soldiers and 120 cannon captured. The skies of every state in the North redden with victory bonfires. A committee of "Christian gentlemen" chooses that very moment to approach Lincoln and ask him if it is true—oh, childish fanaticism!—that Grant is given to drink. "I really cannot say," replies Lincoln, stroking his beard, "but if he is, I would like to know where he buys his brandy, so I could send a barrel of it to every one of his generals." And the Christian gentlemen go away peevishly. Meanwhile Grant, having been made commander of the entire district, was flying to save the Union troops under siege in Chattanooga, a coveted eminence on the banks of the Tennessee, that gathers together as in a fist all the railroad lines moving from the Southern forces and carrying meat and grain from the valleys to the armies of Virginia; Chattanooga, where the South unmercifully persecutes the brave mountain folk who are loyal to the Union. Chattanooga lies between two bluffs bursting with Confederates who are calmly awaiting its fall. The Federals' only means of escape is the river watched over by their enemies. The road by which they receive reinforcements and supplies is filled with the Confederate advance guard. The summits of Lookout Mountain and Missionary Ridge look down upon Chattanooga like two giants watching a child. Grant arrives at night in a tremendous downpour. He must be carried along in the arms of his soldiers from time to time, because he is crippled by a riding fall. How can one describe those glorious events? Grant deploys his forces over Chattanooga without overlooking a single detail, or relinquishing an inch of valuable ground, or leaving the road behind Chattanooga exposed, or alerting the enemy which, with consummate stupidity and confident of driving the assailants back from their lofty citadels, comes to block the advance of a supporting column bound for Chattanooga. Thomas' plan will be carried out by the troops commanded by Grant with such foresight and dexterity—Thomas, who replies to Grant's order to "hold Chattanooga at all costs," with "I'll hold the city till we starve." The day arrives, a fine day inviting victory. But mist envelops the summit of the higher of the two fortresses. Without the enemy's knowledge, the Federals have crossed the river on pontoons, and have taken a few hills below the mountain from which they begin their attack upon the fortress. Thomas leaves the city and makes a successful frontal assault upon a nearby position. Up Lookout Mountain go the Federals with fixed bayonets shining in the sun. To those below it looks like a silver snake winding its way upward on its belly! The assault is irresistible. A cannonball splits the ranks the way lightning splits clouds; the ranks close again like clouds after a thunderbolt. The attacking troops finally reach the fogshrouded summit and are almost lost to view. The terrified gunners are given the finishing stroke beside their cannon. Entire regiments surrender. The Confederate soldiers flee down the mountainside as their own guns are turned against them by the Federals who win "the battle above the clouds." The other height, Missionary Ridge, remains to be won, and they do so at bayonet point. The steep slope is covered with redoubts, trenches, rifle pits, and blinds. Farther up the slope Sheridan's troops break ranks. Flags wave against the blue sky in a hundred places at once. The soldiers leap and bound like Alvarado,[38] ditch over ditch, trench over trench, attacking everything in Confederate hands at once. Missionary Ridge, taken at the crest itself, surrenders to the Federals. They count their dead: 7,000 in this battle alone!

The rivers of the West are won; now to the rivers of the East.

38. Pedro de Alvarado (1485-1541), Spanish Cavalier, companion to Hernando Cortes in the conquest of Mexico. During an attack on the Spanish forces by the Indians, Alvarado saved his life, according to tradition, by leaping across the great gap in the causeway in Mexico, at the spot later called "Alvarado's Leap."

Applauded by the nation, Congress revives in Grant's honor the rank of lieutenant-general, and bestows upon him the distinction held in the United States by Washington alone. Lincoln promised him full support, "as God is my witness," and places Grant in command of all the Union forces, scattered at the time,. because of bad tactics of former commanders, into isolated armies that harry the enemy and hold it at bay but never enter its camps or reduce the field of operations, or disrupt its communication systems, or divide its forces, or prevent it from defending several positions with the same soldiers, or break its fighting spirit, which as long as it lasts will keep the destiny undecided.

The Mississippi and Tennessee are open, but the banks of the Potomac and James are still bristling with Confederate tents; Richmond still stands defiant ninety miles from Washington; Lee and his undefeated army of 80,000 still operate between Washington and Richmond; Johnston still commands a formidable army in defense of Atlanta and her railroads that still move the men and supplies of the Confederacy; there are still nine million men obeying the laws of Richmond, a city being defended by more than half a million soldiers within an area of 800,000 square miles. The roads of war converge on Virginia and Georgia, protecting Atlanta to the west. The land between is filled with Southern marauders and the disengaged columns pursuing them.

7

Grant does not return to the West as Sherman asks him to do "for the love of God," lest the conspirators in Washington strip him of his fame. He does not tarry in Washington where the battlefield is far away and he fears he may be defeated by "those in my own house." No, he goes off "to water my horse in the Potomac and the James." Lee's Army of the Potomac has never been defeated; Grant sets out to defeat it.

No more uncoordinated attacks; no more periods of leisure when the enemy is free to help the plantation Negroes sow summer crops to provide provisions for the following winter; no more useless assaults on villages, or even on Richmond. "The military might of the South must be broken once and for all" to pursue the enemy, harass it, bottle it up, drain it of resources, exhaust it. The Union forces must attack in a body, from everywhere at once, and destroy the Confederate armies still redoubtable for their bravery and numbers. He must march against them incessantly, in all seasons; keep constant pressure upon them from all sides, so that no sooner could they use their forces to defend one position than they would have to use them to protect another. Not a day without fighting; not a day without moving a step forward. Sherman advances on the confederate nucleus of Georgia so that when he is victorious, he will be able to join the nucleus facing Lee in the east. An army from the north descends upon Lee in the east, and another cuts off his retreat in the south. Grant now has everything planned, and he made the secretary of war understand and respect this most emphatically before leaving Washington. Against Lee, then, from every quarter, always keeping Washington protected during the march on Richmond! "I am going to subdue him, cut off all his retreats, pound him with repeated strikes, hit him incessantly like a hammer." Whereupon he attacks Lee[39] with his 130,000 men from May of one year to June of the next. Seated on a log, he orders all corps to begin marching as the first battle commences. And at the height of the Wilderness battle where the generals, confused in the midst of unfamiliar territory, suffered casualties of 2,261 dead and 8,758 wounded, news arrives from all the generals of the divisions: the

39. Robert Edward Lee (1807-1870), Confederate general who resigned from the U.S. army to become commander of Virginia's forces at the outbreak of the Civil War and rose to be general-in-chief of the Confederate army. The final battles between Grant and Lee were among the most decisive of the war.

march that leads Sherman from victory to victory all the way to the sea, and that leads Grant to the gates of Richmond, has begun! Never did a general move so large an army as did Grant at that time. Rawlins was no longer at his side, and Grant's attacks were less brilliant; but not his talent for organizing, or his endless patience, or his ability to dictate each night from his tent the following day's orders for four armies, and this sometimes in defeat.

Grant fights Lee not like a general who plans, but like a huge advancing mass. Lee may come out to meet him, as he does, each time Grant tries to force his hand. Grant cannot make a move that Lee does not anticipate; and when he thinks he has outwitted him, there is Lee, ready and waiting, but each time more exhausted than the time before. This campaign is unprecedented! What kind of warmaking is this? When Grant sets out to do something, he does it. Once, a dozen times, Lee's courageous and spirited forces repulse him; Grant turns his horse around, and a little farther downstream he tries again, never looking back at the 50,000 dead he leaves behind in slightly over a month. And in the long run he can say: "What I attempted to do, I did."

Grant's entire campaign against Lee's Army of the Potomac, which ended the war, used this type of strategy. Onward, onward; no spectacular battles, just bewildering strikes. Today one river, tomorrow another; a trench today, another tomorrow. Lee is gradually forced to retreat to Richmond, defended by the improvised fortifications that he erects wherever he makes camp. But how can the South, disheartened and demoralized, with the enemy closing in on all sides, with Atlanta in Sherman's hands and the four railroad lines converging upon Richmond either taken or soon to be taken, give to its leader, eager to avoid useless bloodshed, those hundreds of thousands of fresh strong men whom the North, determined like Grant to end the war as quickly as possible, puts so generously at his disposal? Grant is now at Petersburg, a bulwark for Richmond. He has lost 100,000 men in less than a year, it is true, but Lee's lines have dwindled to such an extent that "there are barely enough men for sentry duty." Grant assaults the last of the Confederate strongholds, outside Petersburg, hoping to bring Lee to his knees before he can join forces with Johnston, who is leading his defeated army north from Georgia. Lee attempts one last drive upon Washington to lift the siege that is strangling him, and Sheridan, who always sleeps fully clothed and with a map in his hand, flies on horseback to his already retreating troops. "It's nothing! It's nothing!" he tells a soldier who has just received a bullet in the brain; and the dying man replies: "No, General; it's nothing," and struggles onward. Lee's cavalry falls back in defeat; Five Forks is the final battle. Jefferson Davis is at a church service in Richmond when he receives the news from Lee that Richmond and Petersburg must be evacuated that very night. Some days later on the ninth of April, Lee goes sadly at the head of his generals to surrender his sword, so often victorious, to Grant who treats him as a friend and refuses to accept it.

Grant had no patience with the arts of war, nor did it seem that in attacks requiring imagination and brilliance he had many to use. But he never intended to wage a war "based upon book learning"; his purpose was to save lives, finish quickly, and annihilate the military power of the South. They called him "butcher" because he watched his men die by the thousands without withdrawing from his positions, to which he would reply that to prolong the war because of these considerations would bring about a greater loss of life in the long run. He realized that if he set his enormous force against a debilitated enemy, he could bring it to its knees, and that is just what he did. Is the object of war to fight brilliantly or to defeat the enemy? He was lacking in instruction, was little endowed with imagination and slow in conception, yet he saw the overall picture, the great contours, the reasons for enemy strength, the new approaches demanded by a kind of war never before experienced. So he destroyed the enemy's strength with that perceptiveness, his one objective being to deliver to the Union the rebels defeated once and for all, while at the same time never staining a victory with a single act of inclemency or injustice. At Appomattox, because of the modesty of his attire and bearing, and the humility of his remarks, it seemed that he and not Lee was the defeated. He arranged the terms of peace as he had conducted the war: unenthusiastically and without rancor. He sensed his accomplishments, but in his still undeveloped pride, all he saw at the time was that he had done "what I set out to do."

8

It is true that at the beginning of the war Grant had Rawlins to advise him, ponder situations, put down intrigue, propose plans of action, and direct battles. It is true that, whether due to Rawlins' good counsel or his own, he no sooner had taken command than he surrounded himself with men of character like himself—men who owed nothing to intrigue and hated it as he did, which fact, in addition to Grant's fine qualities, drew them to him. It is true that in Washington he had Lincoln, a child of Nature more than any other, a soul "beloved of man" who always knew how to distinguish between him and the jealous generals and politicians who, without Lincoln's influence, and caring little for their country, might have relieved him of his command. It is true that he was backed by a nation having the same origin and inclinations as himself, and that supplied his ranks with the generosity and determination in keeping with the size of the struggle, and pleased to recognize its own spirit in that man who had advanced and conquered. It is true, as his most sympathetic biographers point out, that fate was lavish with that man who did not always show the foresight expected of him, or save the blood he should have saved, or hesitate to compensate for his oversights and blunders by victories won sometimes at the cost of horrendous sacrifice. Yet looking at

that astounding war with the higher sensitivity gained from
intimate knowledge of it, one observes nothing supernatural,
and it emerges as one of the most complete and spontaneous
of human expressions, perhaps achieved with the most consummate artistry thus far known to man, inasmuch as in that
war the elements of the struggle, with its agents and methods
in perfect analogy, had been powerfully developed in the
warmth of a limited freedom.

Truly historical events are those which not only reflect all
of human nature, but most particularly the characteristics of
the age and nation in which they occur. Take the events out
of their age and nation and they cease to be fruitful or even
grandiose.

Neither men nor events achieve permanent greatness unless
they assimilate an age or a nation.

In its wise and cautious determination, in the sudden and
awesome assembling of its armies, in the trust in facts instead
of theory that characterized the men who gained renown in
them; in the initially disorganized and almost unprofessional
(and later blind and brutal) way the war was conducted; in
the very magnanimity of its leader at the height of combat
and during the bloodiest victory—there never ceased to be an
absolute analogy between the spirit, methods, and formation
of the North and the spirit, methods, and formation of the
war. Attempts to introduce unnatural or exotic elements
were eclipsed by this relationship. A meteoric country of
immense size and tolerant, industrial habits quite naturally
gave rise to a meteoric war, brought on more by humanitarian aims than by the powerful internal dissatisfaction with
the political differences that influenced it. It was a war regarded throughout its course and in its conclusion in terms of
public interest, and carried on with all the enormous resources consistent with the magnitude of the struggle and its
combatants, but without the cruelty still frequent in those
more artistic and literary nations which have not yet been
shaped by the constant and orderly expression of free will, so
ennobling and strengthening to men's character.

The North waged a war that was enormous, improvised, unschooled, original, and noble, as was the nation responsible for it in those days—a nation born of poverty and deprivation as were its people, as was the leader who gave it his natural and ingenuous spirit and freed it from the extraneous and academic. Like his nation he devoted more time and energy to direct and productive efforts than to ineffective and secondary book learning. He replaced imported and conventional ideas with new ideas that Nature suggested to him in virgin fields of interest and in local conditions. And like his people he always threw himself fully into the object of his desires, firm and unyielding as the mountains.

Like his nation and to a far greater extent, he sullied his glory with unsound political practices. Since his tannery days he had won such honors through his own efforts that to properly recognize them, Congress created the title of general, never attained even by Washington, in spite of what he represented in the United States.

This was not love but a kind of frenzied worship. Here was a man regarded by his fellow citizens as lord and savior of their home, so that Grant accumulated such a supply of affection that his greatest mistakes were soon pardoned. It seemed as if his country were encouraging his mistakes for the sheer pleasure of forgiving them. He lacked that virile aloofness that men in public life should probably have, although it would have been difficult for him to maintain it, since the entire nation held him in such deep affection. Cities and citizens competed with gifts and donations for the savior of the Union; New York gave him a hundred thousand dollars, Philadelphia twenty thousand; Galena presented him with a beautifully furnished house which Boston filled with books. Wherever he went his path was strewn with roses. During the war, when they wanted to draft him to run against Lincoln, he said that his only political desire was to be mayor of his own city so he could repair the sidewalk leading from the railroad station to his house. When he arrived in Galena, the entire town was at the station to meet

him, and with the greatest enthusiasm he was escorted to his
new home on the repaired sidewalk.

9

Whoever imagined that Grant would be satisfied with those
tranquil honors did not know the silent floorpacer of five
years before. A man's mood in times of peace is more
troublesome than in the fortunes of war. The pent-up energy,
the repressed activity, the very different personality, and the
confused animosity against the good turn of events that went
unrecognized or counter to those who, willingly or not, aided
the bad turn of events, had now found ample outlets and
natural employment. That violent and expansive nature of his
was not suited to repose; it had to be constantly supplied
with attack and conquest—never with speech, of course,
where in both war and peace he was always much too tight-
lipped with anyone who did not enjoy his intimate confidence, but with action. He no longer found politics disagreeable, since he never had to pursue it; this would have been
against his nature. On the contrary, politics came knocking
on his door. President Johnson asked him to put back into
order the war machine he had had in his hands; Republicans
and Democrats alike proposed to use his prestige to win the
presidential elections, then soon to come. After the assassination of the man whose name will always be spoken in rever-
ent praise, he served in Johnson's cabinet[40] until the Senate,
at odds with the president, refused to confirm the appointment. His subsequent withdrawal earned him the respect of

40. Abraham Lincoln was assassinated by John Wilkes Booth at the
Ford Theater, Washington, D.C., and died the next day, April 15, 1865.
He was succeeded in the presidency by Andrew Johnson (1808-1875),
who had been elected Vice-President on the Union-Republican ticket in
1864.

the governing body and enhanced his glory. By thus bowing to the nation's will through its legislative organ, his candidacy was assured. The Democratic nomination was his for the asking, but the shrewd politician Thurlow Weed,[41] as the principal item on a luncheon agenda, offered him the Republican nomination. For now that Lincoln was dead, "the only way to definitively stamp out the spirit of secession is to head the Union government with the man who had just saved it with his sword." President he became, under the Republican banner,[42] although in the election before the war he had voted for that most uncompromising Democrat, Buchanan.

Who is this curious and changeable man, ignorant of the most elementary laws of the Republic and of the graces and courtesies of government; totally oblivious to the difference between the private rights and the public authority of the president of a nation; incapable of understanding the indispensable relationship between positions of national importance and the individuals appointed to fill them? Who is this dictatorial and defiant man who brings to the administration of a country, jealous of its freedom and self-respect, all the frankness and ill-humored informality that the special nature and purposes of war permit and even demand? It is Grant, who wears his campaign boots in the White House, and does wrong. There is no more complicated and subtle task than governing, nor one requiring more experience in world affairs, demanding more compliance and wisdom. Instinct alone is not enough; one must have knowledge and a genius for detail. Genius is accumulated knowledge. A president should have experienced all kinds of conditions in order to be kindly and just, according to different norms, with men of all classes and circumstances.

There should be the highest degree of awareness of one's

41. Thurlow Weed (1797-1882), journalist and New York Republican leader, editor of the *New York Commercial Advertiser*.
42. Grant was elected in 1868, defeating the Democratic candidate, Horatio Seymour.

own rights as well as respect for the rights of others; and the latter should awaken a livelier and more delicate sense than the former. Abuse of the first can only result in weakness, but abuse of the second can lead to despotism.

It goes without saying that the president does not use funds from the national treasury for the benefit of his family and friends, or shape the nation to his own liking, or numb the spirit of the laws by neglect or misapplication. He must govern with integrity, applying the laws his people give him, without taking for himself or for his friends and relatives what the nation entrusts to him for safekeeping. Government is obedience.

All that lives expresses itself. Whatever is repressed over-flows. Let us look into this man's character. That he was someone to contend with was quite obvious in the war. He complemented his own qualities with the judgment, wisdom, and eloquence of others, but while he pretended not to understand them, he built upon their suggestions and freely borrowed or rejected what he considered prudent; this to such a degree that no sooner was he somewhat free of that excellent Rawlins than his individuality began to assert itself. As early as Chattanooga he was starting to be annoyed by the contrast between his adjutant's noble qualities and his own lack of them. He gave orders incessantly, without effort or ostentation, as if it were a natural thing to do. He neither sought nor heeded advice, as if he wanted to prove he had no need of it. And just as in the war where he conceived the simple and effective idea of winning by means of numbers, thus obtaining the troops he required, so he admired and was pleased with himself, taking it for granted that men should compare him with the greatest military leaders of all time, sometimes even placing him above them. Who had commanded more soldiers? Who had defeated such a powerful enemy with fewer ideas borrowed from outside sources? Who in a war had produced so many freed men on the one hand, and such a prosperous nation on the other? Throughout the war—and several incidents confirm this—he had won his victories fearing and speaking ill of "those in Washington," of those who were unfair to the fighting man, of the armchair strategists in league with the professional politicians, of the politicians themselves. He had ample cause to speak ill of them, but he did this without the necessary ingredient of justice. He failed to see that Lincoln was a "politician"; "politicians" to him were men who wanted to put Rosecrans[43] or McClellan above him. Sherman, a man passionately fond of justice and like Grant a product of Nature, exacerbated his horror of those who gave preferential positions to people ill-equipped to fulfill them. When they passed through Washington during the war, Grant made himself perfectly plain. "No, this time the commander-in-chief is going to direct the war; Washington has done nothing but delay and hamper it at every turn." And it was a fact.

10

In the war his command brooked no contradiction. He had to be very fond of anyone who contradicted him, to tolerate it. Little by little the members of his staff, anxious to stay in his good graces, made it a rule never to contradict him. Rawlins was the exception, and this irked Grant. Once peace had come, the greatest nation in peace and the noblest in war in the world of his day sang his praises continuously as they had never been sung of any man before, and he felt he deserved them.

So Grant became President of the Republic, the highest political post in the land, with these qualities: an abomination of politics and an accumulated animosity toward all who

43. William Starke Rosecrans (1819-1898), aide-de-camp to General George B. McClellan, succeeded McClellan as commanding general of the department of the Ohio and later as chief of the new department of western Virginia.

embodied it; an overcomplacent personality and a constant desire for expansion, conquest, and action; a pampered habit of giving orders without opposition, and a total lack of the habit of obedience; contempt for every well-defined and progressive law, and a meteoric career outside of the natural and orderly operation of law; the habit of seeing everything from his own point of view and as if accomplished by his will and in conformity with it.

This was the man of instinct who, because of an uninhibited personality or an excessive attachment to Nature, stemming from sincerity or crudity, refused to benefit from the civilizing effects of man's work throughout history. Carried along by his natural strength and by timely strokes of luck to the complexities of government, which include in precise and active practice the most perfect discoveries and results of human culture, he broke to pieces against it, since he was unable to shatter a country skilled in defending its interests and stronger than he.

There are other primary and natural characters, born directly or indirectly from Nature, who have something more than mere strength, as in Grant's case, and a certain generosity that always accompanies it. Lincoln, Garfield,[44] and even Rawlins shone brightly among primary characters, for they had intellect and beauty and from these qualities the capacity and active need of assimilating the whole of human accomplishment. The ultimate greatness in these superior characters is the inevitable result of the union of these qualities with an extraordinary will; whereas in characters of strength alone, it is simply an accident and as blind as strength itself, requiring for its realization adventitious circumstances outside the nature of the individual.

It is quite normal for a man to think of himself; his exis-

44. James Abram Garfield (1831-1881), Union brigadier-general during the Civil War, Republican leader after the war, and elected president on the Republican ticket in 1880. Garfield was shot by Charles Guiteau on July 2, 1881, and died September 9, 1881.

tence inexorably and cruelly forces him to do so. Some men develop a "self-centeredness," when fortune is on their side, that is odious in its scope and tenacity, for it engenders egoists in private life and despots in government. Yet there are others who view themselves as a message to be communicated, an indignation to be vented, or a charitable act to be done. They give their precedent in their lives to human betterment, and only then begin thinking of themselves; and suffer sharply, as if conscience-stricken, until they have made their message known, vented their indignation, or done their charitable act openly.

But even when primary characters are not disinterested, a bond of originality draws them closer to those who are disinterested than to the general run of men. Although they usually abominate and combat by all possible means those whose strength is embellished by intellectuality and beauty, who in turn detest and censure as monstrosities persons possessed of strength alone, these nevertheless have a capacity for moments of personal and conscious greatness that seems to be denied them through most of their lives. But no sooner are they exposed to disinterested characters or to some favorable condition, than an intellectual and spiritual greatness emerges from its opaque and rudimentary state, as if simple energy were the raw material out of which intelligence and beauty are made. Then careers based on strength shine with a fresh, soft, and penetrating light that men of good will and purpose leave in their wake, ennobling and expanding them.

And what a country Grant was about to govern with the disdain for others, the self-indulgence, and the headstrong mind he had developed from the plain hard facts of war! Certainly a nation in danger where the consciousness of power and the hunger for wealth imperil national decorum, the independence of neighboring countries, and even the human spirit itself. But nonetheless a great country where man realizes his potential and fulfills himself with nothing to hinder him beyond the natural limits imposed by coexistence with his fellow beings; where the sublime spectacle of a peaceful nation embarking upon a tremendous war for the sake of human decency had just been witnessed; where Grant himself saw 250,000 men march back to their homes through the streets of Washington with their flags in tatters, their uniforms torn, their arms and legs maimed, yet glowing with victory. It is a nation where questions are asked and answered, where no man is above public scrutiny; for his every act is probed to the core, and if he should be found wanting, it will go hard with him. It is a nation of prayer meetings where men and women are taught in church to confess their sins before the congregation, to denounce the sins of their neighbors, and to ask the pastor to clarify their doubts on points of dogma. It is a land where newspapers are living things, and no sooner does a cause emerge than it has its organ to which all who are interested have equal access. Therefore there is no injustice or suspicion without a voice, and a newspaper to publish it, and a body of opinion ready to censure it. A nation infatuated, it is true, with a man as martial, stubborn, and aggressive as itself, which had crushed its rivals and opened the way to the greatest prosperity the world has ever known; but above all, a nation that denounces and overthrows whoever curtails or threatens its rights.

The political career with which Grant tarnished the memory of his magnanimous deeds during the war was distressing, from its violent beginnings all through the compromises and transgressions that followed.

11

From the very first he behaved in keeping with his hatred for politics and his animosity toward the men who represented it, convinced that he was doing the right thing; yet by his manner of proceeding, he gave childish proof of his ignorance of the laws and the sense of decency inspiring them. Because he wanted to surround himself with advisers who were not professional politicians, he appointed a well-known businessman as secretary of the treasury.[45] The loyal friend who had him named brigadier and restored to the command of his army became secretary of state.[46] He named an obscure businessman secretary of the navy,[47] and a certain Williams, who by some shady means rose from village judge to senator, became attorney general.[48] But in the terrible and unfamiliar loneliness of supreme power, where Grant realized he was both ignorant and under scrutiny, he turned to his faithful friend of perpetually sound advice: Rawlins, whose nearness to death, which overtook him soon afterward, did not prevent him from gallantly responding to the call and acting as intimate adviser to his chief while he lived near him as secretary of war. And as long as Rawlins remained in the cabinet, thieves and bad advisers never crossed the threshold, although

45. The reference is to A. T. Stewart, the department store king of New York and the nation's greatest merchant, with a fortune of nearly fifty millions, a lavish contributor to his campaign fund and one of the principal donors of a $65,000 house for Grant. But it was discovered that a law of 1789 forbade persons engaged in commerce to hold that post. The Senate refused a request by Grant that Stewart be excepted from the law, and his name had to be withdrawn.

46. Elihu Benjamin Washburne (1816-1887) had helped forward the military fortunes of Grant during the Civil War and was appointed Secretary of State. However, it was mainly a gesture since, appointed March 5, 1869, Washburne resigned March 10 and vacated the office on March 26 to become Minister to France. He was replaced by Hamilton Fish.

47. Adolph E. Borie, a wealthy retired merchant enriched by the East India trade and one of the leading contributors to a house for Grant in Philadelphia, was appointed Secretary of the Navy even though he knew nothing of the position and made it clear he did not want the appointment.

48. Martí is in error here. Ebenezer Rockwood Hoar (1816-1895) who was appointed the first Attorney-General had been for ten years a justice of the Massachusetts Supreme Court. Martí is referring to the later appointment of George H. Williams of Oregon, a relatively obscure lame-duck senator, as Attorney-General.

they did wait for a propitious time from afar. After Rawlins had gone, how was that man who scorned such complicated matters and knew nothing about them going to govern? He drifted with the wind like a lost ship. He frowned upon those who sought to give him advice, and rejected their proposals, but in spite of himself he had to seek opinions on matters outside his sphere of knowledge—matters upon which he had to be informed. By so doing he inadvertently became the tool of men who gave him biased advice and convinced him that their ideas originated with him.

Vanity has sensitive vitals, flattery some incredible arts. The man who praised Grant controlled him; he could not endure anyone who did not. He gave everything that was asked to those who pretended to believe in him, and being a man guided by instinct, he gave it with a singular loyalty, even at the risk of his honor. What can a man ignorant in the ways of government be but the natural prey of those who are aware of his defects and play upon them?

His self-complacency persuaded him that the government belonged to him as well as to the nation, which could not exist without him; that there would be no guidance unless he were the guide. He saw all his henchmen and all who defended his person and desires as extensions of himself. As if obeying a national edict, he saw to it that no relative, or friend of a relative, was left without a high position, which soon earned his government the title of "the government of in-laws." Some men out of admiration too freely bestowed, and others out of a desire to curry favor, followed his wishes to the letter, and zealously carried out his novel and autocratic orders, as long as they remained within the law. Or they catered to the desires of his powerful flatterers who used him to overthrow their political enemies in the North, or to establish there the fear of a resumption of war in the South, and of the elections assuring it. Even his natural magnanimity toward the rebels, which could not have been greater, was poisoned by those who represented the legitimate resistance of the defeated states to abuses in federal policies. To such an extent did they encourage Grant's habit of command and reluctance to heed advice or duty, that he went as far as to adopt an iniquitous plan—discovered in time and stopped—to muzzle the free press that criticized him, by establishing in Washington a special court of tractable judges to pass upon cases of "crimes" in the political press throughout the nation.

Spurred on by his desire for expansion and advance, and in keeping with his ignorance of the form and spirit of the laws, he ordered his private secretary, on the pretext of inspecting the Bay of Samana, to sign a treaty of annexation with the government of Santo Domingo,[49] circumventing regular diplomatic channels. In the Senate Sumner protested indignantly both against the violence of such a plan,[50] which would make

49. An effort to annex the Negro republic of Santo Domingo had been made during Johnson's administration, but, despite the pressure of businessmen who were deeply interested in exploiting the resources of the island, it had ended in failure. Grant, an advocate of national expansion, sent General Orville E. Babcock, private secretary to the Chief Executive, to Santo Domingo on a warship with definite instructions to resume negotiations for annexation. Babcock was connected with American businessmen who held speculative concessions in Santo Domingo, the value of which would be greatly enhanced by annexation. He met with President Buenaventura Báez according to instructions and, on September 4, 1869, signed an agreement providing for a treaty of annexation between the United States and the Dominican Republic. The agreement contained a specific promise that Grant would "use all his influence, in order that the idea of annexing the Dominican Republic to the United States may acquire such a degree of popularity among members of Congress as will be necessary for accomplishment; and he offers to make no communications to that body on the subject until he shall be certain that it will be approved by a majority."

50. On September 6, 1869, Babcock left the Dominican Republic. When he arrived in Washington with his plan for a definitive treaty of annexation, Grant immediately set out to line up senatorial support. With this in mind, he visited Sumner, then chairman of the Senate Committee on Foreign Relations, and returned to the White House fully convinced that Sumner would back the treaty of annexation. But

it appear that a weak country had been subjected to the ambitions of a powerful expansionist, and against the danger to a government of republican institutions when the president usurps the authority that rightfully belongs to the nation alone. To gain support for this plan of usurpation, Grant entered into secret agreements with both houses of Congress, and secretly promised to support certain reprehensible projects in exchange for the votes he needed in support of annexation and his method of handling it.[51] It was a sorry affair in more ways than one. Not only was there the spectacle of the nation that stands for freedom in this world being prepared to violate—as in fact she did violate—the freedom of a gallant albeit small country, but there was the logical suspicion that a ring of speculators, familiar with Grant's spirit of conquest and expansion, had inspired him with the idea of annexation, intending to reap the profits for themselves while leaving him out of it.

Sumner began to see the motives of the business interests behind the treaty of annexation and became convinced that the Dominicans did not want to surrender their independence. He maintained that the independence of Santo Domingo was of vital importance to the Negro people the world over, and he feared that Haiti's independence would be menaced by the annexation of the Dominican Republic.

51. Since Sumner's views were supported by a large group of senators, it soon became evident that Grant would encounter difficulty in securing ratification of the treaty and he tried by every possible means, including promises to support pet projects of senators, to win the necessary votes. But he was unsuccessful. On June 30, 1870, when the vote was taken in the Senate, it resulted in a tie—twenty-eight to twenty-eight. Since a two-thirds vote was required for ratification, the treaty was defeated. Hitting back at Sumner, Grant ordered John Lathrop Motley, minister to England and one of Sumner's closest associates, to give up his post. Later Grant's senatorial friends retaliated further by stripping Sumner of his post as chairman of the Senate Foreign Relations Committee.

12

And so during Grant's first term of office, and again during his second, the government drifted along without a compass. He was reelected because of his personal candor which made him appear innocent, as indeed he was, of the abuses his enemies committed because of his blind attachment to his loyal supporters, and because of the deeprooted love his nation felt for him as its most valued hero. It felt secure with his presence in the White House, since the South still seethed with resentment. But for all that, when following his second election there was talk of assuring him of a third, an outcry of fear and anger arose that cowed even his boldest adherents. The public was adamant in refusing to blame Grant for his secretaries' scandalous frauds, in which his own brother and his nearest relatives appeared to be implicated on occasion; for the thefts of public monies authorized to the major corporations by Treasury officials who stood to gain by the scheme; for transgressions later revealed by the swindlers themselves, who claimed that their tax payments had not been made to the national treasury because they had been applied to the campaign expenses of Grant's third term.[52] As long as Grant lived, the American people persist-

52. During the 1872 campaign the Crédit Mobilier scandal broke out, revealing that shares in that railroad holding company had been distributed among senators and congressmen; this was followed during Grant's second term by the uncovering of the "Whisky Ring" in St. Louis which had defrauded the government of millions of dollars in internal revenue, and led to the trial of Orville Babcock, Grant's private secretary. This then was followed by the revelation of corruption in the appropriation of funds for the Indians and led to the resignation of Secretary of War W. E. Belknap. Finally there was the "Salary Grab Act" of 1873 by which congressmen raised their own salaries and those of the president, the Cabinet and Supreme Court justices while millions were unemployed as a result of the economic depression which followed the Panic of 1873.

Despite the scandals of his administrations and the air of corruption

ently championed their president, even in more deplorable instances, because of his candor as a soldier and loyalty as a friend. The subservience of the public trust to his own interests did not matter; nor the defilement of public offices by unfit henchmen and objectionable acquaintances; nor the outrageous stupidity shown in selecting obscure men with shady reputations to fill the most important and representative positions in the Republic; nor those slovenly attempts of his, more substantiated than contradicted in his letter of explanation, to institute a permanent power which, by all indications, his close advisers had in mind. His nation forgave him for his discourteous silence, his unconcealed disregard for the sincere opinions of his cabinet, his determination to have everyone around him freely bow to his wishes in public affairs, whether those wishes were original with him or came from others. Those characteristics were excused because of the austere politeness noted in his manner and speech, his humble way of treating his subordinates, the superficial modesty which in him, as in so many others, was actually a skillful cover for the dangerous lack of modesty within. Yet in spite of this, not even all the splendor of his ostentatious trip around the world, in which he epitomized his nation's greatness, could move his people to elect him president of the Republic for a third term. He lost his own majesty because of having jeopardized the majesty of the law.

How wretched were his later years! Since his longing for power never flagged, he now turned to the needless pursuit of wealth, despite the assurance from his friends of a lifelong income from a two hundred and fifty thousand dollar fortune. With no slackening in his urge to be on the march and to conquer, his mysterious quality of hero-businessman led him to poke about Cuba and Mexico, and to recommend a project, headed by himself, for the extension of North Amer-

in Washington, Grant was all but given a third presidential nomination in 1880.

ica's railroad network into Mexico.[53] His nation never tired of blaming Grant's associates for his business catastrophes, although even a cursory glance showed the blame to be his. Those who knew him best kept a close watch upon him at all times, as if they had discovered that he was the center of a powerful group which, at the slightest provocation, might rise above the laws of the Republic with the support of the enormous monopolies that must protect themselves against the lower classes whose well-being and future they oppose.

At first glance this North American nation appears to be thoughtless and selfish, but it is actually profoundly generous, or decent, or discreet. If not, then how to explain its persistent good will in refusing to blame Grant for the scandalous mismangement, the colossal fraud, of the business establishment that misused his name, secured his signature on important documents, and walked the same tightrope as did the government during his years in office? Would it not have been natural for people to assume that he was to blame, since circumstances so similar occurred in the government as well? But not so; he was not guilty. He may have sanctioned some half-understood scheme that he considered useful, but he could never knowingly profit from filthy gains. His blame lay in his overpowering desire for visible preeminence; his constant urge for leadership and command; his lack of the intellect and beauty that could have added to the strength of his basic character; and his deplorable inability to recognize the gentle dignity of modesty and the greater influence exerted, even in practical matters, by those who in true republics do not use the trust placed in them to set themselves above these republics.

In the end it was illness which brought a luminous and

53. Grant left the presidency with little in the way of financial resources and his business friends and associates set up a fund for his needs. However, the fund lost its value over the years and Grant turned to a number of deals to support himself.

memorable conclusion to that life of pure strength that was sometimes brilliant, sometimes sordid; yet the vast scope of the services he rendered made it undeniably and definitively a distinguished one. Some people will consider the spectacular funeral given to Grant by his nation, when his body was carried from the mortuary to his tomb on Riverside Drive (covered now by the clinging tendrils from a cutting of a vine from Napoleon's tomb on St. Helena), an appropriate conclusion to the existence that preserved without cruelty the greatest political system devised by man. They no doubt see a fitting end to that productive life in the funeral train winding down the proud mountain, with the black curtains waving in the rainfilled breezes; in the ranks of New York militiamen accompanying the body through the still wet streets from the railroad station to City Hall where the vestibule had been turned into a funeral crypt. There are probably those who consider it quite suitable that there should be an endless throng of men and women, both black and white; of workmen on their way home; of soldiers who had fought in his armies; of the curious who for two days and nights formed an unbroken line over the mile-long route from City Hall coming to view his body. The day of the solemn burial was declared a day of prayer for the entire nation. It was the day on which the enormous hearse drawn by twenty-four black horses carried his remains to the tomb through streets hung with crepe and packed with people, many of whom had been huddled in doorways since the dawn of the day before. Spectators clung to the rooftops, perched on telegraph poles, crowded on balconies where they paid dearly to see General Hancock[54] pass by with the general staff, including one Southerner; the spruce regiment of militiamen; the Virginia battalion that Grant drove before him, and another com-

54. Winfield Scott Hancock (1825-1886), Union general who served brilliantly at Gettysburg. After the war he became a leading Democratic politician and was the unsuccessful candidate for president on the Democratic ticket in 1880.

posed of men who drove it under Grant's command; the deceased, at whose passing all heads were bared; the President of the Republic[55] in a coach drawn by black horses, and two ex-presidents; five hundred carriages filled with notables, secretaries of state, governors, bishops, and generals; and the daughter and daughters-in-law of the great man, veiled in deep mourning.

But it was not all this that brought Grant's life to such a brilliant conclusion; it was the magnificent spirit he showed in the long-drawn-out days before his death, days endured with singular fortitude by that wasted old man, days in which he revealed by words and acts of great tenderness the best of his natural energies, long obscured by the usual appetites and vulgarities of existence. Deep introspection made that man fully aware of his life's true greatness. And in preparing his own wartime memoirs—probably the only bequest he had to leave his children—whose final pages he wrote struggling for breath and sweating in agony on the verge of death, the vanities that with a show of humility he once prized so highly fell at his feet like dust from a timeworn statue. And because of the genuine grace in men of exceptional character, permitting them to rise to a higher sense of spiritual greatness regardless of their class or condition, Grant neither saw nor respected nor remembered anything of his lifework except those essential exploits in which he was great in battle only to be greater in the manner of his triumph.

His deepset eyes, softened by the gratitude he felt for the good people who forgave his blunders and were keeping the death watch with him, looked back with commendable and lofty affection to those mistaken heroes it was his lot to fight without rest, and subdue without anger. And his emaciated hand, held out benevolently to the South from the edge of

55. Grover Cleveland (1837-1908), who had been elected in 1884 on the Democratic ticket, the first Democrat to be elected president after the Civil War.

his tomb, has been grasped in loving admiration, as a treasured national gesture, by his gallant former enemies. A nation of men has begun, and this man, in spite of his serious errors, helped clear the way.

La Nación (Buenos Aires), September 27, 1885

The Great "Buffalo Bill"

"Buffalo Bill" we read printed in large colored letters on every corner, wooden fence, sign post, deadend wall in New York. Sandwich-men—that is what they are called—walk along the streets, stuffed between two large boards which fall front and back, and sway as does the untroubled fellow who carries them, while the crowds laugh and read the bright letters shining in the sun: "The Great Buffalo Bill."

"Buffalo Bill" is the nickname of a Western hero. He has lived many years in the wilderness among rough miners, and buffaloes less fearful than the miners. He knows how to chase buffaloes and tumble them and how to approach them, stun them, mock them, confound them, and lasso them. He knows how to dazzle ruffians and make them recognize him as boss; because no sooner does one of these jump on Buffalo Bill wielding a knife, then he falls with Buffalo Bill's knife between the ribs, or if Buffalo Bill is shot at, his bullet meets the other in mid-air and bounces back against the aggressor, for Buffalo Bill is such a crackshooter that he can shoot at a flying bullet, stop it, and disintegrate it. He knows all there is to know about Indians, their customs, tricks, ways of fight-

1. William Frederick Cody (1846-1917), American scout, Indian fighter, and showman. He obtained his reputation as "Buffalo Bill" by killing some 4,000 buffaloes in eighteen months as a hunter for the Kansas Pacific Railroad.

ing, and, like them, he can see in the dark and can tell by
putting his ear to the ground how many enemies are approaching, how far away they are and if on foot or horseback. As to fighting, he would just as soon shoot it out in a
saloon with troublesome cowboys who are not satisfied if
they haven't buried, with boots and spurs on, some neighboring cowboy or unwary traveler, as with howling, agile Indians
who, leaning against their mounts' necks, flourishing their
deadly rifles, swarm down fiercely upon the white man, himself forced to take shelter under his horse's belly or behind a
nearby tree. All such terrors and victories can be read in
Buffalo Bill's clear, melancholic, sparkling eyes. Women love
him; they find him handsome and desirable. Never is he to be
found alone on the streets. He is always accompanied by a
beautiful woman. Boys gaze upon him as though he were a
sun god, high and brilliant, who charms them with his skill
and pluck. His brown, graying hair hangs long over his powerful shoulders. He wears a widebrimmed, white felt hat, and
boots.

Now he is cashing in on his reputation and tours the
United States at the head of a large troupe of cowboys,
Indian sharpshooters, horses, bucks, stags, and buffaloes.
Either in the afternoon, by sunlight, or in the evening, by
electric light, in a tent as spacious as a prairie, they put on a
show presenting all the scenes full of risk and romance that
have made the West famous. In real, live tableaux he presents
to wide-eyed New Yorkers the marvels and dangers of that
restless, wild life. We can see the cowboys approaching with
their leather trousers fringed at the seam, their short jackets,
neckerchiefs, dashing Mexican sombreros, flung rather than
seated on their spirited steeds, their lariats rolled on the
saddle horns ready to be whirled in the air, their guns, with
which they settle their smallest disagreements, ready to be
drawn from their crude holsters. The brave rascals—homeless,
childless—look upon death as though it were a mug of beer:
they give it or take it: they bury their victims or, with a
bullet in their breast, they roll up in their blankets to die.

Then the cowboys move on after showing off their persons and tricks, and the Indians appear close behind a white traveler who seems unaware of being followed. The Indians advance single-file, facing front, at a slow gait, holding back their restless ponies, which the moment the wild men cease to rein them in, will charge against the white enemy as though it were up to them to avenge their riders' people. One would say men's grievances had seeped into the earth in such a manner that everything that sprouted from that earth brought those grievances back to life again! Thus the Indian pony is, like its master, slender and nervous, crafty and resentful. Like an arrow come to life, this pony is a weapon that does not seem invented casually by the men who use it, but is the expression, concretion, and symbol of the race's physical and spiritual traits, and of the episodes of its history. The slender Indians come, singing a dragging, monotonous, piercing song that penetrates the soul and saddens it. It is a song as of something which is departing to sink dolefully into the bosom of the earth. When it is over it continues vibrating in our ear like a twig on which a pigeon has just died.

Suddenly there is smoke all around; the plaintive wail is followed by a diabolical outburst of cries. The ponies charge, the heads of the Indians on a level with the ponies' heads. If one could swing a great knife under the horses' hoofs, not one hoof would be touched. Screaming and shooting, in a cloud of dust reddened now and then by powder flashes, they fall upon the white man who kneels and empties all his cartridges like grapeshot. While loading he uses both hands and holds his gun between his teeth. The Indians shoot between their horses' ears or under their bellies. They are like ghosts through whom bullets pass without harming them. The white man, who is Buffalo Bill, runs out of ammunition; by the way he sways it seems he is badly wounded. The Indians encircle him as vultures would an eagle still alive. He embraces the neck of his horse, which he has used as a parapet, and dies.

The war cries now become cries of victory. You would not

say they had killed one white man but all of them. It's just a
circus show for the benefit of Easterners, but this is so deeprooted in their souls that the show seems real. They take him
away hanging across the saddle of a horse belonging to an
Indian fallen in the fray. Off they go elated, yelling, when,
amid screams and lashing of whips, there appears a stagecoach full of white men, and drawn by small mules with
many bells on their harness. The fight is on! The old coach
becomes a barricade, the coach box a castle's battlement,
every window a loophole for firing. The savages in vain try to
defend their dead prey. Again there is smoke, flashes, bullets,
powder everywhere; at last the ponies stampede away and the
brave avengers carry the traveler's body to the stagecoach.
The public applauds frantically. This much we have advanced
since Rome; then the throngs applauded the gladiator who
slew, now they applaud those who save. The whip cracks,
music is heard, hymns rumble, and the rickety stagecoach
disappears in a thick cloud of dust.

Thus Buffalo Bill's men represent the scenes which are still
being enacted out West. A horseman appears flying. A shot is
heard. He undoes the pouches, hanging against the horse's
rump, disengages both feet from the stirrups and, as he rides
past another horse already saddled which a man holds by the
bridle, he jumps on its back with his leather bags and continues on his way to a fresh mount, while they blanket and
revive the tired one. Such was postal service in yesteryear;
before railways, men did the work of railways.

Or again it is a herd of buffaloes, charging with their
muzzles sweeping the ground. The cowboys on their horses
swiftly surround them, dazzle them with their shouts, lasso
them with their skillful lariats around the horns or by whatever leg the public chooses, or tumble them or ride them in
spite of the beasts' efforts to shake the riders off. And sometimes a very able cowboy will lasso the beast by the horns,
speed up on his mount so that the rope will slacken; then,
with a jerk, he will make a noose in the air, land it on the

animal's muzzle and, with a strong wrench, fasten it there like a halter.

The show comes to an end amidst thousands of shots, as the sharpshooters break clay pigeons in the air, and choruses of hurrahs that die down as the crowds board the trains homeward-bound; then the electric lights, shedding their brightness on the empty circus, mimic one of those magnificent spectacles that surely take place in the very bowels of Nature.

La América (New York), July 1884
La Nación (Buenos Aires), October 1, 1884

Jesse James, the Great Bandit

These Easter days, so festive in New York, have been exciting ones in Missouri where there lived a bandit of noble brow, handsome features, and a hand made for death's work. He robbed banks, not pockets; ransacked towns, not houses; waylaid trains, not travelers. He was a hero of the West. His boldness dazzled his countrymen and drew their eyes from his crimes. He was well-born, the son of a clergyman, looked like a gentleman, not a villain, and married a schoolteacher, not a bawd. And there are those who say that during one of his law-abiding spells he was a political leader and attended the last Democratic Convention under an assumed name, influencing the nomination of the presidential candidate. But the lands of Missouri and Kansas are full of dense woodlands and craggy places. Jesse James and his men knew each nook and cranny of these wilds, every bend in the road, swamp trail, and hollow tree. His house was an armory and his waist became another when he strapped on his two great gunbelts bristling with revolvers. He went to fight in the war as a youth, and before his cheeks lost their down he sent more

1. Jesse Woodson James (1847-1882), desperado, born in Missouri, fought as a guerrilla with his brother Frank in the Civil War on the side of the Confederacy, and after the war became leader of a band of outlaws who robbed trains and banks in the West until he was killed by a member of his band.

than one bearded man to his grave. In times of Alba[2] he would have been a captain in Flanders; in times of Pizarro,[3] his able lieutenant; in these times, he was first a soldier and then a bandit. He was not one of Sheridan's magnificent soldiers who fought that slaves might live free in a united land and planted the Union colors atop the embattled breastworks of the Confederacy. Nor one of those hardy soldiers under silent Grant who stalked the bristling Rebels to the final battleground, as the patient hunter stalks the ravenous boar. He was a trooper of the Southern stripe, of those who saw in the battle flag a license for plunder. His hand was an instrument of death. He left his victims unburied, and rode off with the booty he generously shared with his companions in crime, the tiger cubs who licked the hand of the great tiger.[4]

The war ended and a great contest began. On one side were the young bandits. They would appear in the cities on horseback, knock at the doors of the bank, empty the vaults of money in broad daylight, and drunk with danger, which goes to the head like wine, gallop off shouting through the startled communities, aware of the crime only after it was accomplished. There would be a halfhearted chase, and the townsfolk would gather again in front of the empty bank, from where it seemed they could still see the bold horsemen, golden against the horizon with the aura of daring. On the other side were the sheriffs, helpless in those regions of small towns and great distances; the soldiers of the territory, who always returned wounded, or never returned; and the uneasy communities, sometimes dazzled by the trailing splendor of boldness, which transfigured the audacious robber into a

2. Fernando Alvarez de Toledo, Duke of Alba (1507-1582), who, as brilliant military leader in Spain's days of glory under Charles V and Philip II, was noted for demanding of his troops strict discipline and courage.

3. Francisco Pizarro (c. 1475-1541), Spanish conqueror of Peru.

4. After the Civil War ended, Jesse James and his brother Frank roamed the countryside killing and looting.

prince of plunder, and made hearts beat faster, as hearts heedless of the soul's good counsel ever will in the presence of an extraordinary act, however vile. So it is that in the bloody rings where men kill bulls, the beauties of Spain fling their wide fans in the air, applaud wildly, and shower the matador with silken slippers from their tiny feet, and red roses from their hair, in token of esteem! Once, Missouri was celebrating its state fair, with at least thirty thousand men at the grounds, betting, carousing, gambling, and watching the races. Panic suddenly swept through the crowd. Jesse James had appeared, and while all eyes were on the swift racehorses, he and his desperadoes burst into the counting room, shot down the guards, and fled with all the receipts. For its magnitude and daring it seemed to many in Missouri that this crime merited pardon. But other times these villains would sink their arms elbow-deep in blood, as when they would tear up the railroad tracks on a curve and lie in wait with their swift horses in the thickets. The train would come and jump the track. Then came the killing of any who resisted the wicked robbery. Then the removal of money by the sackful. Then the loading of horses with bullion. And then the murder of all who could make the train run anew. If there was a wealthy barroom in the territory where a local bully held sway, the bandits went there spoiling for trouble, that no one might say that a man lived who was quicker on the draw and harder in the saddle than Jesse James' boys. If they danced the quadrille at a Texas ranch with all the beauties from near and far, Jesse James would knock at the door with his pistol butts, and as he was the bravest, to him belonged the fairest. A famous agent was commissioned to track him down, and they found the agent's body riddled with bullets and this note pinned to his chest: *Fair warning to all who would hunt Jesse James.*

    The strange life men lead in the remote regions of this country exposed to the raw wilderness develops in them all the appetites, magnificence, impulses, and elegance of the wild beast! It is fitting that the buffalo hunter, who challenges the powerful beast and sits at ease, as in his own chair, on the flanks of the fallen bull, should let his hair hang to his shoulders, and that his foot should be made to overstep forests, his hand to uproot trees, with his heart tuned to the tempest and his eyes filled with that solemn and melancholy look of one who has looked long on Nature and the unknown.

But where in the life of that bloodier of the highways are those noble deeds of a Don Quixote, which the newspapers insist on finding? It is true he was shot in the back by a friend in the Governor's hire. It is true that the State House should be rid of a Governor who pays an assassin with the hand that should be holding the scales of justice.[5] It is horrifying and shameful that in the dark of night by a side door of the executive mansion, the Governor and a young gunman should settle on the price for a bandit's life. What respect can a judge command who commits the same crime as the criminal? The shadows that shrouded the thicket where James and his men awaited the train stretched into the Governor's council when the price on his head was fixed. The peacemakers who pursued him in life buried him in a magnificent coffin, which they paid for out of their own pocket, or was it the state's? The body was taken on a special train, for no ordinary train would do, for burial in the earth of his mother's people. The coffin was carried by the lawmakers of the region and thousands of persons turned out, their eyes red from crying, to see the earth thrown over that bandit who

5. In 1881 the railway and express companies put pressure on the Governor of Missouri to take action against the outlaws. Governor Crittenden offered a reward of $10,000, much of it furnished by the companies, for the capture of Jesse James, dead or alive. The high price placed on his head led one of his own men, Robert Ford, to shoot Jesse in the back for the reward. The killing of Jesse James took place in his own home at St. Joseph, Missouri, on April 3, 1882.

shattered so many skulls with the quiet unconcern of a squirrel cracking hazelnuts. The swift mare on which the bandit rode fell into the hands of a turnkey.

La Opinión Nacional (Caracas), 1882

III

North American Scenes

Dedication of the Statue of Liberty

For him who enjoys thee not, Liberty, it is difficult to speak of thee. His anger is as great as that of a wild beast forced to bend his knees before his tamer. He knows the depths of hell while glancing up toward the man who lives arrogantly in the sun. He bites the air as a hyena bites the bars of his cage. Spirit writhes within his body as though it were poisoned.

The wretched man who lives without liberty feels that only a garment made of mud from the streets would benefit him. Those who have thee, oh Liberty! know thee not. Those who have thee not should not speak of thee but conquer thee.

1. Following a visit to the United States, French historian Édouard de Laboulaye proposed that the French people present a monument to the American people as a symbol of friendship between the two countries. The French people volunteered to raise the funds and the famous French sculptor Bartholdi agreed to undertake the project. He came to America, selected the site, returned to France, and in 1874 started work on the future Statue of Liberty. It was made chiefly of copper and other materials and stood 151 feet and 1 inch tall. The frame was designed by Gustav Eiffel, the creator of the Eiffel Tower.

When the statue was finished it was packed in 214 cases and shipped to the United States, but because of lack of funds the base on which to erect the statue could not be built and the statue itself had to be stored in a basement for several years. Then Joseph Pulitzer, the famous news-

133

But rise, oh insect, for the city swarms with eagles! Walk or at least crawl: look around, even if your eyes fill with shame. Like a smitten lackey, squirm among the hosts of brilliant lords. Walk, though you feel the flesh stripped off your body! Ah! if they only knew how you wept, they would pick you up, and you too, dying, would know how to lift your arms toward eternity!

Arise, oh insect, for the city is like an ode! Souls ring out like well-tuned instruments. If it is dark and there is no sun in the sky, it is because all light is in the souls; it flowers within men's breasts.

Liberty, it is thine hour of arrival! The whole world, pulling the victorious chariot, has brought thee to these shores. Here thou art like the poet's dream, as great as space, spanning heaven and earth!

That noise we hear—it is triumph resting.

That darkness we see—it is not the rainy day, nor gloomy October; it is the dust, tinted by death, thy chariot has raised up in its wake.

I can see them with drawn swords, holding their heads in their hands, their limbs a formless pile of bones, their bodies girded with flames, the stream of life oozing out of their broken foreheads like wings. Tunics, armor, scrolls of parchment, shields, books gather resplendently at thy feet, and thou commandest at last over the cities of interests and the phalanxes of war, oh aroma of the world! Oh goddess, daughter of man!

---

paper publisher, undertook to raise the necessary money. He announced a contest for an appropriate inscription to be placed at the base. A great many writers and poets submitted material, including a young Jewish-American poetess, Emma Lazarus, who won the contest with her entry, "The New Colossus." Her sonnet expressed America's concern for the poor and oppressed, eloquently pleading, "Give me your tired, your poor, your huddled masses yearning to breathe free" and concluding, "Send those, the homeless, tempest-tossed to me; I lift my lamp beside the golden door."

Man grows. Behold he has outgrown churches and chosen the sky as the only temple worthy of sheltering his deity! But thou, o marvelous one! growest with man; and armies, the whole city, the emblazoned ships about to exalt thee approach thy mist-veiled feet, like variegated shells dashed on the rocks by the somber sea when the fiend of tempest, wrapped in lightning, rides across the sky on a black cloud.

Thou hast done well, Liberty, in revealing thyself to the world on a dark day, for thou canst not yet be satisfied with thyself! Now you, my feastless heart, sing of the feast!

It was yesterday, October 28, that the United States solemnly accepted the Statue of Liberty which the people of France have donated to them in memory of the Fourth of July, 1776, when they declared their independence from England, won with the help of French blood.[2] It was a raw day: the air was ashy, the streets muddy, the rain relentless; but seldom was man's rejoicing so great.

One felt a peaceful joy as though a balm soothed one's soul. From brows to which light is not lacking, light seemed to shine more brightly, and that fair instinct of human decency which illumines the dullest faces emerged even from opaque spirits, like a wave's surge.

The emotion was immense. The movement resembled a mountain chain. Not an empty spot remained on the streets. The two rivers seemed like solid land. The steamers, pearly in the fog, maneuvered crowded from wheel to wheel. Brooklyn Bridge groaned under its load of people. New York and its suburbs, as though invited to a wedding, had risen early. Among the happy crowds that filled the streets there were

---

2. On March 4, 1778, Congress ratified the treaty with France concluded by Benjamin Franklin and Silas Deane. In case war broke out between Britain and France—Britain did declare war in June 1778—the United States and France agreed "to make it a common cause," and neither party would make peace without consulting the other. In 1778 and again in 1780, French fleets arrived in America with troops to aid the American cause.

none as beautiful—not the workmen forgetful of their troubles, nor the women, nor the children—as those old men who had come from the country with their flying cravats and greatcoats to salute, in the commemorative statue, the heroic spirit of the Marquis de Lafayette,[3] whom they as children had greeted with waving hands and boughs, because he loved Washington and helped him make this country free.

A grain of poetry suffices to season a century. Who can forget that beautiful friendship? Washington was the graver and older of the two. There was scarcely a down on Lafayette's upper lip. But they shared, under different appearances, the same blind determination and capacity of ascent common to all great personalities. That noble child had left wife and king to help the humble troops that in America were pushing the English king to the sea and phrasing in sublime words the teachings of the Encyclopedists, words through which the human race announced its coming of age with no less clatter than that which had accompanied the revelation of its infancy on Mount Sinai.

That blond hero kept company with the dawn. His strong soul preferred marching men to the iniquitous pomp with which his monarch paraded, shining opalescently on the shoulders of his hungry vassals like a saint carried on a litter by barefoot porters. His king persecuted him, England persecuted him, but his wife helped him.

God pity the heroic heart whose noble enterprises found no welcome at home! He left his house and regal wealth, armed his ship, wrote from his ship: "The happiness of America is intimately bound up with the happiness of Humanity. She is going to become a cherished and safe asylum of virtue, of tolerance, of equality, and of peaceful lib-

3. Marquis Marie Joseph de Lafayette (1757-1834), French general and statesman who served in the American Revolution as major-general in the Continental army and associate of George Washington, went to France to aid the American cause, and returned to serve at Yorktown and Virginia in 1781.

erty." How great his soul, ready to give up all the privileges of fortune to follow a handful of poorly clad rebels on their march through the snow! He jumped off his ship, flew to the Continental Congress: "I wish to serve America as a volunteer and without pay."[4] Sometimes things happen on earth that shed a heavenly splendor over it.

Manhood seemed to have matured within that youthful body. He proved to be a generals' general. As he clutched his wound with the one hand, with the other he commanded his fleeing soldiers to turn about and win. With a flash of his sword he mustered a column that a traitor had dispersed.[5]

If his soldiers were on foot, he was on foot. If the Republic had no money, he who was offering her his life, advanced his fortune. Behold a man who glittered as though he were all gold! When his fame restored to him his king's affection, he realized France's hatred toward England could be helpful in chasing the exhausted English out of America.

The Continental Congress girded on him a sword of honor and wrote to the King of France: "We recommend this noble man to Your Majesty's notice, as one whom we know to be wise in counsel, gallant in the field, and patient under the hardships of war." He borrowed the wings of the sea. France, the vanguard of nations, bedecked herself with roses to receive her hero.

"It is a wonder Lafayette is not taking with him to his America the furniture of Versailles,"[6] exclaimed the French

4. In a letter to the President of Congress, Lafayette, "acting on one of those impulses that sometimes served him," wrote: "After the sacrifices that I have made, I have the right to demand two favours; one is to serve at my own expense; the other is to begin my service as a volunteer." (Brand Whitlock, *Lafayette* [New York, 1929], Vol. I, p. 80.)

5. The reference is to Benedict Arnold (1741-1801), revolutionary general traitor, who plotted to surrender his army to the British, was discovered and forced to flee to the enemy.

6. In his biography of Lafayette, Brand Whitlock writes: "He was always at Versailles, closeted with Maurepas and Vergennes, pleading the American cause. Old Maurepas complained that, to clothe the

Minister, as Lafayette crossed the ocean with France's help to the newborn republic, with Rochambeau's[7] army and de Grasse's[8] navy.

Even Washington was at the time despairing of victory. But French noblemen and American farmers closed against Cornwallis[9] and routed him at Yorktown.[10]

Thus did the United States assure with France's help the independence they had learned to wish for in terms of French thinking. The prestige of a heroic deed is such that this svelte marquis has sufficed to keep united during a century two nations that differ in spiritual warmth, in the idea of life, and in the very concept of liberty—egotistical and selfish in the United States, and generous and expansive in France. Blessed be the country that radiates its light!

Let us follow the throngs that fill the streets, coming from every direction. It is the day of the unveiling of the monu-

---

American army, the Marquis would gladly have stripped the palace at Versailles." (Op. cit., Vol. I, p. 190.) Jean Frédéric Maurepas (1701-1781) was a French minister.

7. Count Jean Baptiste de Rochambeau (1725-1807), French soldier, commander-in-chief of the troops that were sent to America. He participated in the actions that led to the capitulation of the British at Yorktown.

8. Count François Joseph Paul de Grasse (1722-1788), French naval officer, in command of the French fleet during the American War for Independence.

9. Charles Cornwallis (1734-1805), second Earl and first Marquis Cornwallis, commander-in-chief of the British forces during the American War for Independence, and later governor-general of India.

10. The battle of Yorktown was the final battle of the American Revolution. Cornwallis, attacked from the sea by the French fleet under de Grasse, while Washington rapidly moved south with Rochambeau, was placed in a very difficult position. Washington moved the combined Franco-American army in on Cornwallis, whose retreat by water was blocked off. On October 19, 1783, while the bands played "The World Turned Upside Down," Cornwallis surrendered his 7,247 troops to Washington.

ment consecrating the friendship between Washington and Lafayette. People of all tongues are present at the ceremony. The rejoicing is to be found among the common people. Banners flourish in men's hearts; few on men's houses. The emblazoned grandstand where the procession is to pass awaits the President of the Republic, the delegates from France, the diplomatic corps, the state governors, the army generals.

Sidewalks, portals, balconies, roofs begin to seethe with a joyous mass of people. Many fill the wharves to await the naval procession. The war ships, the fleet of steamers, the prattling tugboats which will carry the invited guests to Bedloe's Island, where the statue stands waiting on her Cyclopean pedestal, her face covered by the French flag. But most gather along the route of the grand parade.

Here comes a band. Here comes a fire brigade with its ancient fire engine raised on stilts. The firemen wear black trousers and red shirts. The crowds make room for a group of deliriously happy Frenchmen. Then comes another group in beautiful uniforms garnished with gold braid, full, striped trousers, plumed cap, fierce mustachios, slender figures, bubbling palaver, and very black eyes: they are a company of Italian volunteers. From around a corner juts the elevated railroad. Up above, a crowded train; down below policemen branching out to their beats, their blue frock coats well buttoned up with gilt buttons. The rain fails to wipe out everyone's smiles.

Now the crowds step back onto the sidewalk, as the mounted police advance pushing against them with their horses' haunches. A woman crosses the street, her oilcloth coat filled with commemorative medals bearing on one side the monument, on the other the sculptor Bartholdi's[11] pleas-

11. Frédéric Auguste Bartholdi (1834-1904), French sculptor of the Statue of Liberty on Bedlowe's Island in New York harbor which was titled in full: "Liberty Enlightening the World." Bartholdi's masterpiece is considered to be the "Lion of Belfort" in Belfort, France, inspired by France's defeat in the Franco-Prussian War of 1870-1871.

ing likeness. There goes an anxious-looking man making notes as he walks.

But what about France? Here there is not much talk of France, nor of Lafayette. Little do they know of him. No one is aware of the fact that a magnificent gift of the modern French people to the American people is being celebrated.

There is another statue of Lafayette in Union Square: also the work of Bartholdi, a gift of France. Only the men of letters and the old men with the cravats remember the admirable marquis. There is a new life boiling in the enormous cauldron. This country where each man lives and toils for himself has really not much love for that other country which has fertilized every human seed with its blood.

"France—says one ingrate—only helped us because her king was an enemy of England." "France—ruminates another in his corner—gives us the Statue of Liberty so that we will let her finish the Panama Canal in peace."

"It is Laboulaye[12]—says another—who gave us the statue. He would apply English brakes to French liberty. Even as Jefferson learned from the Encyclopedists the principles of the Declaration of Independence, so did Laboulaye and Henri Martin[13] try to take to France the methods of government the United States had inherited from the Magna Carta."

Not so at the dedication: a small man (Lesseps[14]), who would fit in the hollow of the Statue of Liberty's hand, started to speak. His voice was so firm and fresh that the illustrious gathering, fascinated, enraptured, hailed that human monument with an interminable cheer. Compared to this man, accustomed to severing continents in order to join

12. Édouard René Lefebvre de Laboulaye (1811-1883), French jurist, historian, and politician.

13. Henri Martin (1810-1883), French historian, author of the fifteen-volume *Histoire de France* (1833-1836).

14. Viscount Ferdinand Marie de Lesseps (1805-1894), French diplomat and financier, was successful in building a canal across the Isthmus of Suez (Suez Canal), but failed in his effort to build a canal across Panama.

seas, what was all that clatter, the clamor of machines, the cannonade from the ships, the monument which towered above him? Why, he even provoked laughter there in front of the statue with his first words! "That steam, American citizens, which has done so much good to the world, at this moment I find very obnoxious and harmful."

Marvelous old man! Americans do not like him because he is doing in spite of them what they have not had the courage to do. But with his first words he won them over. Then he read his speech written in his own hand on big, white, loose sheets of paper. He spoke familiarly or gave familiar form to graver matters. From the way he phrases his sentences we can see how it has been easy for him to reshape the earth. Within his every idea, no bigger than a nutshell, is contained a mountain.

As he speaks he moves incessantly; he turns to every side so as to face everyone. When he utters some phrases he drives them home with a movement of his head. He speaks a martial French, resonant like bronze. His favorite gesture is to raise his arm rapidly. He knows the land should be trodden victoriously. His voice as he talks on grows stronger instead of weaker. His short phrases are wavy and pointed like pennants. He was invited by the American government as the foremost Frenchman of his time.

"I have hastened to come," he says as he lays his hand on the flag of France draped in front of the rostrum; "the idea of erecting the Statue of Liberty does honor to those who conceived it as it likewise does to those who with understanding have received it."[15] To him France is the mother of na-

15. The Statue of Liberty was dedicated on October 28, 1886. The *New York Times* headline the following day over page one, column seven, read: "France's Gift Accepted. Liberty's Statue Unveiled On Bedloe's Island. A Great Holiday To Be Remembered In This City." The opening sentences read: "Liberty! A hundred Fourths of July broke loose yesterday to exalt her name, and despite the calendar rolled themselves into a delirious and glorious one."

tions and with exceptional skill he mentions without contradiction the opinion expressed by Hepworth Dixon[16]: "An English historian, Hepworth Dixon, in his book *New America,* after having said of your constitution that it is not a product of the soil, and that it does not emanate from the English idea, adds it can on the contrary be regarded as an exotic plant born in the atmosphere of France."

He does not deal in symbols but in objects. Things exist, in his opinion, according to what they are good for. The Statue of Liberty leads him to his Panama Canal. "You like men who dare and persevere. I say, like you, 'Go ahead!' We understand each other when I use that term!"

"Yes, indeed, it was Laboulaye who inspired Bartholdi. It was his idea: Go, he said, and propose to the United States the construction, jointly with us, of a superb monument in commemoration of their independence. Yes, the statue was to signify the prudent Frenchman's admiration of the peaceful practices of American liberty."[17]

The *Times* reported Lesseps as saying: "I come to bring to you a tribute of fraternity with America. I hastened to avail myself of the gracious invitation which was given to me by the great American Republic. The idea of erecting the Statue of Liberty was a generous one. It does honor to those who conceived it, as it likewise does honor to those who executed it. Liberty lighting the world! A great lighthouse raised in the midst of a fleet on the threshold of free America. In landing beneath its rays, people will know that they have reached a land where individual initiative is developed in all its power; where progress is a religion; where great fortunes become popular by the charity they bestow and by encouraging instruction and science and casting their influence into the future. You are right, American citizens, to be proud of your 'go ahead.' You have made great headway in a hundred years, thanks to that cry, because you have been intrepid. . . ." (*New York Times,* October 29, 1886.)

16. William Hepworth Dixon (1821-1879), English historian and traveler. His book *New America* was published in 1867.

17. Lesseps did not use the exact words quoted by Martí, but he did, as indicated above, refer to the "go ahead" spirit in the United

Thus (says he) was born the idea which grew like the streamlet that swells along its course from the mountaintop until at last it reaches the sea. On the grandstand sit the delegates from France, the sculptor, the orator, the journalist, the general, the admiral, and this man who joins the seas and cleaves the land. French tunes flitter over the city; French flags flap against balconies and wave on the tops of buildings. But what livens all eyes and gladdens all souls is not the gift of a generous land, received perhaps with insufficient enthusiasm, but the brimming over of human pleasure on seeing the instinct of our own majesty, which resides in the marrow of our bones and constitutes the root and glory of our life, rise with stupendous firmness, a symbol of captivating beauty.

Behold, they all reveal the exhilaration of being reborn! Is not this nation, in spite of its rawness, the hospitable home of the oppressed? The voices that impel and counsel come from within, from deeper than the will. Flags are reflected on faces, heartstrings are plucked by a sweet love, a superior sense of sovereignty brings to countenances a look of peace, nay of beauty. And all these luckless Irishmen, Poles, Italians, Bohemians, Germans, redeemed from oppression or misery, hail the monument to Liberty because they feel that through it they themselves are uplifted and restored.

Behold how they run toward the wharves from which the

States, and he concluded his speech: "Very soon, gentlemen, we shall find ourselves together to celebrate another pacific conquest. I say *au revoir* until we meet at Panama, where the 38 Stars of North America will soon float at the side of the banners of the Independent States of South America, and will form in the New World, for the benefit of mankind, the peaceful and prolific alliance of the Franco-Latin and Anglo-Saxon race." (*New York Times,* October 29, 1886.) Ironically, the United States was to replace France in the construction of the Panama Canal, sponsor a revolt against Colombia under President Theodore Roosevelt, and establish the new Republic of Panama as a virtual colony of the United States.

statue can be seen, elated as shipwrecked people who descry a hopeful sail! These are the humblest, those who fear the main streets and the clean people: pale tobacco workers, humpbacked stevedores, Italian women with their colored shawls. They do not run brutally, disorderly as on ordinary holidays, but in friendly equable groups. They come from the east side, the west side, the congested alleys of the poor neighborhoods. Sweethearts act like married couples, husbands offer their arms to their wives, mothers drag their young along. They question each other, encourage each other; cram into the positions from where they think they will see better.

In the meantime, among the crowd's hurrahs, the lavishly decorated gun carriages roll along the broad streets; buildings seem to speak and hail each other with their flags; the elevated trains, like an aerial, disciplined, steaming cavalry seem to stop, paw, unload their riders on the beach; the steamers restlessly test the ties that hold them to their moorings, and out there, in the distance, wrapped in smoke, the enormous statue rises, greeted by all the incense burners on earth, crowned with clouds, like a mountain.

The greatest celebration is at Madison Square where, facing the impious monument of Farragut[18] which commemorates the North Americans' inglorious victory over Mexico, rises from the grandstand bedecked with United States and French flags from where the President is to watch the parade. He has not yet arrived, but everyone is anxious. The brown helmets of policemen protrude above the dark mass. Tricolored festoons hang from house fronts.

The stand is like a bunch of roses on a black background. Now and then a murmur spreads over the nearby groups as though their collective soul had suddenly been enriched, for

18. David Glasgow Farragut (1801-1870), commander of the sloop *Saratoga* during the Mexican War, naval hero of the Union Navy during the Civil War, and first to hold the ranks of vice-admiral and admiral in the U.S. Navy. There are many statues of Farragut.

Lesseps has walked up, and then come: Spuller, Gambetta's[19] friend, with his steely eyes and powerful head; bold Jaurès who gloriously led twelve thousand soldiers, closely pursued by the Germans, out of the battle of Mamers; Pellisier who although wounded at Nogent-sur-Marne applied his pale hand to the wheels of his cannon; Lieutenant Ney who, when his Frenchmen fled in panic from a trench on fire, opened his arms, steadied his feet firmly on the ground, his face embellished by the bronze-hued glare, pushed the cowards through the hellish mouth and then followed; Laussédat, the gray-haired Colonel who with youthful hands built barriers against the Prussian arms; Bureaux de Pussy who kept his great-grandfather Lafayette's sword from falling to the enemy; Deschamps, the Mayor of Paris, who three times fell prisoner to the Germans and three times got away; Villegente, the young naval officer like a figure out of a Neuville painting; Caubert, lawyer and soldier, who wanted to organize a legion of lawyers and judges to hold Prussia back; Bigot, Meunier, Desmons, Hielard, and Giroud, who have served the Fatherland bravely with purse or pen; and Bartholdi the creator of the statue, who planted on the buttress of Fort Belfort his sublime lion and cast in silver for Gambetta that pathetic, cursing Alsace, whose eyes, melancholy as great men's eyes are, reveal all the sadness of the standard bearer dying on his Alsace's bosom, and all the faith of the child by her side in whom the Motherland is reborn.

Familiarity with what is enormous cannot but engender light. The habit of conquering matter imparts to sculptors' faces an air of triumph and rebellion. The very capacity to admire what is great makes one great, much more so to model it, caress it, give wings to it, to extract from our mind the idea which, by means of our arms, our deep glances, our

19. Jacquese Eugène Spuller (1835-1896), French politician and journalist. Léon Michel Gambetta (1838-1882), French lawyer and statesman, one of the founders of the Third Republic.

loving strokes, gradually curves and illumines the marble or the bronze.

This creator of mountains was born a free soul in the Alsatian city of Colmar, stolen from him later by the German foe,[20] and in his eyes, inured to the sight of Egyptian colossi, liberty's beauty and grandeur took on the gigantic proportions and eminent majesty to which the Fatherland rises in the minds of those who live bereft of her. Bartholdi wrought his sovereign statue out of all his Fatherland's hopes.

Never did man create anything of real beauty without deep suffering. That is why the statue advances as though to step onto the promised land; that is why she bows her head and there is a widow's expression on her face; that is why she stretches her arm, as though to command and to guide, fiercely toward the sky.

Alsace! Alsace! cries every inch of her. The sorrowing virgin has come more to ask for a French Alsace than to light the way for world liberty.

Smiles and thoughts are but an abominable disguise, a tombstone when one lives without a Fatherland or when a part of it falls prey to the enemy's clutch. An atmosphere of drunkenness perturbs judgment, shackles words, quenches verses, and then whatever a nation's minds produce is deformed and empty, unless it expresses the soul's craving. Who feels more deeply the absence of a good than he who has possessed it and lost it? From the vehemence of sorrows stems the greatness of their representation.

There is Bartholdi, greeted lovingly by his comrades as he takes his place on the grandstand. A vague sadness veils his face; in his eyes shines a chaste grief; he walks as in a daze; looks where there is nothing to see; his unruly locks falling across his forehead bring to mind cypresses and shattered banners.

And there are the deputies: all have been chosen from

20. Germany took over Alsace-Lorraine after defeating France in the Franco-Prussian War.

those who fought most bravely in the war in which Alsace was lost to France.

Over there sits Spuller, Gambetta's friend. At the reception given by the French Circle of Harmony in honor of their compatriots there had been vague talk full of compliments, talk of historic brotherhood, of generous abstractions. Then Spuller appeared, a veritable lion. At first his speech was like a prayer, he spoke slowly, sadly as one burdened with some pain. Over the august, tearful silence he gradually draped his flaming words; when he drew them to a close the whole audience sprang to its feet; Spuller was sheathed in an invisible flag; the air seemed to vibrate like a smitten sword: Alsace! Alsace!

Now Spuller moves with bowed head, as always do those who are preparing to charge.

The French delegates gathered on that grandstand together with President Cleveland and the country's personages surrounding him watched the gala parade with which New York celebrated the dedication of the statue: rivers of bayonets, miles of red shirts, gray, blue, and green militiamen, a spot of white naval caps, a miniature model of the *Monitor* on a truck led by a boy in navy uniform.

The artillery in its blue uniforms passes by; the police, marching heavily; the cavalry, with their yellow lapels; on either hand the sidewalks black with people. The "hurrah!" raised at the foot of Central Park passed on from mouth to mouth and died amid the rumble of the Battery. Then pass Columbia University students wearing their square caps; then carriages bearing invalids, veterans, and judges; and then Negro groups. Bands are heard; an anthem follows them all the way.

The gallant 7th Regiment militia gets applause from the grandstand; the 22nd Regiment militiamen are handsome in their campaign capes; two German girls who came with one company hand the President two baskets of flowers; almost speechless, a child dressed in blue presents Lesseps with a silk banner for Bartholdi; the golden clarion notes of the "Mar-

seillaise" fly over the procession; the President salutes bareheaded the tattered flags; as they pass the grandstand each
company dips its colors and each French militia officer kisses
the hilt of his sword. There are frantic cheers from the stand,
sidewalks, and balconies when armless sleeves, bullet-riddled
flags, wooden legs pass by.

An old man in a dovecolored cloak drags himself along.
Everyone wants to shake his hand. There was a time in his
youth when he was a volunteer and pulled a fire engine as
bravely as now he drags his old bones. He had broken his
arms catching in them a child in flames, and his legs trying to
protect an old man from a falling wall. He is followed by
firemen dressed as in days of old and pulling their engines by
means of ropes. Just as the oldest engine of all, lovingly cared
for, brightly polished and laden with flowers, comes shaking
on its fragile wheels behind the young redcoats, one of the
formidable new engines dashes through the crowd to put out
a fire nearby. It leaves the air stricken and warm in its wake.
The smoke is black, the horses black. It knocks down carts,
runs over people. Puffs of sparks redden its smoky mane.
Then the hook-and-ladder wagon flies by followed by the
enormous pumper as noisy as the artillery.

A bell sounding like an order is heard and the masses
respectfully step aside to allow the passage of an ambulance
with a wounded person. The regiments can still be heard far
away. The golden clarion notes of the "Marseillaise" still
hover over the city.

Then, when the hour came to draw away the flag that
veiled the statue's face, everyone's heart swelled and it
seemed as though the sky had become covered with a canopy
of eagle wings. People rushed to the boats as impatiently as
would bridegrooms. Even the steamers, dressed to look like
great wreaths, seemed to smile, chatter, and bustle about as
merrily as girls at a wedding feast.

Everyone's thoughts were uplifted by a deep feeling of
respect as though the festival of liberty evoked all those who
have died in its quest. Over our heads a ghostly battle was

being waged! Oh, the lances, the shields, the statuesque dead, the superb agonies! One fighter's shadow alone was as great as a public square. They stood up straight, stretched out their arms, glanced down on men as if they were creating them, and then vanished.

The brightness which suddenly cleaved the dark atmosphere was not from the rays of the sun, but caused by clefts between the shields through which the splendor of the battle pierced the mist. They fought, they fell, they died singing. Such is the triumphal hymn which, better than the sounds of bells and cannon, becomes this statue made, rather than of bronze, of all the sunshine and poetry in the human soul.

From the time the parade was over, until dusk brought an end to the celebrations on the island where the monument stands, New York City and its bay were like one great cannon volley, a ringing of bells, a column of smoke. . . .

In her presence eyes once again knew what tears are. It was as though souls opened and flew to take refuge among the folds of her tunic, to whisper in her ear, to perch on her shoulders, to die like butterflies in her light. She seemed alive, wrapped in clouds of smoke, crowned by a vague brightness, truly like an altar with streamers kneeling at her feet! Not even Rhodes' Apollo,[21] with the urn of fire on his head and the dart of light in his hand, was higher; nor Phidias' all gold-and-ivory Jupiter,[22] son of the age when men were still women; nor the Hindus' statue of Sumnat,[23] inlaid with precious stones like their fancy; nor the two thirsty

21. The bronze statue of the sun god, 105 feet high, on the island of Rhodes in the Aegean Sea, created by Chares (fourth century B.C.), and destroyed by earthquake in 224 A.D., only fifty-six years after its completion. An older idea that it bestrode the harbor at Rhodes has been discredited.

22. Phidias (500-432 B.C.), most famous sculptor of ancient Greece.

23. Sumnat (also spelled Somnath), site of the famous temple of Siva (Shiva) at which a colossal statue was erected. It is in the state of Gujarat, north of Bombay, India.

statues at Thebes,[24] captive as the desert soul on their chiseled pedestals; nor the foul colossi guarding by the mouth of a cavern the temple at Ipsambul.[25] She is greater than the Saint Charles Borromeo in crude bronze on the hill at Arona[26] by the lake; greater than the Virgin at Puy,[27] a low-flighted conception on the mount overlooking the hamlet; greater than the Cheruscian Armenius[28] who rises over the Teutoburg gate summoning with his sword the German tribesmen to rout Varus' legions; greater than the Niderwald "Germania,"[29] a sterile armored beauty who opens not her arms; greater than Schwanthaler's "Bavaria,"[30] who proudly crowns herself on the Munich plain, with a lion at her feet; over and above the churches of all creeds and all the buildings

24. The statues of rams which lined the road leading to the temple in Thebes. The colossi of Memmon stood on the edge of the desert in western Thebes.

25. Another name for Abu Simbel, the sixty-seven-foot seated figures of Ramses II (c. 1250 B.C.) on the west bank of the Nile in Aswan province, Egypt. The four sitting colossi, carved in solid rock, were cut apart and lifted when the Aswan High Dam was built to prevent them from being submerged. The project was sponsored by the United Nations.

26. The colossal, 112-foot statue of Saint Charles Borromeo (1538-1584), cardinal and archbishop, was erected in 1624 near his birthplace on the western shore of Lago Maggiore. The sculptor was Giovanni Battista Crespi.

27. The fifty-foot bronze statue of the Virgin Mary on one of the volcanic peaks at Le Puy in Haute-Loire, France, is the work of Jean Marie Bonnassieux.

28. The statue, commemorating the victory of Armenius over the Roman legions commanded by Varus, was erected in the Teutoburg Forest near Detmold, Germany. It took forty years to erect.

29. A colossal national monument by Johannes Schilling (1829-1920), commemorating the Franco-Prussian War, erected in 1883 near Rüdesheim, Germany.

30. The sixty-foot statue of "Bavaria," near Munich, Germany, was erected by Ludwig von Schwanthaler (1802-1848).

of men. She rises from out of a starshaped pedestal, "Liberty Enlightening the World," without any lion or sword. She is made of all the art there is in the Universe, even as Liberty is made of all the sufferings of mankind.

She has Moses' Tablets of the Law, Minerva's uplifted arm, Apollo's flaming torch, the Sphinx's mysterious expression, Christianity's airy diadem. Even as mountains rise out of the depths of the earth, so has this statue, "an immense idea in an immense form," sprung from the brave aspiration of the human soul.

Man's soul is peace, light, and purity. Simply clad, Liberty seeks heaven as her natural abode. Girdles are painful to Liberty; she disdains crowns that hide her forehead; she loves nakedness as symbolic of nature; Liberty stands pure in the light from which she was born.

Thus the tunic and the peplum become Liberty as a protection against unlove and impure desire. Sadness also becomes her, that sadness which will only leave her eyes when all men love each other. It is right that she be barefoot, as one who only feels life in her heart. The diadem made of the fire of her thoughts emerges naturally from her temples, and even as a mountain ends in its peak so does the statue taper to the torch above in a condensation of light.

At the foot of the statue, the grandstand built for the occasion from fresh pine trees and adorned with virgin flags seemed as small as a poppy. The more favored guests occupied the platform in front of the stand. The whole island was like one human being.

How the people roared when their President, who had come up as they had from the worker's bench, stepped into the official launch to go and accept the image in which every man seems to see himself redeemed and uplifted! Only an earthquake is comparable to such an explosion.

The rumble of cannon smothered out the clamor of men. The steam compressed in the boilers of factories and ships escaped in unison with a mad, stirring, wild jubilation. At times it seemed as though the soul of the Indian charged across the sky yelling its war cry; or that churches knelt, their belfries bent over, their bells pealing; or that from the steamers' chimneys came, now weak, now strident, the cock's crow, the symbol of victory.

At times what was enormous became childlike: steam rushed in the boilers; lighters frolicked through the fog; the crowds on the steamers nagged the bands; stokers, garbed in gold by the glare of the fire, poked coal into the furnaces; through puffs of smoke one could see sailors standing on the yards of navy vessels.

At the grandstand the commander-in-chief of the American army called in vain for silence, waving his black three-cornered hat. Nor did the Reverend Storrs'[31] prayer, lost in the confusion, quiet the bustle. But Lesseps did conquer it, Lesseps with his eighty-year-old head bare in the rain. The magnificent spectacle was unforgettable. The great old man had not simply stood but jumped to his feet.

Oh, benevolent old man! Before he sits down, rewarded by the applause even of his opponents, astounded and won over, let thanks reach him from us "down there," from the America which has not yet had her fiesta, because he remembered our peoples and pronounced our forgotten name on that historic day when America consecrated Liberty, for who have better known how to die for her than we? Or loved her more?

"Until we meet again in Panama, where the thirty-eight stars of North America will soon float at the side of the banners of the independent States of South America, and will form in the New World, for the benefit of all mankind, the peaceful and prolific alliance of the Franco-Latin and the Anglo-Saxon races!"

Good old serpent charmer! Lucid soul who sees the greatness of our hearts under our bloodstained garments! The

31. Richard Salter Storrs (1821-1900), American Congregational minister.

other America loves you because you spoke of Liberty as though she were your daughter!

Before Senator Evarts[32] got up to offer the statue to the President of the United States on behalf of the American Commission, the audience, stirred by Lesseps' words, insisted on greeting Bartholdi, who, with becoming modesty, stood and gratefully acknowledged the tribute from his seat. Senator Evarts' speeches are characterized by noble language and lofty content, and his eloquence, deft and genuine, reaches the heart because it is born of the heart.

But his voice faded when he read from narrow sheets his speech depicting France's generosity in phrases like ribbons and pompons. After Lesseps he seemed a stooping reed: his head is all forehead; his inspiration finds difficulty in shining through his lean, parched face; he is dressed in a frock coat with turned-up collar and a black cap on his head.

Before he concluded his speech someone mistakenly thought the expected moment had arrived when the banner covering the face of the statue would be drawn, and the navy, the ships, the city broke out in a unanimous din that seemed to ascend to high heaven from a shield of resounding bronze. Astounding pomp! Sublime majesty! Never did a people incline with greater reverence before any altar! Men at the foot of the pedestal, stunned by their own smallness, looked at each other as if they had fallen from above. Far away the cannon boomed, masts disappeared in the smoke, the growing clamor spread through the air. In the distance the statue seemed like a huge mother among the clouds.

President Cleveland seemed entirely worthy of speaking in her presence. His style too has marrow, his accent is sincere, his voice warm, clear, and powerful. He suggests more than he explains. He said such broad, lofty things as sound well

32. William Maxwell Evarts (1818-1901), Secretary of State under President Hayes and U.S. Senator from New York (1885-1891). He was President Andrew Johnson's lawyer during his Senate impeachment trial.

before a monument. His left hand rested on the rostrum rail, his right he sank under the lapel of his frock coat. His glance had that challenge which becomes honest winners.

Shall we not forgive for being haughty one who knows he is surrounded by enemies because he is pure? His mind is a compensation for his overflowing fleshiness. He looks what he is, kind and strong. Lesseps glanced upon him affectionately as if wanting to make friends.

He too, like Lesseps, bared his head to speak. His words brought forth applause not so much for the pompous phrase and commanding gesture, as for their vibrating tone and sound sense. If the statue could be melted into words, they would say the same: "This token of the love and esteem of the French people proves the kinship between republics and assures us that we have a firm ally across the Atlantic in our efforts to recommend to all men the excellence of a government built on the will of the people." "We are not here today to bow our heads before the image of a warlike and fearful god, full of wrath and vengeance, but to contemplate joyfully our own goddess guarding the gates of America, greater than all those the ancients worshiped, a goddess who instead of wielding the bolts of terror and death, raises to heaven the beacon that lights the way to man's emancipation." The long applause that rewarded this honest man came from loving hearts.

Then Chauncey Depew,[33] "the silver orator," began the main oration. It must have been good when he was able to hold untiringly the public's attention at a late hour.

Who is Chauncey Depew? All that talent can be without generosity. Railroads are his business, millions his figures, emperors his public, the Vanderbilts[34] his friends and

33. Chauncey Mitchell Depew (1834-1928), American lawyer and railroad manager, and well known as an after-dinner speaker.

34. Depew was attorney for the Vanderbilt railroads. Cornelius Vanderbilt (1794-1877), known as "Commodore" Vanderbilt, was one of the leading Robber Barons of the post-Civil War period.

Maecenas. Men are of little concern to him, railroads of much.[35] He has a preying eye, a broad, haughty brow, a hooked nose, a thin, narrow upper lip, a long, pointed, close-shaven chin. He is idolized here because his speech is brilliant and harmonious, his will aggressive and sharp, his judgment keen and sure. On this occasion his fresh, versatile style did not sparkle as it often does in his much praised after-dinner talks, nor did he present a point with irrefutable logic as when he pleads a case as lawyer and railroad executive, nor had he adversaries to browbeat mercilessly as he is reputed doing at the malignant, fearful performances of political meetings. Instead, he told in fiery phrases the generous life of him who, not satisfied with having helped Washington found his nation, returned—blessed be the Marquis de Lafayette!—to ask the North American Congress to free "his Negro brothers."[36]

In ardent paragraphs he described the friendly talks between Lafayette and Washington at the latter's modest

35. Martí frequently referred to Depew as the representative of the type of Americans who dominated the country after the Civil War in the interest of big business. (See *Obras Completas* [La Habana, 1946], Vol. I, pp. 1193, 1252, 1257, 1276, 1280, 1343, 1776, 1801, 1871, 1877, 1878, 1890, 1952, 1953, 1955, 1974, 1996, 2000.)

36. Lafayette wrote to Washington (and sent a copy to the President of Congress) in which he suggested: "At present my dear General, when you are going to enjoy some repose, permit me to propose to you a plan that may become greatly useful to the black portion of the human race. Let us unite to buy a small property where we can try to free the negroes and to occupy them only as agricultural labourers. Such an example, given by you, might be generally followed and if we succeed in America, I shall with joy devote a part of my time to make that idea fashionable in the West Indies. If it is a bizarre idea, I had rather be judged a fool in that way, than to be considered wise on account of the opposite conduct. ..." (Whitlock, op. cit., Vol. I, p. 276.) Lafayette was also a member of the Society of the Friends of the Blacks in Paris, founded in 1788 with the objective of ending the slave trade in the French West Indian colonies.

Mount Vernon home and the speech with which the Marquis, "purified by battles and privations," took leave of the American Congress, in which he saw "an immense temple of liberty, a lesson to all the oppressors and a hope to all the oppressed of the world." [37]

The year of 1793 did not appall him, nor the dungeon at Olmütz tame him, nor Napoleon's victory convince him. To one who really feels liberty in his heart, what are persecutions but challenges, or unjust empires but soap bubbles? It is such men of instinct that guide the world. They act first and reason after. Thought corrects their errors, but lacks the virtue of sudden action. They feel and push. Thus by the will of nature it is written that things should be in the history of man!

Chauncey Depew looked like a magistrate when, shaking his arm and a trembling forefinger over his head covered with a silk cap, he summarized admirably the benefits man enjoys in this land founded on liberty; and with all the fire of a charger that feels his loins sorely spurred, he transformed his hidden fear into bravery, rose up in the name of free institutions to attack the fanatics who, under their protection, would seek to defeat them, and having learned the lesson of the social problem spreading over the United States, this "silver-worded" gentleman humbled the pride for which he is noted and drew out inspired strains to utter as his own the very phrases which are the gospel of the workers' revolution.

Oh, Liberty, how convincing is thy shadow: those who hate thee or use thee bow before the commanding gesture!

Then a bishop appeared on the rostrum. He raised an age-bitten hand; all around the men of genius and of power stood up. There was a magnificent silence while he blessed in the name of God the redeeming statue. Guided by the bishop the

37. The *New York Times* summarized Depew's address, which it said "was a long historical review of the story of the French alliance with the struggling American colonies during the Revolution, which he characterized as the Romance of History." (October 29, 1886.)

audience intoned a slow, soft hymn, a mystic doxology. A sign from the top of the torch indicated the ceremony was over.

Streams of people, fearful of grim night, rushed to the narrow wharves, without concern for age or rank. Bands were heard vaguely as though lulled by the evening twilight.

The weight of joy rather than the weight of people seemed to load down the ships. Cannon smoke covered the official launch that carried the president back to the city. High above, the astonished birds circled fearfully around the statue as though it were the top of a new mountain. Men felt their hearts were firmer within their breasts.

When, among shadows, the last boats left the shores of the island, now transformed into an altar, a crystal-clear voice breathed out a popular melody which passed from ship to ship. Garlands of lights, reddening the sky's canopy, shone from the cornices of buildings. A song, at once soft and formidable, spread at the statue's feet and along the river. A united people, pressed together on the sterns of ships, gazing toward the island, with an unction fortified by night, sang: "Farewell, my only love!"

La Nación (Buenos Aires), January 1, 1887
Dated New York, October 29, 1886

New York Under the Snow

The first oriole had already been spied hanging its nest from a cedar in Central Park; the bare poplars were putting forth their plush of spring; and the leaves of the chestnut were burgeoning, like chattering women poking their heads out of their hoods after a storm. Notified by the cheeping of the birds, the brooks were coming out from under their icy covering to see the sun's return, and winter, defeated by the flowers, had fled away, covering its retreat with the month of winds. The first straw hats made their appearance, and the streets of New York were gay with Easter attire, when, on opening its eyes after the hurricane had spent its force, the city found itself silent, deserted, shrouded, buried under the snow. Doughty Italians, braving the icy winds, load their streetcleaning carts with fine, glittering snow, which they empty into the river to the accompaniment of neighs, songs, jokes, and oaths. The elevated train, stranded in a two-day death vigil beside the body of the engineer who set out to defy the blizzard, is running again, creaking and shivering,

1. The headline in the *New York Times* of March 14, 1888, the same day Martí wrote this dispatch, read: "Crushed Under The Snow. Struggling To Throw Off Its Heavy Burden. The City Still In A Paralyzed Condition." The *Times* predicted that the great blizzard of 1888 would continue to hamper the city for days to come, and that "if New York recovers within a week it may consider itself in good luck."

158

over the clogged rails that glitter and flash. Sleigh bells jingle, the news vendors cry their papers; snow plows, drawn by stout Percherons, throw up banks of snow on both sides of the street as they clear the horsecar's path; through the breast-high snow, the city makes its way back to the trains, paralyzed on the white plains; to the rivers, become bridges; to the silent wharves.

The clash of the combatants echoes through the vaultlike streets of the city. For two days the snow has had New York in its power, encircled, terrified, like a prize fighter driven to the canvas by a sneak punch. But the moment the attack of the enemy slackened, as soon as the blizzard had spent its first fury, New York, like the victim of an outrage, goes about freeing itself of its shroud. Through the white hummocks move leagues of men. The snow already runs in dirty rivers in the busiest streets under the onslaught of its assailants. With spades, with shovels, with their own chests and those of the horses, they push back the snow, which retreats to the rivers.

Man's defeat was great, but so was his triumph. The city is still white; the Sound remains white and frozen. There have been deaths, cruelties, kindness, fatigue, and bravery. Man has given a good account of himself in this disaster.

At no time in this century has New York experienced a storm like that of March 13. It had rained the preceding Sunday, and the writer working into the dawn, the newspaper vendor at the railroad station, the milkman on his round of the sleeping houses, could hear the whiplash of the wind that had descended on the city against the chimneys, against walls and roofs, as it vented its fury on slate and mortar, shattered windows, demolished porches, clutched and uprooted trees, and howled, as though ambushed, as it fled down the narrow streets. Electric wires, snapping under its impact, sputtered and died. Telegraph lines, which had withstood so many storms, were wrenched from their posts. And when the sun should have appeared, it could not be seen, for like a shrieking, panic-stricken army, with its broken squadrons, gun carriages and infantry, the snow whirled past the darkened windows, without interruption, day and night. Man refused to be vanquished. He came out to defy the storm.

But by this time the overpowered streetcar lay horseless beneath the storm; the elevated train, which paid in blood for its first attempt to brave the elements, let the steam escape from its helpless engine; the suburban train, halted en route by the tempest or stalled by the drifting snow, higher than the engines, struggled in vain to reach its destination. The streetcars attempted one trip, and the horses plunged and reared, defending themselves with their hoofs from the suffocating storm. The elevated train took on a load of passengers, and ground to a halt halfway through the trip, paralyzed by the snow; after six hours of waiting, the men and women climbed down by ladder from their wind-tossed prison. The wealthy, or those faced with an emergency, paid twenty-five or fifty dollars for carriages drawn by stout horses to carry them a short distance, step by step. The angry wind, heavy with snow, buffeted them, pounded them, hurled them to the ground.

It was impossible to see the sidewalks. Intersections could no longer be distinguished, and one street looked like the next. On Twenty-third Street, one of the busiest thoroughfares, a thoughtful merchant put a sign on a cornerpost: "This is 23rd Street." The snow was knee-deep, and the drifts, waist-high. The angry wind nipped at the hands of pedestrians, knifed through their clothing, froze their noses and ears, blinded them, hurled them backward into the slippery snow, its fury making it impossible for them to get to their feet, flung them hatless and groping for support against the walls, or left them to sleep, to sleep forever, under the snow. A shopkeeper, a man in the prime of life, was found buried today, with only a hand sticking from the snow to show where he lay. A messenger boy, as blue as his uniform, was dug out of a white, cool tomb, a fit resting place for his innocent soul, and lifted up in the compassionate arms of his comrades. Another, buried to the neck, sleeps with two red patches on his white cheeks, his eyes a filmy blue.

The old, the young, women, children inch along Broadway and the avenues on their way to work. Some fall, and struggle to their feet. Some, exhausted, sink into a doorway, their only desire to struggle no more; others, generous souls take them by the arm, encouraging them, shouting and singing. An old woman, who had made herself a kind of mask of her handkerchief with two slits for the eyes, leans against a wall and bursts into tears; the president of a neighboring bank, making his way on foot, carries her in his arms to a nearby pharmacy, which can be made out through the driving snow by its yellow and green lights. "I'm not going any further," said one. "I don't care if I lose my job." "I'm going on," says another. "I need my day's pay." The clerk takes the working girl by the arm; she helps her weary friend with an arm around his waist. At the entrance to the Brooklyn Bridge, a new bank clerk pleads with the policeman to let him pass, although at that moment only death can cross the bridge. "I will lose the job it has taken me three years to find," he supplicates. He starts across, and the wind reaches a terrible height, throws him to the ground with one gust, lifts him up again, snatches off his hat, rips open his coat, knocks him down at every step; he falls back, clutches at the railing, drags himself along. Notified by telegraph from Brooklyn, the police on the New York side of the bridge pick him up, utterly spent.

But why all this effort, when hardly a store is open, when the whole city has surrendered, huddled like a mole in its burrow, when if they reach the factory or office they will find the iron doors locked? Only a fellow man's pity, or the power of money, or the happy accident of living beside the only train which is running in one section of the city, valiantly inching along from hour to hour, can give comfort to so many faithful employees, so many courageous old men, so many heroic factory girls on this terrible day. From corner to corner they make their way, sheltering themselves in doorways until one opens to the feeble knocking of their numbed hands, like sparrows tapping against the window panes. Suddenly the fury of the wind mounts; it hurls the group fleeing for shelter against the wall; the poor working women cling to one another in the middle of the street until the snarling, screeching wind puts them to flight again. Men and women fight their way uptown, struggling against the gale, clearing the snow from their eyes, shielding them with their hands to find their way through the storm. Hotels? The chairs have been rented out for beds, and the baths for rooms. Drinks? Not even the men can find anything to drink; the saloons have exhausted their stock; and the women, dragging their numb feet homeward, have only their tears to drink.

After the first surprise of the dawn, people find ways to adjust their clothing so the fury of the tempest will not do them so much harm. There is an overturned wagon at every step; a shade, hanging from its spring, flaps against the wall like the wing of a dying bird; an awning is torn to ribbons; a cornice dangles from its wall; an eave lies in the street. Walls, hallways, windows are all banked with snow. And the blizzard blows without respite, piling up drifts, scattering destruction, whistling and howling. And men and women keep walking with the snow to their armpits.

One has made a mask of silk from his umbrella, with two holes for the eyes, and another for the mouth, and thus, with his hands behind his back, he cuts his way through the wind. Others have tied stockings over their shoes, or bags of salt, or wrapping paper, or strips of rubber, fastened with twine. Others protect themselves with leggings, with fur caps; another, half dead, is being carried, wrapped in his buffalo-hide overcoat. "Sir," pleads the voice of a child, who cannot be seen for the snow, "help me out of here, I am dying." It is a messenger boy whom some heartless employer has sent out in this storm. There are many on horseback; one, who came out in a sled, is carried away with it at the first gust, and nearly loses his life. A determined old lady, who set out to buy a

wreath of orange blossoms for her daughter's marriage, loses
the wreath to the wind. Night fell over the arctic waste of
New York, and terror took over. The postman on his round
fell face down, blinded and benumbed, protecting his leather
bag with his body. Families trapped in the roofless houses
sought madly and in vain to find a way out through the
snow-banked doors. When water hydrants lay buried under
five feet of snow, a raging fire broke out, lighting up the
snowy landscape like the Northern Lights, and swiftly burned
three apartment houses to the ground. The fire wagons arrived! The firemen dug with their hands, and found the
hydrant. The walls and the snowy street were scarlet, and the
sky was blue velvet. Although the water they played against
the flames was hurled back in their faces in stinging pellets by
the fury of the wind, although the tongues of crimson flame
leaped higher than the cross on the church steeple, although
the wind-tossed columns of smoke bearing golden sparks
singed their beards, there, without giving an inch, the firemen
fought the fire with the snow at their breasts, brought it
under control, and vanquished it. And then, with their arms,
they opened a path for the engine through the snow.

Without milk, without coal, without mail, without newspapers, without streetcars, without telephone, without telegraph, the city arose today. What eagerness on the part of
those living uptown to read the newspapers, which thanks to
the intrepidity of the poor newsboys, finally came up from
the downtown presses! There were four theaters open last
night, but all the stores and offices are closed, and the elevated struggles in vain to carry the unwitting crowds that
gather at its station to their places of work.

The trains and their human cargoes stand snowbound on
the tracks. The city is cut off from the rest of the country
and no news goes in or out. The rivers are ice, and the courageous cross them on foot; suddenly the ice gives way, and
cakes of it float aimlessly with men aboard them; a tug goes
out to rescue them, skirting the ice cake, nosing it toward the
bank, edging it to a nearby dock. They are saved. What a

cheer goes up from both sides of the river! There are also cheers as the fireman passes, the policeman, and the brave postman. What can have happened to the trains that never arrive? The railroad companies, with admirable despatch, send out food and coal, hauled by their most powerful engines. What of those at sea? How many bodies lie buried under the snow?

Like a routed army that unexpectedly turns on its vanquisher, the snow had come in the night and covered the proud city with death.

These unpredictable onslaughts show utilitarian countries to advantage more than any others, for as was amply proven yesterday, in the hour of stress, the virtues that work heightens completely overshadowed those which selfishness withers. How brave the children, how loyal the workers, how uncomplaining and noble the women, how generous the men! The whole city spoke in loud voices today, as though it were afraid of finding itself alone. Those who unfeelingly push and jostle one another all the rest of the year, smile on each other today, tell of the dangers they escaped, exchange addresses, and walk along with new friends. The squares are mountains of snow, over which the icy lacework clinging like filigree to the branches of the trees glitters in the morning sun.

Houses of snow crown the rooftops, where the merry sparrows dig fragile nests. It is amazing and frightening, as though a shroud should suddenly flower in blood, to see the red roofs of the houses reappear in this city of snow. The telegraph poles ruefully contemplate the destruction, their tangled, fallen wires like unkempt heads. The city digs out, buries its dead, and with men, horses, and machines all working together, clears away the snow with streams of boiling water, with shovels, plows, and bonfires. But one is touched by a sense of great humility and a sudden rush of kindness, as though the dread hand had touched the shoulders of all men.

La Nación (Buenos Aires), April 27, 1888
Dated New York, March 15, 1888

Two Views of Coney Island

1

Nothing in the history of mankind has ever equaled the marvelous prosperity of the United States. Time will tell whether deep roots are lacking here; whether the ties of sacrifice and common sorrow that bind some people together are stronger than those of common interests; whether this colossal nation carries in its entrails ferocious, tremendous elements; whether a lack of that femininity which is the origin of the artistic sense and the complement of nationality, hardens and corrupts the heart of this wonderful country.

For the present, the fact is that never has a happier, a jollier, a better equipped, more compact, more jovial, and more frenzied multitude living anywhere on earth, while engaged in useful labors, created and enjoyed greater wealth, nor covered rivers and seas with more gaily dressed ships, nor overflown lovely shores, gigantic wharves, and brilliant, fantastic promenades with more bustling order, more childlike glee.

United States newspapers are full of hyperbolic descriptions of the unusual beauty and singular attraction of one of these summer resorts, with crowds of people, numerous luxurious hotels, crossed by an elevated railroad, studded with gardens, kiosks, small theaters, saloons, circuses, tents, a multitude of carriages, picturesque assemblies, vending wagons, stands, and fountains.

French newspapers echo its fame. From all over the Union come legions of fearless ladies and country beaux to admire the splendid scenery, lavish wealth, blinding variety, Herculean push, and surprising aspect of famous Coney Island, an island which four years ago was nothing but an abandoned heap of earth and is now an ample place for rest, seclusion, or entertainment for the one hundred thousand New Yorkers who visit its shores daily.

It is composed of four hamlets joined by carriage, tram, and steam railroads. One is Manhattan Beach, where, in the dining room of one hotel, four thousand people can comfortably sit at the same time; another, Rockaway, has arisen, as Minerva arose with lance and helmet, armed with steamers, squares, piers, murmuring orchestras, hotels big as cities, nay, as nations; still another, less important, takes its name from its hotel, the vast, heavy Brighton. But the most attractive place on the island is neither far-off Rockaway, nor monotonous Brighton, nor aristocratic, stuffy Manhattan Beach, but Cable, smiling Cable with its elevator, higher than Trinity Church steeple in New York, twice as high as the steeples of our Cathedral, to the top of which people are carried in a tiny, fragile cage to a dizzying height; Cable, with its two iron piers projecting on elegant piles three blocks into the sea, its Sea Beach Palace, now only a hotel, but which in the Philadelphia Fair was the famous Agricultural Building, transported to New York and reassembled as if by magic, without a piece missing, on the shores of Coney Island; Cable, with its fifty-cent museums where human monsters, freakish fish, bearded ladies, melancholy dwarfs, and rickety elephants, ballyhooed as the biggest elephants in the world, are shown; Cable with its one hundred orchestras, its lively dances, its battalions of baby carriages, its gigantic cow being perpetually milked, its fresh cider at twenty-five cents a glass, its countless couples of loving pilgrims which bring back to our lips García Gutiérrez's[1] tender cries:

1. Antonio García Gutiérrez (1812-1884), Spanish romantic dra-

In pairs they go
Over the hillocks
The crested larks,
The turtle-doves

Cable, where families resort in search of wholesome, invigorating sea breezes instead of New York's foul and nauseating air; where poor mothers, as they open great lunch baskets with provisions for the whole family press against their breasts their unfortunate babes who seem consumed, emaciated, gnawed by that terrible summer sickness which mows down children as a sickle does wheat, *cholera infantum.*

Steamers come and go, trains whistle and smoke, leave and arrive emptying their serpent belly full of people on the shore. Women wear rented blue flannel suits and coarse straw hats which they tie under their chins; men in still simpler suits lead them to the sea, while barefooted children at the water's edge await the roaring breakers and run back when the waves are about to wet them, disguising their fear with laughter. Then, relieved of the smoldering heat of an hour ago, they charge, tirelessly, against the enemy, or, like marine butterflies, they brave the fresh waves, play at filling each other's pails with shovelfuls of burning sand, or, after bathing—imitating in this the behavior of grown-up people of both sexes who do not heed the censure and surprise of those who feel as we do in our countries—they lie on the sand and allow themselves to be buried, patted down, kneaded into the burning sand. This practice, considered a wholesome exercise, lends itself to a certain superficial, vulgar, and boisterous intimacy to which these prosperous people seem so inclined.

But the most surprising thing there is not the way they go bathing, nor the children's cadaverous faces, nor the odd headdresses and incomprehensible attire of those girls noted for their extravagance, their eccentricity, and their inordi-

---

matic and lyric poet, author of *El Trovador,* from which the libretto for Verdi's opera *Il Trovatore* was taken.

nate inclinations to merrymaking, nor the spooners, nor the bathing booths, nor the operas that are sung at café tables in the guise of *Edgar* and *Romeo,* and *Lucia* and *Juliet,* nor the grimaces and screams of Negro minstrels, surely not like the Scottish minstrels, alas!, nor the majestic beach, nor the soft, serene sun. The surprising thing there is the size, the quantity, the sudden outburst of human activity, that immense valve of pleasure open to an immense people, those dining rooms which, seen from afar, look like bivouacked armies, those roads which, from two miles away, do not seem like roads but like carpets of heads, that daily outpouring of a portentous people upon a portentous beach, that mobility, that change of form, that fighting spirit, that push, that feverish rivalry of wealth, that monumental appearance of the whole place which makes a bathing establishment worthy of competing with the majesty of the country that supports it, the sea that caresses it and the sky that crowns it, that swelling tide, that dumbfounding, overwhelming, steady, frenzied expansiveness, and that simplicity in the marvelous; *that* is the surprising thing.

Other peoples—we among them—live devoured by a sublime inner demon who pushes us tirelessly on in search of an ideal of love or glory. When we hold the measure of the ideal we were after, delighted as though we were holding an eagle, a new quest makes us restless, a new ambition spurs us, a new aspiration heads us toward a new vehement desire, and out of the captive eagle emerges a rebel, free butterfly, daring us to follow it, chaining us to her circuitous flight.

Not so these tranquil souls, only disturbed by the craving of owning a fortune. Our eyes scan the reverberating beaches, we go in and out of those halls as vast as pampas,[2] we climb to the peak of those colossal structures as tall as mountains. Promenaders in comfortable chairs by the seaside fill their

2. Martí's article, "La Pampa," a description of the vast prairies of South America, appears in the third volume of this collection.

lungs with that bracing, benign air. But a melancholy sadness, as it were, takes hold of the men of our Latin American countries who live here, for they seek each other in vain and no matter how much first impressions may have lured their senses, charmed their eyes, dazzled and puzzled their reason, they are finally possessed by the anguish of solitude, while the homesickness for a superior spiritual world invades them and grieves them. They feel like stray sheep without their mothers or their shepherd. Tears may or may not flow to their eyes, but their astounded souls break in bitter weeping, because this great land is devoid of spirit.

What a bustle! What flow of money! What facilities for pleasure! What absolute absence of all sadness or visible poverty! Everything is in the open air; the noisy groups, the vast dining halls, that peculiar courtship of North Americans into which enter almost none of the elements which make up the modest, tender, exalted love found in our lands. The theater, the photographic studio, the bathing booths; everything in the open. Some get weighed, for to North Americans to weigh a pound more or less is a matter of positive joy or real grief; for fifty cents, others receive from a stout German woman an envelope containing their fortune; still others, with incomprehensible delight, drink certain unsavory mineral waters out of tall, narrow glasses like mortar shells.

Some ride in roomy carriages from Manhattan to Brighton at the soft twilight time. One fellow shores his boat, in which he had been rowing with his smiling girlfriend, who holds on to his shoulder as she jumps, frolicking like a child, onto the bustling beach. A group of people admire an artist who cuts silhouettes out of black paper of whoever wishes to have this kind of portrait of himself and glues them on white cards. Another group watch a woman in a tiny shop less than a yard wide and praise her skill at fashioning strange flowers out of fish skins. Others laugh uproariously when one fellow succeeds in hitting a Negro on the nose with a ball, a poor Negro who, for a miserable wage, sticks his head out of a hole in a cloth and is busied day and night eluding with grotesque movements the balls pitched at him.[3] Bearded, venerable citizens ride gravely on wooden tigers, hippogriffs, sphinxes, and boa constrictors that turn like horses around a central pole where a band of would-be musicians play unharmonious sonatas. The less well-to-do eat crabs and oysters on the beach or pies and meats on tables that some large hotels offer free for such purpose. The wealthier people lavish large sums on fuchsin infusions passed off as wine and on strange, massive dishes which our palates, fond of the artistic and light, would certainly reject. To these people eating is a matter of quantity; to ours, of quality.

And this lavishing, this bustle, these crowds, this astounding anthill lasts from June to October, from morning till midnight, without respite, without interruption, without change.

What a beautiful spectacle at night! True enough, a thinking man is surprised at seeing so many married women without their husbands and so many mothers strolling by the humid seaside, concerned with their pleasure, and heedless of the piercing wind that might harm the squalid constitution of the babies they hold against their shoulder.

But no city offers a more splendid view than Cable Beach by night. More lights shine at night than heads could be seen by day. When descried from a distance offshore the four towns shine in the darkness as though the stars of heaven had suddenly gathered and fallen to the sea.

The electric lights that bathe with magic brightness the approaches to the hotels, the lawns, the concert pavilions, even the beach whose every grain of sand can be counted, seem from afar like restless sprites, like blithe, diabolic spirits romping about the sickly gas jets, the garlands of red lanterns, the Chinese globes, the Venetian chandeliers. One can

3. Martí here reveals a keen perception of the degraded status to which racism reduced Negroes in the North where, employment opportunities being so limited, they were forced to seek such humiliating work at Coney Island and other resort areas.

read everywhere, as though it were day: newspapers, billboards, announcements, letters. All is heavenly: the orchestras, the dances, the clamor, the rumble of the waves, the noise of men, the ringing of laughter, the air's caresses, the loud calls, the rapid trains, the stately carriages, until the time comes to return home. Then, as a monster emptying its entrails into the hungry gullet of another monster, the colossal, crushed, compact crowds rush to catch the trains, which, bursting under their weight, seem to pant in their ride through solitude, until they deliver their motley load onto gigantic ships. These latter, livened by harps and violins, take the exhausted tourists to the piers of New York and distribute them in the thousand cars and along the thousand tracks that like veins of steel traverse the sleeping city.

La Pluma (Bogotá), December 3, 1881

2

Coney Island, New York's summer watering place, is not primarily for bathing and neither are its hotels, for those beaches look like mosaic armies or rivers, and those kitchens the stomach of a monster, and the whole island with its three neighboring towns a gigantic glass of champagne in whose sparkling bubbles the joyous sun breaks into a myriad of colors. Alas! back in the city, in the infected slums where one can see thin and filthy hands appearing above the roofs of tenements, like the ragged flags of some tremendous army on the march; in the damp streets where men and women crowd together and mill about, with neither air nor space, much as beneath the surface of roots the ugly and deformed worms, in which vegetal life is being transformed, are lazily unrolling; there in the dark and rambling buildings where people in the dregs of poverty live in stinking cells filled with dank and impure air; there, like young corn in a plague of locusts, the children of the poor are dying by the hundreds in the plague of summer; there, as ogres do to children in story books, the *cholera infantum* sucks the children's lives away. A boa constrictor would leave the children of the poor in no worse condition than the New York summer leaves them—withered, wasted, cadaverous, all skin and bones. Their little eyes resemble caverns, their heads are bald like the heads of old men, their hands are bunches of dry twigs. They drag themselves about like worms, exhale in groans. And I say that it is a national crime, and that abolishing this unnecessary misery is an obligation of the state! At times a compassionate ship takes them to some nearby beach for a breath of fresh air, at the cost of a few good people and a hundred mothers. Oh, those poor children! They look like broken lilies pulled out of the mire. Housing is dear, mothers uneducated, fathers given to prize fights and drink. There are too few industries for the industrialists; the factories are glutted with goods and have no need of new workers. The prohibitive tariff, which gives rise to high and unrealistic salaries, burdens raw materials in such a way that when domestic consumption is supplied, the manufacturers cannot go out and compete with rival products that are cheaper in other countries. And so, due to the mistakes of the legislators, and to the hardheartedness and indifference of the well-to-do, the poor are isolated, angered, offended, and debased. And because of sullen parents and fetid air, the children are dying.

Coney Island in summer is like a flowered pillow upon which, every afternoon, the city rests its fevered head where the swollen brain is pounding. From the account books one goes to the docks that lead to Coney Island. Every hour has no more minutes than there are steamboats. What a joy for the eyes to meet upon the river, like its noble secular gods, those majestic white steamboats; the joy of not seeing in the lively, twofold highway of land and water either slovenly beaches or filthy villages or dismal and abandoned roads! What strength and dignity that broad river, that vast sky, those tilled fields, that winged railroad, those clean cities put into one's character! What wholesome commerce between man and Nature, after the petty and painful incidents of daily life!

New York pours into Coney Island; by day it is an immense midway; by night it seems that every star has agreed to meet in one corner of the sky, and torn out of it has suddenly fallen in three gigantic baskets of light upon the island. Happy Hoffman![4] Railroad trains run from one little town to the next; along the ocean is a broad highway, above the edge of the waves a boardwalk. In front of every hotel a noisy orchestra, covered by a huge shell, sometimes plays *Lohengrin,* sometimes mimics a crying child or a clucking hen, to loud applause from the common people; at times it is accompanied by cannon, at others by anvils. I do not consider this latter kind of music bad! And each little town of the island's three, having no hotels or strolling people, cries out, entices, splatters its charms, squanders its colors, is out of place. Gay flags wave from blue towers; along the damp white sand, shouting for joy, their blowing clothes gathered up, thousands of barefoot children run to the waves and then flee from them. Beneath a red umbrella two jovial lovers devise a corner of their own, as if nobody could see them. At the crowded railing lazy spectators laugh at the comical bathers.

This machine is for making silk cloth; see the thread, the weft, the dye vats, the stamping process, the finished handkerchief made before our eyes; we can buy it for a few silver coins. This fellow hawking his wares and gesticulating calls the passersby to see a pretty young girl from Madras wearing silver rings upon the toes of her small feet, and richly wrought and not unhandsome gold filigree earrings covering her ears. She has swarthy skin, curving outlines, straight and very glossy hair, and kindly eyes. Inside that little painted den a frail girl—oh, what a poor caricature of the gypsy

4. John Thompson Hoffman (1828-1888), lawyer, politician, mayor and governor of New York.

people!—takes out of a little machine an envelope containing
the fortune of those who pay for it, a fortune told by a
silverplated fairy surmounting the machine. Some people
weigh themselves, others fall off of their velocipedes, others
practice rifle shooting. Those over there, both men and
women, are going to bet on the horses, as if dying of hunger
and thirst. This way and that, dispensers of aromatic soda,
cloudy beer, mock champagne, or cider that is healthful and
real, for there one can see how it is pressed out of red apples.
Some serious, comely, nimble-fingered women gently squeeze
the springs of the mechanical udders of a big, rawhide, imitation cow from which come fountains of milk, like a vine-
crowned Bacchus.

Here go the children and young people to see how the
island, with all of its crowds and colors, is reflected in a
pinhole camera. There go some people ascending almost one
hundred yards above the ground in an elevator that takes
them to the top of a colossal iron skeleton—people who, with
such an excess of life, find the ground too limiting. By that
pier, which extends like a tongue to make a treacherous
highway of insects, a monstrous anthill, the island pours running people into streets two hundred meters over the water.
They buy soft drinks, applaud the puppets, laugh, cheer,
wander from place to place. Here the young people, and the
servants who take a myriad of little children there, hang onto
a wooden griffon, ride a rooster, sit between the two humps
of a camel, mount the tail of a fish, going round and round to
the sound of music.

All is moving cars, flying ribbons, sparkling glass, sounds of
the sea of humanity, dense physical merriment.

And there at last, behind those wooden barriers, before ten
thousand fictional characters, the longhaired men of the West
with implacable hands, elegant felt hats, and nervous bodies,
and with their cohorts of cowboys and Indians, pretend to
have brought from the forests, amid volcanic hurrahs, those
terrible and romantic deeds that snatched virgin territory in
the face of buffalo humps and the rancorous teeth of Indians.

Over there you see men hunting the stag! This fellow comes at full gallop, firing at fifty-odd flying pigeons that he is shooting down. Here come some Indians singing their wild and doleful chant to the slow gait of their warhorses, and suddenly, like an invisible wall, a departing throng of partisans shouting warcries that vibrate in the air like bloodthirsty swords, disband in helter-skelter flight. Stretched over the necks of their horses, they surround against a lone tree trunk a dying white man who empties his pistol into those feathered heads and yellow breasts. Quickly! Quickly! The brave explorers launch an attack to rescue their surprised companions, and the Indians wind in and out among their avengers, escaping from their clutches and hanging onto their animals' flanks by their nails. They flee in the black smoke and hail of bullets, fearfully clinging to the undersides of their swift horses. Hurrah, hurrah! For now the Indians and explorers and cowboys, peacefully arm in arm, tie up by the forelegs and hindlegs and head the buffalo buck whose imposing snout strikes the ground like a stout warclub, while the band plays, the longhaired gentlemen wave their handsome hats in the healthful sea air, the lamblike Indians sell their portraits among the crowd, and the resplendent and snorting locomotive huffs and puffs and squeaks at the hippodrome gates, its crest of smoke rising above men like a salute!

La Nación (Buenos Aires), October 21, 1883
Dated New York, September 1, 1883

Prize Fight

The pen soars when it has grand things to relate, but it plods, as it does now, when it must give account of brutal things, devoid of beauty and nobility. The pen should be spotless like a virgin. It writhes like a slave, it flees the paper like a fugitive, it swoons in the hand that holds it as though it shared in the wrong it describes. There are men here who fight like bulls, running together, skull against skull. They bite and claw one another during the fight, and when it is over, one of the combatants, streaming blood, his gums depopulated, his forehead bruised and knuckles raw, staggers through the crowd that swirls around him, scaling hats in the air and shouting its acclaim, to collect the purse that is his reward for victory. At the same moment, his opponent lies senseless in the arms of his handlers, his vertebrae shattered, and women's hands arrange bouquets of flowers to perfume the crowded dressing rooms of these base ruffians.

These fights are national holidays, setting trains and telegraphs in motion, paralyzing business for hours, and bringing together knots of laborers and bankers in the streets. Bets are laid to the clink of glasses, and the newspapers, which editorialize against the practice, fill their pages with accounts of the comings and goings, the comments, private life, training, feuds, triumphs, and defeats of the rivals. Every heartbeat of these low fellows is recorded as though the blood of martyrs flowed in their veins. Their physiques are described minutely,

176

and the whiteness and smoothness of their skin. Their muscles and limbs are measured and compared. Their dress, their meals, their most trivial remarks, their weights, are reported daily. Their battle colors are blazoned. Their footgear for the ring is sketched.

That is a prize fight. With such preparations, the Giant of Troy and the Boston Strong Man have just fought.[1] In this manner, the Giant was sent reeling to the ground, senseless and gory, while two thousand spectators roared. That is what has kept New Orleans at carnival pitch, every hamlet in the country on tenterhooks, and Boston, New York, and Philadelphia in visible excitement. I can still see the city urchins, who are like green fruit withered on the vine, clinging to the wheels and sides of the newspaper wagon like an angry swarm of bees. The customers crowd around the wagon, which pulls away, drawn by the dray horse to which it is hitched, leaving behind a welter of newspaper peddlers fighting over the bundles of newspaper dropped off by the wagon. They are miserable little girls, or fierce Irish ragamuffins who get up from the mud cursing the hats they lost in the scuffle. New wagons arrive and the fighting breaks out anew. Those who are fortunate enough to get newspapers cannot sell them fast enough to satisfy customers who besiege them. Great crowds shiver in the rain and peer up at the bulletin boards the leading newspapers post in front of their offices with the latest particulars on the fight. The children learn from the newspaper their father brings home which blow closed which eye, whose right bloodied whose nose, and how a fighter can kill his opponent by politely pushing back his face with one hand while hitting him on the back of the neck with the other. Pictures of the fighters, drawings of their pennants, and sketches of the fighting are published by their news-

1. John L. Sullivan (1850-1918), known as the "Boston Strong Man" (and the "Great John"), knocked out Paddy Ryan ("Giant of Troy") in the ninth round, February 7, 1882, for the heavyweight championship, a fight conducted with bare knuckles.

papers. The conversation around the family dinner table is of how this friend lost a hundred dollars while another won a thousand, and yet another a thousand more, because some bet on the Giant, and others on the victorious Strong Man. That was New York the afternoon of the fight.

But what of the fight itself? It was off in the South beside the sea, beneath cedars and live oak. These are not squabbles between knaves, inflamed or cooled by circumstances, and governed by caprice. They are contests between brutes under contract, in which, as in the days of jousting, the field is divided according to the sun, and the weight of the combatants and rules of the contest are formally agreed upon in the greatest detail, as in a horse race. The contestants will fight on foot, without rocks or irons in their hands, and with no more than three cleats, rounded at the ends and not to exceed a half-inch in length, on the soles of their shoes. It is agreed, with an eye to decorum, that this time there will be no biting or scratching, and that no blows are to be struck while an opponent has a knee and a hand touching the ground, nor while he is held by the neck against the ropes or ringposts, which are to mark out an area of level ground no more than twenty-four feet square. Furthermore, the battle colors of the rivals are to be hoisted atop the main post for all to see, in this case, a harp, a sun, a moon, and a shield, with a broadwinged eagle perched on a starspangled sphere for the Giant of Troy, and an eagle holding an American shield flanked by American and Irish flags aloft in the clouds, for the Boston Strong Man. For it was from Ireland, with the great migration, that this barbarous sport came to this country.

The ages of men are simply this: a transition from the man-beast to the man-man. There are moments when the beast in man gets the upper hand, and teeth feel a need to bite, a murderous thirst consumes the throat, eyes become flames, and clenched fists must find bodies on which to rain their blows. The human victory consists in restraining the beast and placing over it an angel. But while the industrious

Aztecs and cultivated Incas were building roads over the
mountains, channeling their rivers through immense conduits,
and fashioning delicate rings for the fingers of their women,
the men of those northern lands, like the Cain of Cormon,
who opposed their hairy chests and hidecovered backs to the
spears of Caesar's legions, pitched their nomad tents in the
craggy highlands, and tore the half-cooked flesh from the
steer roasted in the hide, which they had throttled in their
arms of steel. Their arms seemed mountainsides, their legs
tree trunks, their hands maces, and their heads forests. Living
was once a struggle with the beasts for control of the forests.
Life is no longer a wild mountain, but a statue carved out of
the mountain.

So it is, that one's eyes start, as if one saw Cain lumbering
through the streets of a modern city, to see how the arts of
illustration and printing abjectly lick the horned feet of these
human beasts, represent and celebrate the magnificent brutes,
and breathlessly seize on the instant in which, naked to the
waist and flexing his trunklike arm, he propels a leather ball
toward the ceiling from which it hangs with the same blows
he will later loose, to the sound of hurrahs and cheers, against
the creaking skull, the swollen lips, and the trembling body
of his terrified opponent. They train for the fight, build up
their strength, work off the superfluous flesh that burdens
and does not withstand assault; they retire with a camp reti-
nue to isolated training sites where their coaches teach them
excellent blows, forbid them excesses of the flesh, and show
them off to the professional gamblers, who demand to see
the fighter in action before betting because "this is strictly
business," and they want to bet on "the best man." It is
strictly business with the fighters, too, who often have never
laid eyes on each other before meeting face to face in the
ring. A promoter, with two thousand dollars backing one
fighter, and a newspaperman, with two thousand on the
other, have arranged the match for the "heavyweight championship of America." The fighters are delighted, for the win-
ner of the bloody fight stands to gain fame and fortune by

shattering the bones and rattling the brains of his opponent. There are 130-pound runts who battle for the honor of being the wealthiest fighter among the lightweights, and there are 200-pounders who fight for the title of heavyweight champion.

As soon as the match is set, those who train the boxer, his "seconds," take charge, making sure that the "fighting man" does not jeopardize the investment of his "backer" by drinking and wenching. The nation becomes the pit for a cockfight. The two men tour the country and box with gloves, naked to the waist, in theaters, squares, and casinos, where their colors are displayed. The managers mingle with the crowds, boast of their fighter's accomplishments, let the spectators feel their muscles, argue the odds, and take bets from the local gamblers. Factions develop in every town, and often as not, the exhibition ends in a riot with the rival gangs leaping onto the ring or the stage with pistols and knives drawn. Troy loves its Giant, who is the owner of a theater, a family man, and a prodigy of the ring; it burns with envy of Boston, which boasts that no man ever measured himself against the Strong Man without being carried all bloody from the ring. Do not ask who halts this barbarous practice, for it occurs in public places month after month, and no one lifts a finger. There are laws to be sure, but it is the same as in Mexico with the bullfights, which serve to make bulls out of men. Bullfighting is prohibited in the Tenochtitlán, but it is permitted in nearby Tlalnepantla, where Netzahualcoyotl, the poet king, once prayed in his tower, and now men born to better things because of the greatness of the land that bred them, affect the costume of the bullfighter and slaughter beasts in the ring.

As the day of the fight draws near, the fighters keep one jump ahead of the law, for each state has different statutes, and there are many distinguished lawmakers who are strongly opposed to prize fighting. But there are states that will take them in, and their arrival touches off a general celebration. The trains come from every direction loaded with bettors, who have closed down their businesses, widowed their wives, orphaned their children, and come thousands of miles to stand in the midst of the turbulent multitude that will crowd around the ring with burning faces, flailing arms, and hats pushed back on their heads, the morning of the long-awaited fight. It is not only riffraff and touts who attend these fights; there are bankers, judges, men of position, pillars of the church in their communities, and young bucks, whose money should be cast into a yoke to bow their brazen necks. Every city has a boxing club, and some cities have many. Every club sends a representative; every bettor commissions an observer; every enthusiast goes to experience the thrills of the encounter. The doors of the hotels and saloons never stop swinging. The free-spending gamblers with their extravagant ways, and the boxers with their bulging muscles, have the ladies and girls of the city agog. They do not shun them as abhorrent beings, but watch them with curiosity and delight, as if they were great men and privileged beings.

In New Orleans, near the scene of the fight, the old families unearthed their savings, hidden away since the days of the terrible war, and staked the tarnished coins on the courage of one or the other of the brutes. The streets were filled day and night, and it was like a family affair. Everywhere one heard the clink of glasses, boisterous talking, heated discussions in stores and on street corners of the respective merits of the fighters, and the rush of feet as droves of people hurried to satisfy their hungry eyes with a glimpse of the broad back, sloping shoulders, and whipcord thighs of the athletes. Some came away crestfallen because their idol seemed fleshy about the ribs, and others came away elated because their man was all muscle and bone. Physicians went in groups to examine these rare physical specimens. Ladies went to touch the gnarled fists of the heroes with their slender fingers.

The whole city seemed in preparation for a journey during the night that preceded the dawn excursion. People slept in chairs, in sofas, and elbow to elbow in balconies, fearful that the train might leave without them and render useless the ten dollars they had paid for a place from which to watch the fight. They emptied their pockets of valuables and stripped the rings from their fingers and had them deposited in hotel safes so they would not be robbed on the journey, for deft pickpockets were known to be abroad. At last the train speeds across the bayou country of Louisiana, with the fighters, the seconds, the sponges, liniments, and salves, and the purse for the fight; with the railway coaches filled to the top, and the overflow clinging to the roofs. Now comes the drinking, the shouting, and the laying of bets. Now the agreement that a good fighter must be fearless, agile, and game. Now the reminiscing about the good old days in New York when electoral campaigns were bare-knuckle affairs in the alleys; the stories retold of how a certain McCoy killed Chris Lilly in the ring, and how the bonfires burned along Park Row after Hyer defeated Sullivan "in a whirlwind fight," and how the huge sign hung for months on the famous old street where the post office now stands: "Tom Hyer, champion of America." Between swigs of burning liquor, some recall how Morrisey left Heenan for dead; others remember the blow to the forehead with which McCool felled Jones, that left him vomiting as if his brain had been shaken from its moorings; others remember Mace as a great slugger, who threw punches like a windmill and broke Allen's neck with one good blow.[2] The morning sunlight streams through the coach windows!

At the scene of the fight, which was the city of Mississippi, the approaches to the ring site are already filled with people. Men are roosting in the trees, the curious peer from every balcony, and spectators stand embattled on the rooftops. The train unburdens itself of its human cargo. The ring is set up, with another larger surrounding ring, within which only the privileged may come. Singing happily, the newspapermen take their seats at ringside in a gleeful band, when suddenly

2. James ("Jem") Mace (1831-1910), English heavyweight, defeated Tom Allen in ten rounds on May 10, 1870, at Kennerville, Louisiana.

hurrahs rend the air, and every hand is waving a hat, as the scowling Sullivan enters the ring in short pants and a green jersey, and the handsome Ryan, the Giant of Troy, takes his place in the opposite corner, attired in spotless white. There are ladies in the inner circle. The ruffians shake hands, and the blood that will soon stream from their wounds begins to boil. Squatted on the ground, their seconds count the money that has been bet on the two men. Why look at them? In a moment one is down; he is dragged to his corner and feverishly sponged. They rush at each other again and deal each other macelike blows; their skulls resound like anvils beneath the hammer. Ryan's jersey is crimson with gore, and he falls to his knees. The Strong Man skips back to his corner, laughing. The roar is deafening. Ryan rises shakily. Sullivan moves in for the kill with his lips twisted in a smile. They clinch and maul each other's faces; they stumble back against the ropes. Nine times the assault; nine times one goes reeling to the ground. Now the Giant is staggered, now his cleated shoes no longer can help him keep his footing, now he falls like a stone from a blow to the neck, and on seeing him senseless, his second throws the sponge in the air in token of defeat. Some three hundred thousand dollars have been wagered across the country on this fight; telegraph circuits have been set up to every corner of the nation to speed a blow-by-blow account to eager throngs that fill the streets of the great cities and receive the news of the victory with clamorous applause or angry mutterings. The victorious Bostoner has been the toast of balls and parties, and the Strong Man and the Giant have toured the country again to be feted and entertained in theaters and casinos. The sands by the sea are still red and trampled in the city of Mississippi! This nation is like a great tree: perhaps it is Nature's law that grubs must nestle in the roots of great trees.

La Opinión Nacional (Caracas), March 4, 1882
Dated New York, February 17, 1882

The Memorial Meeting
in Honor of Karl Marx

Look at this large hall. Karl Marx is dead.[1] He deserves to be honored for declaring himself on the side of the weak. But the virtuous man is not the one who points out the damage and burns with generous anxiety to put it right; he is the one who teaches a gentle amendment of the injury.

The task of setting men in opposition against men is frightening. The compulsory brutalization of men for the profit of others stirs anger. But an outlet must be found for this anger, so that the brutality might cease before it overflows and terrifies. Look at this hall: dominating the room, surrounded by green leaves, is the picture of that ardent reformer, uniter of men of different peoples, and tireless, powerful organizer. The International was his creation:[2] men of all nations come

1. Karl Marx (1818-1883), founder of scientific socialism, one of the most influential thinkers of all times, died in London on March 14, 1883. In New York City the Cooper Union was thronged on March 20, 1883, to honor his memory. Initiated by the Central Labor Union of Greater New York and Vicinity, it was the outstanding memorial event held anywhere in the world in the weeks immediately following Marx's death. (For a discussion of the reaction to Marx's death, including the full proceedings of the Cooper Union Memorial Meeting, see Philip S. Foner, *When Karl Marx Died: Comments in 1883* [New York, 1973].)

2. Martí is referring to the International Workingmen's Association, the "First International," founded by Marx in 1864 and whose first conference was held in London in September 1865. A number of con-

to honor him. The crowd, made up of valiant workers, the sight of whom affects and comforts, shows more muscles than jewels, and more honest faces than silk underwear. Labor beautifies: it is rejuvenating to see a farmworker, a blacksmith, or a seaman. By manipulating the forces of Nature, they become as beautiful as Nature is.

New York goes on being a kind of vortex: what boils up in the rest of the world, in New York drops down. Here they smile at one who flees; out there, they make him flee. As a result of this kindness, a strength has come to this people. Karl Marx studied the methods of setting the world on new foundations, and wakened those who were asleep, and showed them how to cast down the broken props. But being in a hurry, with his understanding somewhat clouded, he did not see that children who do not have a natural, slow, and painful gestation are not born viable, whether they come from the bosom of the people in history, or from the wombs of women in the home. Here are the good friends of Karl Marx, who was not only a titanic stimulater of the wrath of European workers, but also showed great insight into the causes of human misery and the destiny of men, a man driven by a burning desire to do good. He saw in everyone what he carried in himself: rebellion, the highest ideals, struggle.

Here is Schevitsch,[3] a journalist: see how he speaks: reflections of the sensitive, radiant Bakunin[4] reach him: he begins

---

ferences took place in subsequent years, and after a struggle for control between followers of Marx and the anarchist adherents of Bakunin, its General Council was transferred to the United States, where it continued to exist until 1876.

3. Sergius E. Schevitsch was a Russian-American socialist, leader of the Socialist Labor Party, and editor of the *New Yorker Volkszeitung*, its daily organ. He is called "Lecovitch" in Martí's account, but this may have been a printer's error.

4. Michael Bakunin (1814-1876), Russian anarchist leader. He came to the United States briefly in 1860, but went on to London, which became his main base of operations. In Russia his ideas were associated with "Nihilism."

to speak in English; he addresses others in German. Dah! dah! his compatriots reply enthusiastically from their seats when he speaks to them in Russian.[5] The Russians are the whip of the Reform—no more! these impatient and generous men, tarnished with anger, are not the ones to cement the new world: they are the spur, and prick like the voice of a conscience which might be falling asleep: but the steel of the spur cannot be used as a construction hammer.

Here is Swinton,[6] an old man inflamed by injustice, who saw in Karl Marx the grandeur of mountains and the light of Socrates.[7] Here is the German Johann Most,[8] persistent and unlovable shouter, lighter of bonfires, who does not carry in his right hand the balm to heal the wounds inflicted by his left. So many people have come to hear them that the hall overflows and they spill out into the street. Choral societies are singing. Among so many men, there are many women. With applause, they repeat in chorus quotations from Karl

5. Schevitsch spoke in Russian in order, he said, "to carry out the International idea of the meeting," and closed his address in German after beginning in English.

6. John Swinton had fought with John Brown in Kansas, had been managing editor of the *New York Times* during the Civil War and chief editorial writer for the *New York Sun,* for which he wrote an interview with Karl Marx on September 6, 1880. In 1883, Swinton resigned his lucrative post with the *Sun,* and until August 21, 1887, when it ceased publication, issued *John Swinton's Paper,* the outstanding labor paper of the 1880s. Swinton died in 1901 at the age of seventy-one. He published an autobiography, *Striking for Life* (1894).

7. Socrates (469-399 B.C.), Athenian philosopher and leading figure in Plato's *Dialogues* who suffered death by drinking hemlock, having been accused of fostering impious ideas among the youth of Athens.

8. Johann Joseph Most (1846-1906), a bookbinder by trade, was a socialist who became an anarchist. After having been expelled from the German Social-Democratic Party in 1880, Most went first to England and then in 1883 to the United States where he became the leading anarchist in the country and published the anarchist journal *Freiheit.* For further discussion of Most, see below, p. 304.

Marx on posters hanging on the walls.[9] Millot,[10] a French-man, says something lovely: "Liberty has fallen many times in France, but it has risen more beautiful from each descent." Johann Most speaks fanatic words: "From the time that I read Marx's book in a Saxon prison, I took up the sword against human vampires."[11] Says McGuire:[12] "Rejoice to see united, without hatred, so many men of all countries. All the workers of the world belong to a single nation, and do not quarrel among themselves but are united against those who oppress them. Rejoice to have seen six thousand French and English workers meeting together near what had been the ominous Paris Bastille."[13] A Bohemian speaks.[14] A letter of Henry George[15] is read—the famous economist, friend to the

9. On the walls were large signs, especially one with the famous words "Workingmen of All Countries, Unite!" from *The Communist Manifesto*, written by Karl Marx and Friedrich Engels in 1848.

10. Théodore Millot, a bookbinder, who had been secretary of Section 2 of the First International in the United States.

11. Just what was "fanatic" about these words is not clear.

12. Peter J. McGuire, born in 1852; influenced by German-American socialists, he joined the Lassallean movement, but later supported the trade union principles of the International. He organized the English-speaking branch of the Socialist Labor Party in 1876, and the Brotherhood of Carpenters and Joiners in 1881. He is known as the father of Labor Day, but this is contested by those who favor Matthew MacGuire, a trade unionist in New Jersey. Martí spells his name Magure, but this, too, may have been a printer's error.

13. McGuire was referring to delegates from Manchester and Liverpool, England, sent by the British trade unions to Paris to inform the French workers that the British workers wanted no more war between the two countries. The meeting of 6,000 men, McGuire declared, "was held close by the Bastille."

14. Joseph Bunta, leader of the Bohemian Section of the First International, addressed the meeting in his native language.

15. Henry George (1839-1897), celebrated author of *Progress and Poverty* (1879), which became one of the most widely read books on political economy in the United States and influenced many in Europe.

distressed, loved by the people, famous here and in England. And with salvos of thunderous applause and frenzied hurrahs, the fervent assembly rises in one unanimous movement, while from the platform two men with open countenance and glance of Toledo steel read out in German and English the resolutions with which the whole meeting ends—in which Karl Marx is named the most noble hero and most powerful thinker of the world of labor.[16] Music sounds; choirs resound; but note that these are not the sounds of peace.

La Nación (Buenos Aires), May 13 and 16, 1883
Dated New York, March 29, 1883

George argued that land belonged to society, which created its value and that if it were properly taxed, through the "Single Tax," poverty could be eliminated. In the fall of 1886 George ran for mayor of New York on the United Labor Party ticket and was almost elected. For further discussion of Henry George, see below, p. 264.

16. The resolutions, read by Phillip Van Patten in English and Justus Schwab in German, and adopted unanimously, deplored the death of Marx "as a grievous and irreparable loss to the cause of Labor and Freedom," promised to keep his name and works "ever in remembrance, and to do our utmost for the dissemination of the ideas given by him to the world," and pledged "to dedicate our lives to the cause of which he was the pioneer, the struggle in which he left so noble a record, and never at any moment to forget his grand appeal: *Workingmen of the World, Unite!*"

IV
North American Politics

The First Voting Women of Kansas

The state legislature, composed of Republicans, which is unusual, needed to expand suffrage in such a way that their party would be favored. For this reason, the party agreed to give the right to vote to "native-born" women, thus assuring itself of the feminine vote, since at the same time that it excluded naturalized women of whom the majority are Democrats, it included the black women who look to the Republicans as their liberators and would seize with joy the opportunity of confronting their masters of twenty-five years ago at

1. Kansas gave its women the school vote in 1861 and women won the right to vote in municipal elections in 1887. This was so far advanced that the National Woman Suffrage Association adopted the Kansas state flower, the sunflower, as its emblem in the drive for complete woman suffrage.

In reporting the voting, the *New York Times* headline read: "Women At The Ballot Box. Female Suffrage In The Kansas City." Its reporter from Leavenworth, Kansas, wrote: "The advent of petticoats in politics has occasioned a special warfare here that dwarfs into insignificance the most bitterly contested issues of the older parties." The report from Topeka, Kansas, carried this moving passage: "One old lady, at least 70 years of age, was heard to remark as she deposited her ballot: 'I have belonged to equal suffrage clubs ever since I was a young woman. I have written and talked in favor of woman's rights for years and years. I accompanied Elizabeth Cady Stanton when she made equal rights

the ballot boxes.[2] The people of Kansas, as throughout the South, are Democrats.

Helen Gougar,[3] an agitator of the neighboring state, was the soul of this new enterprise. She fences with a political pen, deals secretly with the party which helps her, eloquently defends "women's rights" and the urgent need to purify, by her intervention, the corrupted suffrage; she propagates, travels, organizes, rehearses her armies, gives points to her lecturers, terrifies her enemies with denunciations. "Nobody can stop me, because the truth is with me." "Filthy lies will be swept away before me like dust before a hurricane." Why would politics frighten this woman? Is politics, as it is practiced today, any different from a woman? Everything done in politics is done in secret, with hints, with rivalries, with gossip; whoever appears in politics with love of country and open speech is bitterly opposed, isolated, intimidated, driven out: a woman who uses politics is not a tough suit of armor, but a flexible corset. A woman does well in this womanly art!

---

speeches in 1860, and today I see my hopes realized. I am now ready to die.' " (*New York Times,* April 7, 1887.)

Elizabeth Cady Stanton (1815-1912), pioneer woman's rights and woman suffrage leader, came to Kansas in the spring of 1867 with her friend and coworker, Susan B. Anthony (1820-1906), to campaign for removing the word "male" from the voting requirements. The women lost, receiving only 9,000 votes out of a total of 30,000. In the election, Susanna M. Salter of Argonia was elected the first woman mayor in the history of the United States.

2. In the exodus of 1879 from the South, many blacks, under the leadership of "Pap" Singleton of Tennessee and Henry Adams of Louisiana, moved to Kansas in the hope of finding a better life than in the white supremacist South. Martí's observations on the role of black voters in the Kansas elections dealt with a phase of the woman suffrage issue which was usually ignored by other reports in the press.

3. Helen Mar Jackson Gougar (1843-1907), Indiana suffrage and temperance reformer, helped revitalize the suffrage movement in Kansas in 1884, and played an important part in the movement for municipal suffrage which finally triumphed in 1887.

Helen Gougar knows her men. "Vote," she says, "in your Republican legislature for this law which I myself wrote, granting suffrage to women, and I will help you to elect the Republican candidates." From afar, these things seem to be marvels; but this one, like all marvels, must be observed close up. The idea of granting the vote to women is making progress, even though it is slow, but in Kansas the law was not passed because of noble humanity, but by virtue of this shabby deal. Is not politics, which ought to be the art of saving the people, the art of reciprocal services?

Helen Gougar fulfilled her promise well. In no way did the organization of the women have to envy the experienced parties. In every city there was a governing council. The leaders visited the saloons and houses of prostitution. They drew up their moral program: the truth is that from time to time men need to feel the burning brand on their shoulders. The manifesto of the leaders says, "The names of those who abandon their homes at night to turn into slobbering brutes should be displayed before the counters of the saloons." "We wish to marry men we can respect, not donkeys! We should publish the names of those who visit the brothels." "We leave the land to our brothers, the men." They created district committees, went from house to house bringing out the vote, assembled in private meetings with women voters before the election, in order to test their strength and get ready to parry the enemy's blows. Since they knew that honor is the dearest thing to a woman, they attacked the honor of their opponents. Hatred, inevitable residue of slavery, envenomed the struggle. The "underdogs," the black women, how could they not take advantage of the opportunity to fraternize with those who once beat them down and even today avoid and scorn them? Those "above," the mistresses, how could they bear the idea of their laundresses, their cooks, yesterday's slaves, having the same rights as they, even for one hour?

So they began to discredit Helen Gougar, questioning her morals, slandering the large number of black women who had joyfully registered for the election, offering their servants help or money in exchange for their votes, fighting for the victory of the Democrats, the masters of yesterday, against the Republicans, supported by the former slaves. This created a tremendous stir. She had no reputation left. "It is *your* morals which are impure," cried Helen Gougar in a speech to them. "My black women wash and iron but their husbands are their husbands; they don't have two doors to their houses—one for the husband who pays the bills and another for good-looking officers!" The insults were choice, from each faction, to the other. Those "above," convinced by anger, finally registered to vote, which they had been resisting from the beginning. The night before the election, the cities hummed with fury, like the buzzing of angry bees.

When the sun came up, the polling places were opened. In Kansas, the area was clear of people, since in order to avoid disputes, the law requires a space of fifty feet between voting booth and voters. This time, there are two lines: one for women and one for men. There is not much talking, they are afraid. There are many exasperated faces, because anger shows the soul's mire on the face. Carriages paid for by the Republicans, filled with black women, come and go. They are ladies and deserve to travel by carriage! The black women show off their Sunday finery in all their glory. The mistresses, arriving in their own carriages, take their places behind their servants in the line.

"Eh, Athanasia!" cries a restless black man to his wife, who is waiting in the other line, "are you voting for the Democrats?" "No, for the Republicans!" "Well, let's go home then, because my vote cancels out yours. Give me your arm, Athanasia!" And they go off happily arm in arm. But Athanasia comes back alone and votes Republican. Two big important ladies try to buy a black woman's vote; some men intervene. Soon fists are punctuating words. The voters disperse them like corn scattered by the air. An old woman of eighty votes. "What am I to do, sir?" a handsome old man smoking a pipe in the doorway, next to an empty chair, answers a reporter. "What am I to do," he repeats, looking at the chair. "My wife came out to vote because the minister told her to."

Applause breaks out. The eloquent orator, a mulatto woman named Stevens, who had spoken from a public platform, is passing, accompanied by two judges and some society women. All women do not feel impelled to keep away from the humble ones, and there are some who take pleasure in raising them up!

Finally, the battle stops. It has not been fought according to prize fight rules, but treacherously—there are some arms which will bear bitemarks for life. Too much rancor has been observed. There was not the noble rapidity of forgetting with which, in common joy over the triumph of liberty, men used to choke off their conflicts. The women as well as the men helped those who helped them. The black women as well as the black men voted for those they saw as their emancipators. In the propaganda, more zeal, more fire, more rancor, more apostolic fervor was observed than is usual among men. The new thing they did—denunciation of the brothels—they did with spirit. Many women won public positions. One ran for mayor. In Stockton, a feminine city council was almost elected. In Garden City, a woman city treasurer was elected for the coming year. A male candidate for the mayoralty, with a proven reputation for gallantry toward women, won the election by a considerable margin.

El Partido Liberal (Mexico), 1887
and *La Nación* (Buenos Aires), May 21, 1887
Dated New York, April 10, 1887

The Boss

... In both parties tenacious and monopolistic political organizations have been formed, directed toward obtaining and enjoying official positions in the government rather than toward achieving political ideals. New York is a doubtful state where at times the Democrats win and at times the Republicans. These controlling organizations, which usually resort to scandalous maneuvers to assure their members of being elected to certain positions in government, prevent wise and austere men from taking part in party administration, for these are men with integrity, men who would never permit the customary manipulations, and their competency is feared. Each of these political organizations obeys a chief. The word "boss" is given to these leaders, until now omnipotent and irresponsible, and from it comes the term "bossism," which might be translated by our own term *cacicazgo*, although the organizations producing it, and the spheres of its activity, give it a special connotation and character. The boss does not consult, he commands. The boss becomes irritated; he quarrels, concedes, denies, dismisses; the boss offers jobs, acquires concessions in exchange, has votes at his disposal and manages them; has a certain control over the election campaign. If the election of a president nominated by his party conflicts with his personal preference, or with his interests in the state, he fights that party, for it views matters preferentially because of its plurality in the state. A boss is

194

arrogant, like Conkling,[1] and uses his personal charisma and influence to make his crude, dictatorial, and aggressive policies succeed. Another boss is ambitious, like Kelly,[2] and directs all his efforts to exercising insuperable influence over electoral power, and over the distribution of government positions in the state whose Democratic Party politics he controls. Their vexed and aggrieved henchmen have risen against both of them at once. Conkling, head of the "Stalwarts"[3] (which might be translated as "the best"), has been defeated by the "Halfbreeds,"[4] Republicans who do not aspire to revision of the Constitution, violation of popular rights, absolute centralization of power, the creation of a government by force, or the reelection of General Grant; but who do aspire to govern conservatively, with the redeeming system of short terms in office to insure honesty in government and respect for the law in the persons of those tem-

1. Roscoe Conkling (1829-1888), lawyer and political boss of the New York Republicans, U.S. Senator from New York. Martí wrote a lengthy sketch of him. (See *Obras Completas* [La Habana, 1946] Vol. I, pp. 1162-70.)

2. John Kelly (1822-1886), member of Congress from New York, sheriff of the city and county of New York, and leader of Tammany Hall, was acknowledged to be the leading Democratic boss in New York during the 1880s.

3. The name applied by James G. Blaine to anti-Southern Republicans which was used by Roscoe Conkling to mean a person loyal to the party. It came to be applied to the professional politicians of the Republican Party during the administrations of President Hayes. Led by Conkling, they supported the policies of former President Grant against reformers, sought a third term for Grant in 1880, opposed civil service reform, and supported a strong Reconstruction policy in the South and high tariffs.

4. A term of contempt applied by former Radical Republicans to President Hayes, his Cabinet and Liberal Republicans who favored a conciliatory policy to the South after 1877, advocated civil service reform, opposed the spoils system, and fought against corruption in the Republican Party.

porarily charged with enforcing it. Kelly, chief of "Tammany Hall"[5]—the organization once embodying all the power of the Democratic Party in the state, and named after a wise and brave Indian—has been defeated in a stormy contest by the most illustrious men of his party, men who, being owned rather than directed by Kelly, were unable to curb the abuses, machinations, and betrayals at the heart of Tammany that were beginning to signal the downfall of the Democratic Party in the state. Another rival organization has now rebelled against Kelly's dauntless authority: it is known as "Irving Hall" inasmuch as "hall" here means a large auditorium where meetings are held.[6] But the members of the new organization were not the most respected and powerful members of the party, for in those days they did not consider it wise to reveal to the Republicans the deep split within their ranks, or they did not yet believe themselves strong enough to defeat the able Kelly. When Hancock was defeated,[7] however, a tremendous accusation rose to the surface: with good reason Kelly was accused of having permitted, for his personal advantage and to satisfy his grudges, the Republicans to win New York State, on whose vote the entire presidential

5. Tammany Hall was originally the political headquarters of the Society of Tammany, also known as the Columbian Order, founded in 1783 as a political and benevolent society, but which later became a major symbol of corruption in government. During the reign of Boss William Marcy Tweed, head of the "Tweed Ring" (1861-1871), Tammany Hall gained the reputation of utter and complete corruption, and went into decline. It later reorganized and continued its work under bosses like John Kelly.

6. Irving Hall was a rival faction in the Democratic Party which claimed to advocate simple government free of corruption, but made deals with Tammany Hall and soon united with it in sharing the spoils.

7. Winfield Scott Hancock (1824-1886), famous as a great soldier of the Union Army during the Civil War but without any experience in politics, was nominated for the presidency by the Democratic Party in 1880. He was defeated by James A. Garfield, the Republican candidate.

election depended. When a Democratic slate displeases Kelly, or when Kelly's slate is not accepted meekly and without question, then Kelly, leader of the Democrats, votes against the Democratic slate. Since in the off-year state elections of 1879 it was proved that he gave the Republicans a certain number of votes in one place so that they would give him the votes he needed in another, the river of anger overflowed its banks, quiet indignation took shape and became vocal, and the distinguished figures of the democracy met in public and solemn conclave to appeal to the electorate, which is all-powerful in opposing the treacherous organization. The people's secret ballot upheld the verdict; fifty notables were appointed—later their number grew to a hundred—to direct the work of reorganization and purification of the Democratic Party. Irving Hall merged with the new association; Tammany Hall, unable to conceive of any other power except the absolute power it was beginning to wield, rose in rebellion against the party from which this power stems, and maintained its right to primacy and individuality in managing Democratic affairs. "I will demolish all that is done without me," Kelly exclaimed. "I will defeat every Democratic slate put to the vote without me. All right, let the Democrats lose all their ability to win, for the party depends upon New York for victory. Without my help the party cannot win, so it will come to me." These serious quarrels now found an honorable and graceful solution. Every year each of the parties in the state holds a convention attended by delegates from all the electoral bodies. The purpose of this convention is to nominate the candidates for public office, these men to be submitted on election day to the vote of the party members. Quite decently and without turmoil Conkling was defeated at the Republican Convention, held in the handsome theater of the New York Academy of Music. The Democratic Convention, held in Albany, openly and ignominiously refused to admit to its bosom the traitorous and rebellious delegate from Tammany Hall. The Democratic Party published lofty and eloquent documents to this effect. Its platform is freedom of the ballot for every voter; exposure of the bosses' behavior to the lowliest member of the party; purification of the Democratic Party, so vilified and discredited by the personal interests created under its protection. It desires, and has nominated this year for the people's choice, men for public office selected from the ranks of respectable and independent souls who are alien to the ambitions of partiality, and uncontaminated by pernicious connivance with greedy politicians and voracious and unworthy aspirants to positions in government. It desires, in short, some assurance that a rebellious faction of the city will not gain control of, and abuse, the entire state party; that honest and upright Democrats keep beside them all the faithful and powerful henchmen who threatened to abandon their ranks, and sadly retired to their homes, ashamed of the conduct displayed in party affairs. The seekers and holders of public office, fearful that the Albany convention might not be courageous enough to bar entrance in their precinct to John Kelly's rebellious faction, still surround him with numerous followers who have shared with him the profits of his long control of Tammany Hall. But now, with the horse's head cut off, it is considered certain that Kelly's followers—for selfish reasons and for fear of being exposed to the monarchic rages of the boss—would abandon a tyrannical chief whose skills could not save him from the anger and anathema of a group they did not know how to honor. And this is the present status of both groups: they are open to public investigation, the rival slates are published, and the elections for high positions in the state government are near at hand. Kelly is no longer strong enough to win, but he is still counting on it. Important Democrats are now acknowledging defeat, but they consider this partial defeat in the state elections useful and not very serious if, thanks to it, they can regain the sympathy they were losing, and if they can put aside the daring rebel whose machinations captivated the growing party. So these important Democrats arrive at the next presidential campaign strong, respected, and closely grouped. It is true that in the elections in which

the honored Garfield defeated the chivalrous Hancock, the
Democrats owed their defeat to their own villainy rather than
to forces outside the party.

A town becomes so picturesque at convention time! Hotels
burst at the seams, joyous bands strike up, flags are unfurled,
faraway sounds of cheering and whistling come from the tumultuous meetings. Great groups of noisy people fill the sidewalks, argue in the streets, stop in doorways. One sees
healthy peasant faces; gallant gentlemen and city politicians
appear; there are threats, insults, laughter, joking, and brag-
ging; store counters are stacked with bottles of liquor. And
after the convention's executive board is chosen and the president has delivered his speech outlining the rules of order,
which ends by being a summary of the party platform; after
reading its planks, in which the hopes, aims, and beliefs of
the party are condensed into a small number of resolutions;
after the candidates have been defended for their various
offices by their respective followers and nominated by vote;
and after the definitive list of candidates has been announced—then the martial airs ring out, the extra trains begin
spewing smoke into the stations, the hotels empty, and the
contestants return as quickly as they can to their deserted
lairs, some laden with laurel wreaths, others with dead hopes,
to all work together for the victory of the nominees. Such
nominations are sacred. Enemy must work for enemy. Let
the community serve the general interest, laying personal
satisfaction aside. The disloyal one is booted out with Kelly.
This kind of discipline explains those dense crowds, those
sudden and happy agreements, that quick burying of grudges
that seemed terrible and all-devouring, those admirable victories of suffrage in this nation's great political battles. By
November the parties are convened. . . .

La Opinión Nacional (Caracas), October 26, 1881
Dated New York, October 15, 1881

Political Corruption

1

A certain John Roach is a great friend of the Republicans. He has a shipyard, and a minimum of ten million dollars has been paid to him for nothing more than repairing rusty ships that are never put into service. But in reality, Roach has been receiving even more than this amount, because year after year, in simulated bidding, the Secretary of the Navy has been adjudicating to him, at nominal prices and as if it were scrap iron, all kinds of material and entire lots of machinery from ships in good condition.

And why not, since the Secretary of the Navy was John Roach's lawyer? So it was that when the government let out bids for its new fleet of warships, John Roach, although he offered to build them at suspiciously low prices, was awarded the contract.[1] And in a few months, even before the first ship

---

1. John Roach (1813-1887) was a shipbuilder who, starting as a youth of sixteen with $100, gradually built up a fortune in constructing iron ships. He was a close friend of William E. Chandler, Secretary of the Navy under President Chester A. Arthur (1830-1886), who succeeded to the presidency on the death of Garfield and held office until 1885. Roach had contributed money to Chandler's political campaigns and had made him personal gifts, so Chandler awarded contracts for naval vessels to him without competitive bidding.

was finished—a vessel that turned out to be such that the government could not accept it—Roach's lawyer, the Secretary of the Navy, had paid for it, with the excuse that it was customary to advance a considerable part of the money the ships were worth, sometimes all of it. When Garfield ran for president, it was not for nothing that Roach contributed one hundred thousand dollars for party expenses. And for the campaign of Blaine,[2] whose ruin came with his own,[3] he appears to have given no less. Hence the candidates who would not win without the aid of shady speculators are immorally obligated to them, which is how the parties are able to afford the extraordinary costs of an election campaign. Those speculators make donations in exchange for legislation and assistance that further their interests; public officials give money in exchange for the promise of being kept in office by virtue of their contributions. Collections from this twofold situation, together with limited additional funds from a few enthusiastic followers, pay for the speakers, newspapers, slanders, journeys, uniformed torchlight parades, carloads of printed matter, elaborate banners with portraits and slogans that are held up and carried through the streets, and all the other shifty business of election time. The Republicans defeated, the secretaryship taken out of the hands of their lawyer, and the moment at hand for delivering to an austere and

2. James Gillespie Blaine (1830-1893), leader of the Republican Party in Maine, U.S. Senator (1876-1881), unsuccessful candidate for president on the Republican ticket in 1884, and Secretary of State (1889-1892). For further discussion of Blaine by Martí, see below, pp. 339-67.
   3. Blaine's presidential aspirations were destroyed by a scandal known as the "Mulligan Letters" in which he was exposed as having had a personal stake in advocating private railroad interests. After his nomination in 1884, the Democrats made an issue of the "Mulligan Letters," and on September 15, 1884, the press published additional letters not hitherto made public. This revelation contributed heavily to Blaine's defeat.

unknown secretary the first ship of the series, in accord with the requirements stipulated by the contract, the ship had to be returned to Roach because, despite the fact that every member of the Naval Advisory Board had approved the vessel's plans and specifications, liberal and impartial tests proved that it fell short of the conditions stipulated in the contract, and the government refused to accept it. Roach put his fortune into safekeeping and declared bankruptcy. The list of unjustified advances paid by the former Secretary of the Navy to his client was published, advances for ships that had barely been started.

The Naval Advisory Board had put its stamp of approval on plans that were unacceptable and lacked the proper specifications. Before the contractor unveiled the first vessel, the former Secretary of the Navy had advanced him slightly less than the value of the entire series. The present Secretary has displayed neither severity nor ill-will nor unmerited condescension. He has reproached the Naval Advisory Board before the nation. As for his predecessor in the secretaryship, the people's vote is sufficient reproach. As for Roach, he is to be dealt with as if the government were merely an important creditor in the bankruptcy, as indeed it is. The simplicity and justice of this warning has won an honorable popularity for Secretary Whitney.[4]

4. William Collins Whitney (1841-1904), financier and political leader, traction magnate, owner of a famous racing stable, was the Secretary of the Navy in President Cleveland's cabinet.

Immediately after Cleveland took office, Whitney was informed that the *Dolphin,* the first of Roach's four ships for which he had been awarded a contract by former Secretary of the Navy Chandler, had been completed, and its acceptance recommended by the Naval Advisory Board. Whitney rejected the recommendation and appointed a board of expert examiners, which early in June 1885 reported that the *Dolphin* was in terrible condition. Whitney then canceled the contracts for all four ships on the ground that they had been given for political considerations.

Politics has its pugilists. The physical habits of a nation enter its spirit and form it in their likeness. These are inconsiderate and aggressive men with feet on desks, bulging wallets, insolent speech, fists ready. These are fortunate strongmen—yesterday miners, then persons of consequence, then senators. These are snorting, redfaced, bullnecked individuals with stubby hands and flat Cyclopean feet; adventurers, creatures of the impossible, fatbellied sons of an oversized era, rowdy cattlemen, perpetual cattlemen. These are mercenaries born in one or another place from parents lost to vanity, from generations burning with greed; men who, once in a land that satisfied their desires, cast them aside rather than achieve them, and angrily take revenge on the surfeit of wealth they acquire, wealth they waited for as slaves and soldiers and lackeys for generation upon generation, and that never came. These new Tartars sack and pillage in the modern manner, riding in locomotives. These colossal roughnecks, a dreadful and numerous element in this sanguinary land, are engaging in their pugilistic politics. Recently come out of the woods, they are living on politics here as they did there. When they see a weakling, they feed upon him. They worship power for its own sake, as the only law they respect, and look upon themselves as its high priests and as having an innate right to grab all power within their reach. In Carthage these men installed themselves in Hamilcar's[5] palace. They ate his oxen and drank his wine. They staggered with drunkenness, were filled with the germs of indolence beside his sweetsmelling rosebushes. Covered with gold and drenched in perfume, they wallowed on their bellies and then rose on all fours like sphinxes, their eyes round like the eyes of trilobites, the battered rosebushes held fast between their teeth. Then, loaded with spoils and howling for their wages, they

5. Hamilcar was the commander of the Carthaginian forces in the first Punic War (264-241 B.C.); when Rome finally defeated Carthage in the third Punic War (149-146 B.C.) it annexed its territory and pillaged Hamilcar's dwelling.

went cheek by jowl through the countryside, like the plague, lances poised and scorching the earth with their breath, to oppose the Republic. The tumultuous foreign influx, the fantastic fortune awaiting it in the West, the magical energy and riches that sprang up and overflowed with the war, gave rise in the United States to those new cohorts of birds of prey, a plague on the Republic, who attack and lay waste like the old ones. The good country regards them with rancor, but sometimes, enmeshed in their snares or dazzled by their projects, it trudges after them. Some presidents, such as Grant, created as he was for troops and conquest, accept and support them, and trade their support for acquisitions of foreign territory. These birds of prey form syndicates, offer dividends, buy eloquence and influence, encircle Congress with invisible snares, hold legislation fast by the reins as if it were a newly broken horse, and, colossal robbers all, hoard and divide their gains in secret. They are always the same, sordid, puffed up with pride, coarse, their shirt fronts covered with diamonds. Senators visit them by back doors; cabinet members visit them in the quiet hours after the working day is over; millions of dollars pass through their hands; they are private bankers.

If the times are conducive to domestic intrigue alone, they contrive to assemble a clique of likeminded persons, influence government decrees to further their own purposes, quickly arrange some enterprise, sell it while it inspires a public confidence that is maintained by artificial and filthy means, and then let it drop. If the government only has domestic contracts with which to feed their greed, they pounce upon these and pay munificently the ones who help to corner them. They fall upon governments like vultures that assume their prey is dead, then flee to where they cannot be seen, like vultures that fly away through a cloud bank when they discover the body they thought was dead is alive. They have ready solutions for everything: newspapers, the telegraph, ladies of the evening, florid and rotund persons of consequence, ardent polemicists defending their interests in

Congress with their silver-tongued oratory. They have everything. They can buy anything. When they find something that is not for sale, they band together with all the other persons in like position and walk off with it.

They are a roving garrison of soldiers with whom ladies dance at evening parties, and flirt with the respectable and important men waiting in their anteroom and eating at their table. When this influential clique is discovered in one operation, they reappear in another. They have studied all the possibilities of foreign politics, all the combinations that can result from domestic politics, even the most problematical and unusual ones. Just as the moves are studied well in advance in a game of chess, so these men study events and their outcome and have the right move ready for all possible combinations. They are always animated by an absorbing desire, an ever turning wheel in this tremendous machine: acquiring land, money, subsidies, Peruvian guano, the northern states of Mexico.

This is what the clique wants now, for it thinks it sees in the suspension of subsidies to American railroads, lately decreed by Mexico as a worrisome measure, a good opportunity to stimulate discontent and unloose the Alexandrian appetites which, because the clique itself happens to have them, it assumes the North American nation has toward its Spanish-speaking neighbors. This is what the men in the clique are now proposing: purchase of Mexico's northern frontier for one hundred million dollars.[6] They have not yet found the method of government they found in Blaine's time; the White House is honest now.[7] But they persist and strive, and unscrupulously stir up the subjection and scorn with which the Latin people, including our near neighbors the Mexicans, are

6. See below, p. 323.

7. President Cleveland generally opposed all plans for American expansionism. "If Cleveland detested anything he detested jingoism and imperialism. . . ." (Allen Nevins, *Grover Cleveland* [New York, 1932], p. 304.)

generally regarded here. And they falsely accuse Mexico of treason and allying with the English. Not a day passes that, with Satanic patience, they do not stoke the fires of resentment with another log.

Those fiendish men who amass their fortunes despite the anxieties and hatreds of the people, should be publicly dragged through the streets, barefoot and with shaved heads! Bandits, not bankers!

La Nación (Buenos Aires), October 4, 1885
Dated New York, August 1885

2[8]

How right it is to hold up to public shame those ignominious partnerships between the wealthy or ambitious companies and their representatives who are despoiling the nation by the authority they received at its own hands!

Honesty should be like sun and air, so natural that it need not even be mentioned. But today general theft is becoming so fashionable, and infamous behavior so elegant, that it is embarrassing to be honest! For is it not at this very moment that a minority from the Congressional Board of Examination recognizes that a failing company is distributing shares worth two and a half million dollars out of its capital stock among senators and representatives so that their names and opinions will enhance the value of the remaining two and a half million, which will then become the liquid assets of those who initiated the campaign? For the use of his name and influence, five hundred thousand dollars in shares were received by the same senator who is today Cleveland's

8. This section is an extract from a dispatch by Martí covering a group of subjects.

Attorney-General, to the disgrace of the nation.[9] And since the Justice Department, if not the Attorney-General himself, instituted in the name of the nation, at a cost of three hundred thousand dollars, a demand for the nullification of patent in favor of the company, what matter if the Democratic majority on the Board claims that the Attorney-General was unwilling to serve the company that had bought him, and to make good in the market its half-million shares? It is no wonder that the Republican Senate, now wearing the penitential robes of the opposition, proposes and passes a law forbidding the congressmen of either house to intercede before Congress on behalf of any company whatsoever that holds interests in land.[10]

La Nación (Buenos Aires), August 15, 1886
Dated New York, July 2, 1886

9. August H. Garland (1832-1899), Attorney General in Cleveland's cabinet, had three years before, when senator from Arkansas, been presented with shares with a nominal value of $500,000 in a new corporation called the Pan-Electric Company, and had been made its attorney. The company possessed no capital or credit, and its sole property was the so-called Rogers telephone patent, which was worthless unless the Bell patent was declared invalid. But if Bell's patent could be broken, then the company would become wealthy and Garland's stocks would be worth a fortune. The Pan-Electric promoters also offered gifts of shares to various congressmen. When Garland became Attorney-General, the company asked him to institute a government suit to test the validity of the Bell patent, and while he personally refused, the Solicitor-General did institute such a suit. Furthermore, Secretary of the Interior Lucius Q. Lamar (1825-1893) also decided that the suit should be pressed. An investigation by Congress turned into a whitewash, with the majority of the congressional committee in a report exonerating Garland, but public opinion viewed the entire incident as another example of business control over government.

10. See below, pp. 264-65.

V

Negroes, Indians
and Other Minorities

The Negro Problem

The city is changing, and so is the entire country. Light tan summer bowlers are being discarded in favor of brown ones for autumn. City people are bidding the countryside goodbye with gunshots, killing deer and rabbits in the woods. Idle hammocks are being taken down, waves are breaking against the piers and bathhouses at the resorts, and the rusticating people are returning to the city armed with spirit and inspiration for the battles of winter. September marks an end to the customary meetings: conventions of veterans, clergy, bankers; of reformers who want absolute nationwide suffrage, a system of permanent employment, and a national treasury that does not take from the country more than is needed to honor and defend it. The annual September convocation of the Friends of the Negro, in memory of Lincoln's Emancipation Proclamation,[1] was this year given an old-style interest and sincerity by the anguish felt when one sees the Negroes hunted down, a situation increasing in the South. Not a day passes without an armed clash.[2]

1. The Emancipation Proclamation was issued by President Lincoln on September 23, 1862, and stated that it would go into effect on January 1, 1863, if the Southern states which had seceded did not return to the Union by that time. Hence celebrations took place on that day annually as well as on January 1.

2. After the Democrats returned to power in the South and with the final removal of federal troops from the South by President Hayes,

209

The mustached vigilante, his cartridge belt around his waist, his little dog at his heels, marauds the Negro settlements "demolishing these ghosts of the devil." He enters their villages on horseback as if he were riding into a conquered city, yelling and firing his rifle through the open doors of houses. In the cities those elegant gentlemen with dainty feet and silken beards say that all Negroes are ingrates, that after twenty years of good treatment they are unwilling to show any love for their former masters, or learn the arts and sciences which they would have no way of displaying or cultivating, or go to schools where they are taught by teachers paid by the very ones who applaud and favor and advocate their persecution and slaughter. The Negro population is growing with the fertility of impoverished couples whose only pleasure takes place in the home, and the Negro gives his wife all the love and companionship the world denies him. Man must create: either ideas or children. Negroes are increasing in the South, and the native white man is not increasing as rapidly. The white immigrant does not go South, for he comes back to life only where he is touched by the North. And the white native, rather than be dominated by the Negro, or mixing blood via male or female, decides to exterminate him, drive him away, throw him out of the region as if he were a fox.

What is the use of a school where he is taught that he was born a slave because of the sin of color, and will never be able to enjoy all the human rights on his native soil? What is the purpose of a seminary where they teach that God seats all men at His side equally, when the white ministers of God are more than God himself, and defy His law, and have no desire to sit beside the Negro ministers? Some of the more cultured Negroes form a group apart, aided by Northern Republicans

---

violence was used regularly as the surest means to keep Negroes politically impotent and economically subservient. Raids on blacks by night riders, such as the Ku Klux Klan, White Caps, Red Shirts Brigades, were almost daily occurrences and filled columns of newspapers in the North.

who employ this kind of justice, on the pretext of defending them, to plead with Congress for a law that will assure them of the Southern vote, until now Democratic.[3] Southern anger against the North is reappearing, although it would rather remain out of sight. A large measure of this anger against Negroes lies in the fact that the white South sees them as the instrument the North is using, with the excuse of the federal law favoring the vote of the emancipated, to take away its political freedom. Without this poison from the North, without this fear on the part of the Republicans of losing the power they are using openly and secretly as victors in a land of conquest, they would end by regulating through natural strength, the power of community life, and the work of conscience—facilitated by the growing culture of the emancipated—what is today being regulated as if for a campaign to the death. So says Lee,[4] the arrogant governor of Virginia who would make a bonfire of all Negroes. So say the churchgoing Negroes, now assembled in convention. . . .[5]

La Nación (Buenos Aires), November 10, 1889
Dated New York, September 30, 1889

3. One such proposal would have enforced the second section of the Fourteenth Amendment, which required the reduction of representation in the House in the same proportion as the number of male citizens deprived of the right to vote. But no action was taken on such proposals. Actually, while some Republicans wanted to protect the Negro's right to vote in order to regain Republican control in the South, others believed the best way to achieve this was to abandon the Negro and win the support of white Southerners.

4. The reference is to Fitzhugh Lee, governor of Virginia, 1886-1890.

5. There were two Negro conventions occurring at this time, one the National Colored Convention in Chicago and the other the Convention of Negro Baptists in Indianapolis. Both conventions dealt with an event which Martí does not mention, namely the fact that Negro delegates on the way to the conventions were assaulted and insulted in Mississippi. (See the *New York Times*, September 13, 15, 1889.)

The Negro Race in the United States

... Why, on the very day when the poorest communities were enjoying their simple games and patriotic pursuits; when eager, mountain-encircled villages were gathered before their improvised platforms erected on the grass to hear their pastors read the Declaration of Independence and their local sages speak words of wisdom; why, when the rivers were covered with regattas, the steamboats joyous with music and dancing, the churches ringing with bells, the flagpoles bright with flying flags, the cities gay with smoke, fireworks, celebrations and parades—why was there a somber procession cautiously making its way through the nearby woods of a town in the South? For what war were they carrying guns? They had carbines wedged under their saddle frames, as if wanting to lose no time in attacking the enemy. They looked like bandits, but were in fact the mayor and his gang going out to murder the Negroes of Oak Ridge in retribution for the crime of an Oak Ridge Negro living in sin with a white woman.[1]

1. The reference is to the lynching of a number of Negroes in Oak Ridge, Tennessee, in retaliation for the fact that one Negro was known to be living with a white woman. Neither the governor of Tennessee nor any of the local authorities acted in response to requests for indictment of the leaders of the white mob.

What are the Negroes to do, persecuted everywhere in the South in the same way, and this very day driven from the shores of a Northern religious community simply because the Christians who go there to worship God are annoyed with the sight of them? What can they do other than to tighten racial lines as they are doing, refuse to receive the religion and knowledge of the white man, as they used to do, build Negro schools and Negro seminaries, prepare to live outside the human community, shunned and persecuted in the land of their birth? In these sons of fathers impoverished by slavery, the character and intelligence of the free man shines brightly. Reparation for the offense is due them, most assuredly it is due them; and instead of raising them from the wretchedness imposed upon them, taking away the miserable and disagreeable appearance so criminally given them, we make use of it to refuse them association with mankind.

And they are increasing. The ignorant and poor, deprived of the subtle pleasures of the mind, are fertile fathers. They are buying farms and houses, founding banks, building their own creeds and universities, fortifying themselves in their villages. They are defending themselves, like the hapless ones of Oak Ridge, with guns in their belts. Those attacks and defenses are taking place every day in the South.

The mayor arrived in the town, indicated surrender to the townspeople, and they responded with gunfire. There were dead on all sides. The defeated Negroes scattered; four remained on the field and eight were hanged without a trial. If the mayor is the law, who will punish him?

He is probably cleaning his rifle for another hunt.

Not in vain do we notice a trace of hopelessness in the speech of cultured Negroes, and this moves us to hold out our arms to them. They usually talk gruffly, in the typical campaign manner; the children are born with more determination than their parents; they read books by the Swedish Swedenborg, who uses fiery language to depict the advent of a new Christianity.[2] They hoard their money like Jews, be-

2. See above, pp. 209-11.

cause wealth serves as a country when one has no other.[3] A heartbreaking supplication that neither sleeps nor ceases shines in their eyes, where the banished reveal their agony!

La Nación (Buenos Aires), August 16, 1887
Dated New York, July 8, 1887

3. Negroes were often told by leaders like Booker T. Washington (1856-1915) to emulate the Jews, go into business, pile up wealth, and thus assure themselves of equal treatment in American society. Martí does not comment on the fact that Jews, too, faced discrimination in American society, though not to the same degree as Negroes.

The Indians in the United States

Lake Mohonk is a lovely place in New York State. The forests of the adjacent Adirondacks beckon to grandeur, unsystematically cutting down crude speculators; with forests as with politics, it is unlawful to cut down unless one plants new trees. The lake invites to serenity, and the nearby river quietly enriches the land and flows onward to the sea. Rivers go to the sea, men to the future. When the leaves turned yellow and red this autumn, the friends of the Indians foregathered[1] in that picturesque retreat to calmly discuss some way of attracting them to a peaceful and intelligent life in which they could rise above their present condition of rights mocked, faith betrayed, character corrupted, and frequent, justified revolts. In that conference of benevolent men and women there was a notable absence of the spirit of theory which deforms and makes sterile, or at least retards, the well-meaning efforts of so many reformers—efforts which generally alienate them, because of the repulsion which a lack of empathy and harmony inspires in a healthy mind, from the solicitous support of those modest souls who otherwise

---

1. Since 1883 a group interested in the treatment of the Indians had been meeting in annual conference at Lake Mohonk. The Mohonk Conferences were the most important gatherings dealing with the Indian question.

would be efficient aids in the reformation process. Genius, which explodes and dazzles, need not be divested of the good sense that makes its life on earth so productive. Senators, attorneys, and supervisors shared their generous task there with enthusiastic journalists and Protestant ministers. In the United States a woman opened men's hearts to compassion for the Negroes, and nobody did more to set them free than she. Harriet Beecher Stowe[2] was her name, a woman passionately devoted to justice and therefore not afraid to sully her reputation, with tremendous revelations befitting a Byron, by the prolific success of her *Uncle Tom's Cabin*—a tear that has something to say!

It was also a woman who, with much good sense and sympathy, has worked year after year to alleviate the plight of the Indians. The recently deceased Helen Hunt Jackson,[3] strongminded and with a loving heart, wrote a letter of thanks to President Cleveland for his determination to recognize the Indian's right to manhood and justice.[4] And at the

2. Harriet Beecher Stowe (1811-1896), daughter of Lyman Beecher, reform minister, who became world-famous with her novel *Uncle Tom's Cabin, or Life Among the Lowly,* published in 1852. She was referred to by President Lincoln as the "little lady" who caused the Civil War.

3. Helen Hunt Jackson (1830-1885), poet and writer, whose concern with justice for the Indian resulted in the publication of *A Century of Dishonor* (1881), and of the novel *Ramona* (1884). The Massachusetts versifier and writer of children's books presented in the first a document of 457 pages sketching the dealings of the U.S. government with the Indians, and in the second a more personalized version of an Indian tragedy. She sent her *Century of Dishonor* to each member of Congress at her own expense.

4. President Cleveland received a copy of *A Century of Dishonor,* and to Mrs. Jackson's request that he take up the problem seriously, responded affirmatively. He announced that he favored the Lake Mohonk Conference's proposals for legislation under which the Indian tribes could be dissolved, their members admitted to full citizenship, and their lands distributed to them in severalty or individual ownership.

Lake Mohonk Convention there were people with an apostolic sense of oratory, subsidized by the state. But the inflexible statistics, the exact accounts, the inexorable ciphers did not belong to the supervisors or attorneys or senators, but to a woman named Alice Fletcher,[5] a lively speaker, sure in her reasoning and skilled in debate.

So the Lake Mohonk Convention was not composed of discouraged philanthropists who look at Indians only because they are Indians—seraphic creatures, so to speak—and it was not composed of those butterfly politicians who alight only upon the surface of things, and pass judgment on the basis of mere appearances and results, blind to the fact that the one way to right wrongs is to eradicate their causes.

This was a meeting of men and women of action. One of them, and surely among the most impassioned, "shuddered on recalling the sad scenes on the Indian reservations where they would divide the year's food rations, clothing, and money like wild animals fighting over raw meat." Anyone who has seen these signs of degradation, since he is human,

---

Although it was not until 1924 that the United States granted full citizenship to all the Indians in the country, the Dawes Act (1887) did provide for division of land among the Indians.

The Act, passed in 1887 during Cleveland's administration, reversed Indian policy and won the praise of the friends of the Indians. (It conferred citizenship and ownership of a tract of land upon those Indians who renounced their tribal allegiance.) However, it soon turned out that the Dawes Act did the Indians more harm than good. In dividing land among the Indians, as the Act provided, the poorest territory was usually given to the Indians, and the best was sold to white settlers. Even where he gained good land, inexperience with ownership and with legal matters left the individual Indian vulnerable to the same kind of deceitful practice that had marked the making of tribal treaties.

5. Alice Fletcher (1838-1927), an ethnologist who was born in Cuba, became a pioneer in the study and transcription of the music of the Indians, and an authority on various aspects of Indian life in North America.

must have experienced some shame and a desire to lift those
unfortunate creatures out of their misery. For it is he who is
responsible for all the wrongs he knows about but does nothing to correct. It is a criminal laziness, a passive guilt that is
merely a matter of degree in the scale of crime; apostleship is
a constant daily duty. Another person at the Convention has
seen the Indians huddled in a circle, gambling their year's
salary, betting nine out of every ten dollars, like Chinese
workers in the cigar factory of a Spanish prison, the moment
they receive on a Saturday afternoon the overtime pay that
they have to hand over to the establishment. The Convention
knows that they are not fond of working, because a bad
system of government has accustomed them to being detes-
tably apathetic. The Convention is well aware that, since the
government gives them a yearly stipend, and food and clothing, they will resist any reform that tends to improve their
character by compelling them to earn their living from their
own efforts; that, deprived of the social aspirations and civil
pleasures of white people, they will view with indifference
the public school system available to them but not proceeding from the tribe's savage existence, or seeming to be necessary to it. The Convention knows this. But it also knows that
the Indian is not like that by nature; he has been conditioned
to it by the system of vilification and easy living imposed
upon him for the last hundred years.

Where the Indian has been able to defend himself more
successfully and stay as he was, it can be seen that he is by
race strongminded and strongwilled, courageous, hospitable,
and worthy. Even fierce, like any man or any people close to
Nature. Those same noble conditions of personal pride and
attachment to territory make him spring around like a wild
animal when he is despoiled of his age-old grain fields, when
his sacred trees are felled, when the hot winds from his burning homes scorch the manes of his fleeing horses. The one
who is burned, burns; the one who is hunted, gives chase; the
one who is despoiled of property, despoils in turn. And the
one who is exterminated, exterminates.

Thus reduced to a poor nation of three hundred thousand scattered savages tirelessly fighting a nation of fifty million, the Indian does not enter the cities of his conquerors, does not sit in their schools, is not taught by their industries, is not recognized as a human soul. By means of onerous treaties he is obliged to give up his land. He is taken away from his birthplace, which is like robbing a tree of its roots, and so loses the greatest objective in life. On the pretext of farming, he is forced to buy animals to work the land he does not own. On the pretext of schooling, he is compelled to learn in a strange language, the hated language of his masters, out of textbooks that teach him vague notions of a literature and science whose utility is never explained and whose application he never sees. He is imprisoned in a small space where he moves back and forth among his intimidated companions, his entire horizon filled with the traders who sell him glittering junk and guns and liquor in exchange for the money which, because of the treaties, the government distributes among the reservations every year. Even if he should be possessed by a desire to see the world, he cannot leave that human cattle ranch. He has no land of his own to till, and no incentive to cultivate it carefully so that he may honorably leave it to his children. Nor does he have to, in many of the tribes, because the government, by means of a degrading system of protection that began a century ago, gives him a communal place of land for his livelihood, and furnishes him with food, clothes, medicines, schools, with whatever is a man's natural objective when he works for a wage. If he has no property to improve or trip to take or material needs to satisfy, he spends this money on colored trinkets that cater to his rudimentary artistic taste, or on liquor and gambling that excite and further the brutal pleasures to which he is condemned. With this vile system that snuffs out his personality, the Indian is dead. Man grows by exercising his selfhood, just as a wheel gains velocity as it rolls along. And like the wheel, when a man does not work, he rusts and decays. A sense of disheartened ferocity never entirely distinguished in the enslaved races, the memory of lost homes, the council of old men who have seen freer times in their native forests, the presence of themselves imprisoned, vilified, and idle—all these things burst forth in periodic waves each time the harshness or greed of the government agents is closefisted in supplying the Indians with the benefits stipulated in the treaties. And since by virtue of these treaties, and by them alone, a man is robbed of whatever nobility he has, and is permitted only his bestial qualities, it is only natural that what predominates in these revolts, disfiguring the justice producing them, is the beast developed by the system.

All enslaved peoples respond in like manner, not the Indians alone. That is why revolutions following long periods of tyranny are so cruel. What white man in his right mind fails to understand that he cannot throw in the Indian's face a being such as the white man has made of him? "He is graceful and handsome," said the venerable Erastus Brooks at the Convention.[6] "His speech is loving and meaningful. We have in American history tens, hundreds, of examples to show that the Indian, under the same conditions as the white man, is as mentally, morally, and physically capable as he." But we have turned him into a vagabond, a tavern post, a professional beggar. We do not give him work for himself, work that gladdens and uplifts; at best we force him to earn, with work affording him no direct profit, the cost of the rations and medicines we promise him in exchange for his land, and this in violation of the treaties. We accustom him not to depend upon himself; we habituate him to a life of indolence with only the needs and pleasures of a primitive, naked being. We deprive him of the means of obtaining his necessities through his own efforts, and with hat in hand and bowed head he is obliged to ask the government agent for everything: bread, quinine, clothes for his wife and child. The

6. Erastus Brooks (1815-1886), journalist, member of the New York Assembly, and a regular participant in the Mohonk Conference on the Indian.

white men he knows are the tavern keeper who corrupts him, the peddler who cheats him, the distributor of rations who finds a way of withholding a part of them, the unqualified teacher who drills him in a languge of which he can speak but a few words, unwillingly and without meaning, and the agent who laughs and shouts at him and bids him be off when he appeals to him for justice. Without work or property or hope, deprived of his native land and with no family pleasures other than the purely physical, what can be expected of these reservation Indians but grim, lazy, and sensual men born of parents who saw their own parents crouched in circles on the ground, both pipe and soul snuffed out, weeping for their lost nation, in the shade of the great tree that had witnessed their marriages, their pleas for justice, their councils, and their rejoicing, for a century? A slave is very sad to see, but sadder still is the son of a slave. Even their color is the reflection of mud! Great hotbeds of men are these Indian reservations. Pulling these Indians up by the roots would have been better than vilifying them.

The first treaty was in 1783, and in it the United States government reserved the right to administer the tribes and regulate their trade.[7] And now the three hundred thousand Indians, subdued after a war in which theirs was not the greatest cruelty, are divided among fifty reservations[8] whose only law is the presidential will, and another sixty-nine known as treaty reservations because of an agreement between the tribes and the government. Thirty-nine of these have treaties stipulating the division of reservation lands into individual properties, an ennobling measure that has scarcely been attempted with twelve of the tribes. "The Indians are given the food that Congress orders for them," said Alice

7. The first treaty with the Indians was in 1778 with the Delawares.
8. Under the Indian reservation policy instituted by the United States in 1786, lands were set aside for use by the Indian tribes. The reservations, however, were usually such poor land that the Indians became solely dependent on the government and often starved.

Fletcher, "and because this passes through many hands, there remains in each pair of them some part of it. But the allotment for schools is not distributed, because the employees can obtain from it the paltry teacher's salary, which is then passed along to their wives or daughters for augmenting household supplies. Thus, out of the two million dollars that must have been spent from the years 1871 to 1881, including the obligations of all the agreements, only two hundred thousand dollars has been spent on schools." Many of the tribes have been offered even more than the private property which they are denied, and the schools which have not been established for them: they have been offered citizenship.

All this was heard without contradiction; on the contrary, the Deputy Inspector of Indian Schools, the authors of the House and Senate reservation reform plans, and the members of the Indian Council supported and corroborated it. High government officials supported and corroborated it, too, and applauded the inspired defense of the Indian's character delivered by that fine man, Erastus Brooks. "There is not one of their vices for which we are not responsible! There is no Indian brutality that is not our fault! The agents interested in keeping the Indian brutalized under their control are lying!"

The government defiles the Indian with its system of treaties that condemn him to vice and inertia. And the government agent's greed keeps the government under a false concept of the Indian, or hides the causes of his corruption and rebellions in order to continue whittling away to his heart's content at the funds Congress sets aside for the Indian's maintenance.

Let the governor keep a wary eye on those rapacious employees!

Give President Cleveland high praise; with neither fanatical vanity nor prudery he has made efforts to investigate the Indians' sufferings, and instead of throwing in their faces the ignominy in which they are kept, Cleveland decided to shoulder the blame himself, and raise them by means of a just government to the status of men. This president wants no drunken insects; he wants human beings. "They are drunkards and thieves because we have made them so; therefore we must beg their pardon for having made them drunkards and thieves, and instead of exploiting them and disowning them, let us give them work on *their* lands and encourage in them a desire to live, for they are good people in spite of our having given them the right not to be."

Without a dissenting vote, then, in the shade of the Adirondacks, which beckon to greatness, the Convention recommended those practical reforms of simple justice that can change a grievous crowd of oppressed and restless men and women into a useful and picturesque element of American civilization.

Since they have already been robbed of their rights as freed peoples, for reasons of state, let us not rob the Indians of their rights as men. Since the despoiling of their lands, even when rational and necessary, continues to be a violent act resented by every civilized nation with hatred and with secular wars, it must not be aggravated by further repression and inhuman trading. The unfair and corrupting reservation system must be quickly abolished, and we must gradually make national lands available to the Indians, fusing them with the white population so they may promptly own state lands, enjoying the rights and sharing the responsibilities of the rest of the citizenry. The payment of yearly stipends must be abolished, for this encourages begging and vagrancy, and accustoms the Indians to neglect making use of their own resources. We must train the Indians in accord with their needs and potentialities, and they must be convinced—and when necessary compelled—to learn and to work, even if because of their present life of laziness in learning they may resist. The Indians will have to return to their unblemished souls and rise to citizenship.

To thus convert them into useful men and women, and change the regions which today are no more than extremely costly prisons into a peaceful and prosperous country, says the Convention, the entire stupid, present-day teaching system will have to be changed. We must substitute the working of common lands, which neither stimulates nor permits the worker to see any profit, for the distributing of land into plots of ground for every family, inalienable for twenty-five years, in relation to the kind of terrain and the size of each house. The government should pay a good price for the lands not apportioned, and since these monies are to go right back into its own pocket, because the government is the guardian of the Indians who sell them, the government should retain the funds received from these lands for the industrial education and betterment of the Indians, and open the purchased lands to colonization. Let the tribes themselves revoke those treaties responsible for their wretched condition. Admit to citizenship all tribes which accept individual distribution of their lands, and all Indians who abandon the tribes that refuse to accept them, to comply with the uses of civilization. Stop taking the Indians away from the land of their forefathers and herding them into crowded centers under the self-seeking vigilance of offensive and avaricious government employees. "Spread schools," said the Deputy Inspector of Indian Schools at last, but they must be useful and living schools, for every effort to disseminate instruction is futile if it does not apply to the needs, nature, and future of the one receiving it. Engage no halfhearted teachers who know nothing of what they teach, and are appointed only to augment the family pittance of some employee, or to please the political bigwigs. Competent teachers will be hired and will compel the Indians to envy their children for the schooling they receive, even if the parents have to curtail their household rations for as long as the ominous rationing system persists. No textbook education, which is merely a storehouse of words weighing heavily upon the head to then tell the hands how to work well. Indians should be taught the nature of the fields they are to cultivate, and the nature of their true selves and the village in which they live; in this way they will understand and admire. Teach them something about practical politics so they may reach a suitable state of mutual respect.

Let them know how the country is run, and what are their human rights to possess it and think about it, and how they may exercise those rights. The school should instruct them in making their life a satisfying one: a country school for country people.

No details or fancy theories; only how to raise animals and plant fields, all the tasks that make them useful and self-possessed members of a community of workers. We should not send the Indians or country people teachers of literature alone. Living literature is the teacher. Let us send them teachers of crafts and agriculture.

That Convention held by the friends of the Indians went well and ended well, there by the quiet waters of Lake Mohonk where the mountains are close at hand and where the beautiful square fields, cultivated with scrupulous care, look like colossal green flowers opening to the eyes of men worthy of contemplating them.

La Nación (Buenos Aires), December 4, 1885
Dated New York, October 25, 1885

Indians and Negroes

. . . There is more of that candid and imposing poetry in
Red Cloud's lecture.[1] In it he pours out the sorrow of his
Indian soul to the people who have come in festival dress and
with their triumphal music to the town of Chaldron, to see
the dances performed by the last of the Sioux, the tribe
whose possessions are so few that they can be covered by "a
single deerskin." The people have come to hear what the
medicine man, who teaches how to heal wounds and pacify
enemies, can tell by looking at the sky. His feather headdress
reaching down to his feet, the medicine man crouches and
listens to Red Cloud, who is also crouching, his head sunk
between his knees. It is said that the Indians are being allowed to keep half their land, the only part they have left!
But that half will also be taken away from them, just like the
other half! Why would they want the fourteen million dollars
they were given? "An eagle feather floating freely through

---

1. Red Cloud (1822-1909), Makhipiya-luta to his own people, was a
Sioux Indian who successfully resisted the U.S. government in defending the Sioux hunting grounds from incursions by whites, and then
signed a treaty on April 29, 1868, under which he laid down arms and
agreed to settle in Nebraska. His stand was criticized by other Sioux,
but Red Cloud traveled to Washington to achieve peacefully what he
had previously fought for, only to find the Indians betrayed. While in
New York Red Cloud delivered lectures on the Indian question.

the air," says Red Cloud, "is worth more than your fourteen million!" "If this is a pact, my wolf-hearted ones; if this is a pact, my fox-hearted ones, what can murder be? The snake has been put into my heart too, for I have no courage to tear it out with my hands and cast it at your feet for you to take to the Great Father in Washington so that he may divide among the white people the last thing remaining to us!" Revolvers in hand, the soldiers listen to him; the women and musicians have climbed into the wagons; the Indians, all of them squatting, their heads bowed, pay close attention to Red Cloud's discourse. He holds his head high; the words leave his lips as if compressed, martyred, broken. His left hand tugs at the leather fringe of his trousers; his right gestures violently as if he wanted to push away from him the causes of so much affliction. "I have been sent here to show the white man how the Indians dance. Very good, very good, for that is all today's Indians know how to do. The Indians are dead! These Indians of today are like the shadows of trees that cause fear at night and laughter in the daytime. These Indians of today are bird bones! But I wanted to come, because I still believe what my father told me, that blood is troubling the land and that all white men and Indians are brothers, as if born from the same woman. The Great Father sends me word to sell him my lands, and if I refuse, it will be like water in a pond where the big fish eat up the little fish. It will do me no good to fence my land, for the white men will leap over the fence and take my land away. The Great Father has deceived me as if I were a child, has robbed me as if I were a child. I do not want to sign any more treaties, for the Great Father will then order his soldiers to take away from me what the treaty told me was mine. We no longer own even our own hearts. The Sioux nation is now a nation of women. Let me die in peace, let me die on my own land the way the smoke from burning tree trunks dies in the air!" And the medicine man lifted his feather headdress from the ground and buried his face in it.

Red Cloud covered his face with his arm and started walking to a clump of trees. The warriors remained in a crouching position, their rifles across their knees and the pony reins in one hand. But all had to sign, because they were forced to do so at gunpoint. The white colonizers have been closing in on Sioux territory for twenty years, the way a snake tightens its coils around the vanquished prey, and are already fencing some of their borders, waiting for the command to enter. Those men to whom General Crook said, "By your faith as honest men," as he watched them work and die, have been forced to sell eleven million acres in Montana and Wyoming for fourteen million dollars. "In bravery and intelligence you are the white man's equal; you are as strong and wise as the white man, and you are guilty of nothing but defending your land with the rifles that we ourselves have given you to destroy yourselves in the war against our greater power. You are our brothers by nature, and our superiors because of your courage in misfortune. Why are you denied the dignity of brotherhood in this evil-hearted nation?" You are a good man, Crook, but your people rob and murder! All who had come to the pow-wow put out their peace pipes as a sign of distrust.

In the South the Negroes fare no better. They are persecuted no less, for in a city as influential as Atlanta the people burned the postmaster in effigy, on the scaffold, because he dared employ a courteous and intelligent Negro who would have outranked a young white woman.[2] "What, you expect

2. Charles C. Penny, the Negro appointed to the post office in Atlanta, received his position because he stood at the head of the civil service list of eligibles, and Postmaster Lewis stated that he was "compelled by the law" to appoint him. Penny was assigned to work in a different room than that in which the white young lady was working, so her fear of having to hand letters to a black man had no basis. Nevertheless, both the young lady and her father, who also worked in the post office, resigned. The white population of Atlanta supported their stand and burned the postmaster in effigy.

me to take papers from a black man's hand all day long, on equal terms? You expect me to have to obey and face a black man who is not my equal and is going to be my superior?" The young woman quit; there were indignation meetings in which she was praised for quitting; a scaffold was built in front of the post office, and when night came they strung up the effigy of General Lewis and set it on fire. Six city policemen opened a path through the crowd to make way for the torchbearers. At the club all the members decided to turn their backs on the general if they should meet him on the street, and refuse to give him the time of day. One of the men who had endorsed him withdrew his signature. The local newspaper asked: "How can Lewis accept a public post and offend the firm convictions of those whose aid he has accepted in attaining that post?" Lewis responded that he was a federal employee, that when he had accepted the position he was unaware of there being white men or Negroes, knowing only that there were citizens with the right to employment and recompense from the Republic. "I will not appoint a Negro to an inferior post or as a mere clerk," he said, "when the nation appoints a mulatto, Frederick Douglass, as the United States representative to Haiti."[3] "But Haiti is a Negro republic," was the newspaper's reply. "You Republicans will not need the Negro vote to keep us Southern Democrats in

---

For a discussion of the reaction to the appointment, see the *Atlanta Constitution,* August 14, 1889; *New York Times,* August 14, 15, 1889.

3. Frederick Douglass (1817-1895), born a slave and completely self-taught, escaped to the North in 1838, made his first public speech three years later, and went on to become the foremost black Abolitionist. After breaking with the Garrisonians, he edited his own paper, *The North Star,* which changed its name later to *Frederick Douglass' Paper.* As editor, orator, and politician, Douglass led the black protest movement for almost fifty years. After the Civil War, he was an editor of *New National Era,* Recorder of Deeds for the District of Columbia, and on July 1, 1889, was appointed by President Benjamin Harrison (1833-1901) Minister-Resident and Consul-General to the Republic of Haiti, a post he resigned in August 1891.

check, and we shall see how eager you are to sit down at the table and eat with these African hordes. . . ."

La Nación (Buenos Aires), October 6, 1889
and *El Partido Liberal* (Mexico)
Dated New York, August 15, 1889

The Chinese in the United States

As the railroads' assets have shrunk and they have found themselves with less goods to carry and a too lively competition on the part of rival carriers soliciting to transport the same scanty available cargo, they have had to reduce freight charges and cut the number of men they employ on the lines, in the shops, and in their mines. They have cut wages; reduced coal extraction. To this general conflict another specific conflict has been added.

Chinese have been flowing in torrentially through ill-guarded ports, despite the legislation which practically prohibits their entering the United States.[1] By means of some ruse or other, or through bribery, the American officials themselves help them get around the law. In San Francisco Chinese merchants have a great advantage over German and American merchants.

The Chinese man has no wife, lives on a pittance, dresses cheaply, works hard. He sticks to his customs, but abides by the law of the land. He rarely defends himself, never attacks. He is crafty and because of his sobriety and sharpness he wins over the European workman.

---

1. The Chinese Exclusion Act of 1882 prohibited Chinese laborers from entering the United States for a period of ten years. It was extended for an additional ten years in 1892 by the Greary Act, and extended indefinitely in 1902. The laws were repealed in 1943.

He is not endearing: a people with no women cannot be; a man deserves esteem not for what he does for himself, but for what he gives of himself. A married man induces respect. The man who resists helping another life, displeases. Woman is man's nobility.

But as a worker the Chinese man is frugal, cheap, and efficient. As he lives differently from the white worker, consumes less, and is not concerned to the same extent with the latter's problems—needs, wages, strikes—he is satisfied with what he earns, which at least covers his bare requirements, and avoids intercourse with white workers and knows that they hate him.

Whatever step white labor takes, the Chinese stand in the way: if the white man is not available, there is always the Chinese man.

The Chinese man is also astute and as he will do anything for pay; no sooner does he hear of an opportunity for gain—a soft pit in a mine, a desirable privilege—than he manages to grasp it, which aggravates the white worker, limited as he is by special conditions, who perhaps failed to see the opportunity the Chinese saw.

Since he is tame and meek, though no less skilled and vigorous than workers of other races, the employers are happy to have him. On arrival at a mine the Chinese raise their houses, eating place, laundry, store, theater, and with less money live comfortably, which makes the European miner bitter and jealous.

Then, one day, there is smoke coming from the mine. It has happened in so many places! There has been a fight way down in a pit: four Chinese are killed.

Their panic-stricken comrades leave their work and sound the alarm. All the Chinese gather in their living quarters. The whole mine suspends work. The white workers summon those of the vicinity and armed with rifles, revolvers, axes, and knives march against the Chinese quarter, and order them to leave the mine within the hour. The poor devils obey without protest and have scarcely time to pick up their belongings.

A few minutes elapse and the white miners start shooting at the Chinese, who, in great fright, leave their houses screaming and take to the nearby hills, pursued by the shooting Europeans. Some fall dead on the road, others run on wounded. The houses behind go up in flames. A few Chinese who had lingered are seen running through smoke and fire toward the hills, covering their heads with blankets and quilts held in their extended arms as a protection against bullets. The whites pursue. Few Chinese escape. If one appears, he is hunted down.

One hundred and fifty are killed.

At night the white workers return to the camp and burn all the fifty houses.

The law carries on its task slowly.

Six Chinese commissioners leave San Francisco under guard to investigate the crime.

The white miners go free and confer with the Union Pacific officers. They demand of the company a decision not to employ Chinese in the mines, a proposal the company does not accept.

The coal pits are deserted and the Knights of Labor announce that they will back with all their strength Union Pacific's white workers and will see to it that their demands will be accepted. Either the Chinese are fired or the railroad will be minus coal.[2]

La Nación (Buenos Aires), October 23, 1885
Dated New York, September 19, 1885

2. Martí is referring to the massacre of the Chinese at Rock Springs, Wyoming, during which white miners, members of the Knights of Labor, raided the Chinese section of the town, killed twenty-eight Chinese, wounded fifteen, burned the homes of the Chinese laborers, and pillaged their possessions. Instead of denouncing the terrorists,

Terence V. Powderly, Grand Master Workman of the Knights of Labor, and other leaders of the organization attacked the Chinese laborers and blamed them for the violence. "Exasperated at the success with which the Chinese had evaded the law," Powderly declared, "the white workmen became desperate and wreaked a terrible revenge upon the Chinese." (See Philip S. Foner, *History of the Labor Movement in the United States,* Vol. II [New York, 1955], pp. 58-60.)

For further discussion of the Knights of Labor, see below pp. 253-56.

Mob Violence in New Orleans

From this day on no person who has known pity will set foot in New Orleans without horror. Here and there groups of murderers still appear and disappear, their rifles on their shoulders. Another group made up of lawyers and tradesmen, broadshouldered, blue-eyed, can be seen with guns at their hips and a leaf on their lapels—a leaf from the tree on which they have hanged a dead man, a dead Italian, one of the nineteen Italians that had been jailed under suspicion of having murdered Chief of Police Hennessy.[1] An American jury had acquitted four of the nineteen, the trials of others had been interrupted because of errors, still others had not yet been indicted.

A few hours after the acquittal a committee of worthies appointed by the mayor to assist in punishing the assassination, headed by the leader of one of the city's political factions, called a meeting of citizens by means of printed public

1. Peter Hennessy, chief of police of New Orleans, was killed on October 15, 1890, after he had begun to investigate the acts of violence associated with Italians, including open gang wars and a series of unexplained deaths, all said to be connected with the Mafia, or "black hand," which flourished in Sicily. When the jury dealt gently with the accused, acquitting some and remanding others to a further trial, a group of several thousand citizens broke into the jail in which eleven Italian prisoners were confined and lynched them all.

convocations one day in advance.[2] The meeting was held at the foot of Henry Clay's statue.[3] They attack the parish jail, with scarcely a semblance of resistance on the part of the police, the militia, the mayor, or the governor. The mob tears down the yielding doors of the jail; screaming, they pour into the corridors along which the hunted Italians flee; with their rifle butts they smash in the heads of the Italian political boss and of a banker who was Bolivian consul accused of complicity with a secret band of Mafia assassins . . . others are murdered against the walls, in nooks, on the floor, at guns' end. The deed over, the citizens cheer their leader, the lawyer, and parade him on their shoulders.

Are these the streets of flowery homes with hypnaceae creeping up the white lattices, of mulatto women in turbans and aprons hanging out colored Indian baskets on trellised balconies, of Creole belles on their way to the lake to lunch on pearly, golden fish, a flowerlet pinned to their bodice and in their black tresses an orange blossom? Is this the city of oaks on which the Spanish moss grows like silvery filigree, of honey-distilling date trees, of weeping willows mirrored in the river? Is this the New Orleans of Carnival mirth, all torch and castanets, which on Mardi Gras parades Mexico's romance on a float festooned with lilies and carnations, on another the lovable heroes of Lalla Rookh in bejeweled costumes and on still another Prince Charming in orange satin waking a glittering-gowned Sleeping Beauty?

2. On March 14, 1891, every morning newspaper in New Orleans carried the following notice:

"All good citizens are invited to attend a mass meeting on Saturday, March 14th at 10 o'clock a.m. at Clay statue to take steps to remedy the failure of Justice in the Hennessy Case. Come prepared for action."

This was followed by a list of sixty-two of the most prominent names in the City of New Orleans.

3. About 3,000 people met at Clay's statue and speakers urged the crowd to invade the prison, seize the prisoners, and mete out "justice" —in short, called for coldblooded murder.

Can this be the New Orleans of fishing canoes, of the charming suburbs, of the noisy, beaming marketplace, of dandies with felt hats down to their ears and gray goatees who gather at the Poetry Café to chatter about duels and sweethearts? . . . Shots blast out; Bagnetto, the dead Italian, is hoisted to a limb; they riddle his face with bullets; a policeman tosses his hat into the air; some watch the scene with opera glasses from balconies and rooftops.

The governor "cannot be reached." The militia, "no one has called it out." A branch is sawed down, another is cut down with an ax; they shake off the leaves which fall upon the compact crowd gathered to take home as souvenirs a splinter of wood or a leaf still fresh at the foot of the oak tree from which an Italian covered with blood hangs swinging.

The city of New Orleans, for the pleasure of it or through cowardice, headed by its leading lawyers and businessmen, marched to the jail from which were to be released the recently acquitted prisoners. . . . The city led by lawyers, journalists, bankers, judges . . . struck down . . . the acquitted Italians: a New Orleaner of Italian descent; a rich man of the world who controlled the votes of the Italian colony; a father of six sons, wealthy partner of a well-known firm; a spirited Sicilian who a few months back had been fired at by an Irishman; a shoemaker who was influential in his neighborhood; a cobbler under suspicion of having killed a compatriot of his; several fruit vendors.

Italians are prone to fight among themselves, as are the feuding gangs in Kansas, where no governor has been able to bring peace in half a century, as are the Southern Creoles, who inherit their family hatreds. Twenty years ago the father of this Hennessy had fallen by the hand of a certain Guerin for meddling in the affairs of the Italians or for wanting to deprive them, on the pretext of their quarrels, of the ascendancy they had gained by their voting power. The killer of the elder Hennessy had been shot to death by a trader in votes who marched as one of the ringleaders in today's assault. The gray-eyed politicians hated the dark-eyed politicians. The Irish, who live mostly on politics, wanted to eliminate the Italians from politics.

They called them "Dagos," a nickname that makes a Sicilian's blood boil. If during these quarrels someone was killed they said he "had been sentenced by the Mafia." They spoke of the political executions by the Mafia when it conspired a century ago against the Bourbons as though they were sheer crimes committed now.

In spite of the fact that Hennessy had once had no better friend with whom "to make the rounds of the gambling tables in the clubs or to partake of a good gumbo" than Macheca, the stylish, wealthy Italian—the one whose head now lies all battered in—our Hennessy then declared war without quarter on the Italians. There had been some killing in the Italian section. The police had followed up the investigation until they got a statement from one Italian, who next morning was found dead, telling them all they wanted to know about a society of assassins called "The Stiletto" and another called "The Stopaliagien." Now, they announced, they held "complete evidence about the terrible Mafia, its death sentences, its thousands of members." One night, at the door of his house—a house with two rose bushes in the hallway—Hennessy fell brandishing his revolver against a band of assassins.

They found eleven bullets in his body. His death was declared "a Mafia vengeance." The most convincing proofs were promised. The mayor himself appointed a committee of fifty citizens—politicians, lawyers, merchants, journalists—to assist the judiciary in its investigations. An impeccable jury was chosen from among the citizens with English family names. A few professional troublemakers among the Sicilians were jailed, along with two men who were the wealthiest and had the greatest control over the Italian voters.

The Italian population, from the Gulf to the Pacific, stood up for them: their press denied, as did their prominent men, that there was a Mafia, or a Stiletto, or a Stopaliagien society, or any possibility of proving such a thing, or any sense in holding for murder men of banker Macheca's or merchant Caruso's position. They insisted that the root of this vicious persecution was to be found in the political rivalries, in the determination to intimidate the Italians who would not submit to the will of their persecutors to get them out of New Orleans and out of the polls. They declared that a devilishly political conspiracy was being hatched.

The jury, after months of public trial, of reciprocal accusations, of witnesses going mad or committing perjury, talk of bribery, of scandal, acquitted the prisoners. Surely enough there were hostile bands among the New Orleans Sicilians. . . . Surely enough the streets were often strewn with Italian blood shed by Italians. But . . . it does not follow that all "Dagos" who live as their burning sun commands, loving and hating each other, giving their life for a kiss or taking a life for an insult, "are an organized school of murderers."

New Orleans received the verdict with ire and threats. . . . But in Chicago the Red Shirts' neighborhood was aglow with lights; in the Providence suburbs they struck work to dance and make merry; the Bowery Italians in New York lined their fruit stands with fresh paper, stuck their flag in the burnished boots that hung to mark their bootblacks' chairs, while women paraded their well-combed hair and their coral earrings—until the telegraph announced the awful news! That New Orleans was in mutiny, that the jail was surrounded, that Bagnetto had been hanged, Macheca killed! Women ran out of shanties and alleys screaming, or set down their babies and sat on the curbs to weep, or untied their tresses and pulled them, or waked their men, insulting them if they tarried, or ran about with their hands on their heads. In front of newspaper buildings the streets teemed with men and women. For the first time their journalists, as a rule disunited, gathered to harangue them; "Let us stand together, Italians, in this grief!" "Revenge, Italians, revenge!"[4] And they read sighing the horrible telegrams. Women fell on their knees in the streets. Men brushed away a tear with their callused hands.

The ringleaders against the court were court people—judges, district attorneys, defenders. The leaders at the killing were delegates of the mayor, who abstained from sending his own forces against the killers. Not a call for pity, not a woman's supplication, not a clergyman's petition, not a protest from the press: just "Kill the Dagos." "To arms, good citizens!" . . . At one o'clock the streets leading to Clay's statue were crowded. They say the militia was with them, that militiamen in plain clothes were around, that there was a house full of picks and axes, that a carload of beams to knock down doors was dumped yesterday behind the jail, that the plan was all laid down yesterday by the committee of fifty, the leaders appointed, the arms distributed. Some cheer Wyckliffe; all, Parkerson. . . . Parkerson, a man of law, a political leader, a young man, speaks: "To arms, citizens! Crimes should be speedily punished, but wherever and whenever courts fail or juries break their oath or bribing appears, it behooves the people to do what courts and juries have left

4. *The New York Times* of March 16, 1891, carried statements of protest from Italian communities in Pittsburgh, Kansas City, New York, St. Louis, and Chicago. Some called for the Italian government to take military action if those responsible were not punished. The Italian Premier, Marquis Rudini, called to his minister in Washington, Baron Fava, demanding punishment of the ringleaders and an indemnity for the victims of the citizens' mob. In the end, Secretary of State Blaine notified the Italian government that he was authorized by President Harrison to offer $25,000 to the families of the victims of the "lamentable massacre" at New Orleans, with the hope that thereby "all memory of the unhappy tragedy" would be obliterated and enduring friendly relations between the two countries restored. (*Foreign Relations of the United States* [Washington, D.C., 1892], p. 728.) The Italian government accepted the indemnity offered and full diplomatic relations were resumed.

undone!" "We're with you, Parkerson!" "What will our resolution be? Action?" "Action! You lead! We're with you!" "Ready?" "Ready!"

Then appears Denegre, a lawyer and proprietor. . . . Then Wyckliffe speaks, a lawyer and newspaper owner. . . .

The column marches at a rapid pace. Parkerson, the Democratic boss, leads. There's also Houston, another boss, the man who twenty years ago killed the first Hennessy's killer. Wyckliffe, former district attorney, is second in command. There are three wagons in the lead with ropes and ladders. From a post on one hangs a noose.

Two hundred men shouldering rifles bring up the rear in warlike formation. They are followed and surrounded by crowds, some carrying shotguns, others revolvers. There is a stamping of feet. "They smile, as on the way to a picnic." When they reach the jail, a masonry building with balconies, each door is stormed by a different picket, evidently following orders. Amidst yelling and whistling the warden denies them the keys. They ram the main door with the beams. Its panels begin to yield and then a Negro hacks them down with an ax. Fifty enter; all would like to. "Here's the key," cries the deputy warden. . . .

The fifty hold council. From an open cell come some prisoners' trembling voices. A deathlike face can be seen through the bars of another. "Those ain't the ones," says one of the custodians politely, "they're upstairs in the women's department," and hands them the appropriate key. "Easy, gentlemen, easy!" cries Parkerson. "Anybody knows them? Only the Dagos." They overrun the empty corridor; the scaly, whitish hand of an eighty-year-old Negress points to a corner and a flight of narrow steps up which the quick stamping of feet is soon heard. "Hurrah, hurrah, hurrah!" cries one of the hunters; the rest, waving their hats, repeat the three hurrahs and follow him up. "Let 'em have it!" yells one. A volley is heard and the last of the fugitives reels in the air and falls with a bullet in his skull. The uproar outside drowns the noise of the shooting: "Hurrah for Parkerson!" "Hurray for

Wyckliffe!" They haven't even time to beg for mercy. Guachi and Caruso fall riddled like sieves. Romero is on his knees, his head touching the ground when he is killed. His hat is like a mesh of ribbons, the back of his jacket is ripped to shreds.

Bullets fly everywhere. Macheca, corraled, falls under a blow on the head and is finished off amidst the feet of men—businessmen, lawyers—who crush him with the butts of their rifles. Angry shouts rang horribly from without: "Bring them outside! Kill them where we can see!" The square is full, the surrounding streets are full. There are women and children: "Bring them out to us! Bring them out!"

A squadron appears at one of the doors pushing before them Polozzi, the mad witness who reels as though he were drunk. They can scarcely hold him on his feet.

Two men insult and strike each other over which can handle the noose better. A cluster of men are strung on one rope. Those standing around empty their revolvers upon them. There are streams of blood on their chests. Bagnetto is carried out, his face covered with wounds. Around his neck, still warm in death, the new noose is placed. They leave him swinging from the branch of a tree. Later the adjoining branches will be pruned off and they will wear the leaves as emblems—women, on their hats; men, on their lapels. One pulls out his watch: "We've made good time: forty-five minutes." From rooftops and balconies people look on through their opera glasses.

La Nación (Buenos Aires), May 20, 1891
Dated New York, March 26, 1891

VI
Capital and Labor

Knights of Labor Strike

... We are at the height of a struggle between capitalists and workers. The first can count on bank credit, funds expected from their debtors, payment of bills on fixed dates, and knowing where they stand at the end of the year. For the workers there is the daily reckoning, the urgent needs that cannot be postponed, the wife and child who eat in the evening what the poor husband worked for in the morning. And the comfortable capitalist compels the poor worker to work at a ruinous wage.

Those who live in luxury, thanks to colossal speculations, are urging Congress, for purposes of keeping the Treasury full at all times, not to lower the enormous duties afflicting production and trade throughout the nation. These excessively high duties, as soon as harvests decline or some product becomes scarce, cause excessively high prices. For the capitalist, a few cents per pound on foodstuffs amount to little on an annual balance sheet. For the worker, whose existence depends upon pennies, these pennies immediate deprive him of the basic necessities. The worker demands a wage that enables him to eat and clothe himself. The capitalist denies it to him.

At other times, impelled by the knowledge of the excessive profits that the capitalist obtains from a position that keeps the worker in extreme poverty, the worker might rebel in demanding a wage that allows him to save the amount needed to apply his skills independently, or to support himself in his old age.

But these uprisings are no longer isolated cases. The labor unions, which are unproductive in Europe and distorted by their own creators for having proposed violent and unjust political remedies together with just ones, are productive in North America because they have proposed to cure the visible and remediable ills of the workers only by peaceful and legal means.

There is no longer a city without as many associations as trade unions. The workers have gathered into a colossal association known as the Knights of Labor.[1] By the thirty thousands, as at this moment in Pittsburgh, they stand with folded arms, steadfast and spirited, before the iron foundries that stubbornly deny them the wages they demand. As in New York, the trains are stopped, the ships are at rest, produce is piled up on the loading platforms of railroad stations, and commerce throughout the nation is suffering a severe slowing down, and all because the freight loaders are asking the railroads for a wage that will let them eat meat.[2]

1. The Noble and Holy Order of the Knights of Labor, founded in 1869 by nine garment cutters in Philadelphia, grew in two decades to an organization of more than 700,000 members. It became the leading rallying point for American workers during the 1880s, and brought into one organization workers of all races and nationalities, except the Chinese, and united workers regardless of sex and religious belief. It sought especially to cut down the distinctions between skilled and unskilled workers. Headed at first by Uriah S. Stephens, its chief leader in the 1880s was Terence V. Powderly.

2. In the summer of 1882 the freight handlers of the New York Central & Hudson River and the New York Lake Erie & Western railroads, members of the Knights of Labor, struck for an increase of pay from 17 to 20 cents an hour. Freight rates for merchandise moving west had recently risen, so the public sympathized with the strikers. At first railroad officials—Jay Gould, Cornelius Vanderbilt, and John Field—brought in inexperienced strikebreakers, especially Italians, who were

They are asking for twenty cents an hour, plus the assurance of two dollars' worth of work per day, because a man who must travel many miles to and from his job, must eat away from home, has a wife and children there, and must live in a costly city in order to work, cannot live a city life on less than two dollars a day.

The railroad companies, caring little for their freight loaders, refused to meet their demands, and for a month now the two hostile forces have been at loggerheads.

The entire city is on the side of the disregarded freight loaders. How courageously they have endured their month of indigence! What a pleasure to see them as if suddenly ennobled, showing their dignity, clean and polite, sometimes appearing in large relays, walking through the streets in a quiet and orderly manner, sometimes coming to meetings held in the middle of squares, on abandoned docks, or in modest assembly rooms! Here they are making a rostrum out of a cart loaned by a lusty Irishman, there out of a pile of crates, in another place out of a slight rise of ground. It is becoming an extremely purposeful battle!

Now it is obvious why the most menial kind of work must not be deprecated. Those trunk-rollers, those sack-pushers have stirred up and hampered the commerce of the entire nation. The railroad companies, taking into account the extreme poverty of the poorer classes, sought and found thousands of other loaders at once. Most were Italians, unaccustomed to this kind of hard labor; some were Germans, far too virile for slavery; some were fugitive Jews from Russia, whose sudden tremendous hardships deprived them of strength and spirit.

---

unable to keep freight from piling up, and the shippers appealed to the courts for help in keeping the freight moving. Strikers were arrested and jailed, and when the railroads hired experienced strikebreakers, freight began to move westward. Even though the Central Labor Union of New York raised $60,000 for the strikers and boycotts were invoked against firms helping the railroads, the strike was broken.

At first it was believed that, since the loaders were being replaced, they would either go back to work again for the same low wages, or would leave their tasks to the newly hired workers. But it turned out that the novices were not such nimble loaders as the rebels, since hundreds of full wagons were waiting in vain at the gates of the colossal warehouses, and since rough young fellows from the neighborhood never tired of harassing the newly hired men who were working in those warehouses, and are still working there, surrounded and protected by heavy detachments of police. And thanks to their patience and practical wisdom, as it now stands the replacement workers are abandoning their employers in a body and bravely joining the rebel freight loaders in their protest. Today all of them—Italians, Germans, and Russian Jews, embracing one another in a brotherly manner on the streets and coming to enthusiastic meetings where all three languages are spoken equally—are demanding the new wage and the new guarantee of the railroad companies, which a short while ago raised their freight rates for no reason.

This marks a great event in the struggle. Formerly, if the country's workers decided to strike, the employers would approach the Italians, who were willing to work for a low wage. But now, since the Italians are resisting because they realize that if better working conditions are achieved for others, they will be achieved for themselves, the employers will have to yield to the just demands of the employed. For it is incredible that because of just demands, a worker whose fortune lies in the strength of his arms should run the risk of leaving his desolate house in hunger and misery.

And this is how things stand: the railroad men arrogant, and the freight loaders confident and aided by generous sums of money given by the work force of the whole nation, by wealthy people of good will. The corps of workers are mingling and establishing intimacy in an astounding fashion.

They are coming together rapidly, like men now ready for the fight. Not only does each work force have its own funds, but all of them together are creating an additional general fund to be used as a permanent treasury for every strike. Up to the present this has been justice. May good fortune grant that once the workers have achieved their ends, justice will not be distorted by rage and jealousy. For in this nation of workers, a workers' league for offensive purposes would be a tremendous thing. They are in it already. The struggle will be such that it will move and stir up the universe. These new laws are seething and bubbling over. Everywhere this is an age of renewal and remolding and putting things back on their hinges. With powerful and vigorous anger, the past century cast out the elements of the old life. This century, hindered in its passage through the ruins which at every instant threaten and incite with galvanic life, deals with particulars and preparations and is accumulating the durable elements of the new life.

La Nación (Buenos Aires), September 15, 1882
Dated New York, July 15, 1882

The Fruits of Protectionism

... It is amazing that serious danger in the condition of the country can be hidden from view. Fortunately, once it is seen, the intelligent of the land, the true priests, the true fathers and leaders, curb their polite hatreds as a sportsman curbs his dogs on the leash, and silently, shoulder to shoulder, consider how to take a common road to the catastrophe. The nation's tenacious industrialists, who still see money in the market, do not want foreign-made articles to enter the country duty free or in a position to compete with domestic products. And the poverty-stricken workers, who think they will be left without work in the domestic plants, or will earn less because everything of domestic manufacture will have to be sold at a lower price, with no parallel reduction in living costs, agree with the producers who employ and incite them,

1. Martí wrote several other articles on how high tariffs adversely affected the living standards of American workers. "The protectionist system hurts nobody more than it hurts the worker," he wrote in one of these articles. "Protectionism strangles industry, gluts the factories with useless goods, changes and damages the law of commerce, and threatens with a tremendous crisis—a crisis of hunger and rage—the countries upholding it. Freedom alone brings wealth and power." ("Liberty, Flank of Industry," *La América* [New York], September 1883. See also "In Trade, To Protect Is To Destroy," ibid., March 1883.)

making strong flanks in the protectionist army. But reason and the fear that serves it are alone filling the enemy flanks, no doubt successfully; permanent strength comes from a just balance. Work and human intelligence are being restricted by precise limits.

Whoever is overendowed with wealth will be poorer than poor. Countries that grow because of accidental conditions, and the illogical laws that profit from those conditions, suddenly weaken like the dogs of Cervantes' madman. In immense, universal harmony, he who abuses and monopolizes soon exhausts the supply and has nothing left to use. The slavery that enriched the slaveowners later drowned them in blood or in vice, and better for them had it been in blood! Protectionism, that sank the country's money boxes with an unexpected surplus, has shattered these money boxes.

The case is simple. It is obvious. The protectionist tariff raised import duties on goods of foreign manufacture so high that it closed the market to all imported articles of the kind made domestically. The nation grew wealthy from its abundant crops. The exclusive owners of the rich domestic market dumped their inferior products upon it at higher prices. The difference between the money being returned by the entire world for overpriced crops exported by the United States, and the cost of articles and produce being imported, kept the market overflowing with wealth, so that little attention was paid to the high prices. The great profits accumulated because of these prices enabled the nation's producers to build tremendously powerful factories, to erect Herculean mills, to smelt iron in cauldrons resembling hollow mountains turned upside down, to attract thousands of workers, to pay them enormous salaries, to create powerful and voracious organizations, to arouse entire cities to life—all these on capricious foundations of froth which would collapse as soon as the tariff props were pulled out from under them. And while the enriched market was being supplied with new products, the producers were flying high on clouds of glory. But the market was glutted, imports increased with the mad desire for luxury, the country needed no more domestic articles than it had, and what it would need would always be far less than the factories produced.

Since the industrialists were making so much money, they did not object to the high taxes which, for the tariff to be logical, were recovered by importing raw materials, so that with the scarcity of raw materials, the high standard of wages, and the interwoven fabric of costs created by the reciprocal laws resulting from the system, the domestic products (most of them run-of-the-mill due to the fact that, since they would be sold at all events, there was no incentive to improve their quality) can neither find anyone in the domestic market to buy them, nor be sent to foreign markets to compete with cheaper and more perfect competitive goods. And the huge, deceptive factory, with its iron belly and its eyes shooting flames, is beginning to throw up its thousands of frightened hands to the sky. Plants are shutting down,[2] looms are no longer weaving, villages of machine makers are letting their forges grow cold. There are labor unions. Factories are discharging their workers for lack of work. This year, with profits accumulated during the long period in which the system was in operation, the industrialists will be able to face paying far more to manufacture their products than the amount realized by their sale. But they are beginning not to be able to do so.

Each of these colossal factories is a veritable town, with thousands of stomachs that want food, voices that threaten, souls that grumble. Maintaining them is like maintaining

2. In 1882 a depression got under way from which the country did not fully recover until 1886. At the depths of this depressed period in 1884 there were close to a million unemployed workers in the United States. Factories closed and wages were reduced. "We could not possibly print all the past week's reports of wage-cutting and discharging of hands in scores of industry all over the country. They would overflow this paper," noted *John Swinton's Paper,* the leading labor journal of the 1880s, on December 7, 1884.

armies. These factories are gigantic affairs, as powerful and terrible as the clashing of winds in the air or of currents in the sea.

And the tycoon's life is a costly one; thirty thousand dollars a year is a niggardly sum for his rent. Soon it will be an elegant thing to paper one's walls with bank notes. Years ago there was an infamous character who covered his bride's wedding gown with bank notes. The problem has reared its head. Protectionism has yielded its harvest. A colossal industrial nation has been created, with no markets for its inferior goods.

That which is suspicion today will be outcry tomorrow. Restlessness is starting, and in its depths, where the surface is shaped, the way is lighted. Slowly at first, the crisis will give rise to deepfelt wrongs. It will be painful, bitter, overcast with gloom. Sudden scornful acts will bring great panic. By keeping the original tariff in force, the monster would grow. By suddenly throwing open the ports to foreign goods, the factories that were able to face expenses from the period of changeover from the manufacturing methods that impose imperfect goods at capricious prices on a forced market, to a manufacturing process that solicits a well-supplied market with perfect goods at low prices, will no longer be able to do so. Manufacturing interests here are so great that suddenly curtailing them would be an incomparable catastrophe.

It seems necessary, then, to keep imported articles within bounds as one sees the imminent danger to domestic producers, so that industry may at least protect the country's consumption. While convinced of fearful mistakes and inevitable competition, factories are improving the quality of their goods in such a way that, with the aid of low duties on imported raw materials and low wages due to a lowering of the usual living costs—both advantages to come from free trade—the latter may finally be established, and the former go out to struggle with competing products in markets abroad.

Whatever is happening today revolves around this problem. . . .

La Nación (Buenos Aires), January 27, 1884
Dated New York, December 21, 1883

An Epidemic of Strikes

Today there are strikes everywhere, appalling strikes. Entire states are striking, entire work regions comprising two or three states.[1] From local chapter to local chapter, or trade union to trade union, the Order of the Knights of Labor has been spreading from its birthplace in Philadelphia throughout the republic: first in the factories of the East, then in the larger cities, then in the railroad centers of the West, and finally among the farmers and miners of the Pacific Coast states.

What a few strongwilled tailors began twenty years ago at a clothcutting table is today a technical association organized along the lines of a tremendously vast Freemasonry by means of which, if a Texas railroad company should dismiss one of its workers without cause, the blacksmiths of Pittsburgh, the

1. In the years 1880-1886 organized labor conducted more strikes than ever before in American history. Until 1886 its efforts were primarily directed to win wage increases, and, as the effects of the industrial depression which started in 1882 became more marked, to prevent wage reductions. By 1886, when recovery was under way, many of the strikes were also for the eight-hour day, a drive which reached a climax on May 1, 1886, when 350,000 workers throughout the country went on strike for the eight-hour day. Although the Knights of Labor leadership was opposed to strikes, most of the strikes conducted during the early 1880s were by members of the organization.

shoe factories of New England, the cigar makers of New York would be prepared to send their share of assistance to the Texas railroad strike until the worker in question has been returned to his post.

If the coal miners feel that they are being paid a ruinous wage for their almost superhuman labors, the Knights of Labor defends them, represents them, and comes to their aid. Six months ago there was little bread and little meat in Monongahela, but the mines were deserted. Some days ago a few of the miners wanted to return to the mines, but their own wives came out to meet them and dumped the household garbage over their heads.

If in New England the manufacturers refuse to give an account of their profits to the Knights of Labor's court, it makes peaceful and sincere inquiries to discover why. To find out whether or not it is true that the colossal shoe factories cannot pay their workers the salary they demand, those colossal factories are left without workers, much to the benefit of those other factories which, in order not to misuse their profits, have a wage policy of turning back to the workers a share of the factories' production.

This system is growing; it may even outnumber other systems as the only fair means of giving a portion of production to both owner and worker. As things now stand, the worker, having had to struggle onward with little success all his life and reckon carefully for fifty years, has to live from the charity he is not always able to find.

And if a great railroad company, such as that in the southeastern part of the country managed by the able millionaire Jay Gould,[2] purposely defaults on its agreements in former contracts and operates counter to what was stipulated in

2. Jay Gould (1836-1892), with James Fish and Daniel Drew, became the classic symbol of the ruthless behavior of the Robber Baron entrepreneurs of the post–Civil War period, manipulating and often wrecking railroads in pursuit of wealth.

them—lowers wages, dismisses men without giving them a month's notice, lengthens the working day, and fails to compensate adequately for the added hours; if time and again the workers vainly ask the company's directors to live up to their agreement and examine the workers' complaints; if patience and moderation are met with challenges and contempt, as unfortunately happened in this case—then the aggrieved railroad union rises in a body, and shortly thereafter, one after another, all the unions working in the company join it: first the stokers, then the machinists, followed immediately by the brakemen and switchmen; in short, ten thousand men, the entire railroad.

Trains do not move. Merchandise piles up in enormous quantities.

Day after day the strike grows.

Goods are not shipped out, imports do not arrive on schedule, sales will not be what they have been.

A railroad system brought to a halt in similar regions is like a glutted aorta.

So it has been for two weeks in Missouri and Kansas.[3]

3. In 1885 the Knights of Labor tied up traffic on the southwestern railroad system operated by Jay Gould and forced the capitalists to settle on terms favorable to the Knights. This spectacular triumph over one of the greatest capitalists of the day brought thousands of new workers into the Knights of Labor. However, it became clear that Gould had no real intention of permitting a union to exist in his empire. In violation of the agreement, railroad workers who joined the Knights were fired; overtime work was not paid for; wages were not restored to the prestrike level, and yardmen, bridgemen, sectionmen, and other semiskilled and unskilled workers were constantly being discriminated against in the matter of wages, hours, and working conditions. When the Gould management refused to live up to its agreement, a strike broke out early in 1886 which spread to the entire southwestern system. Despite the militancy of the strikers the strike was lost. The surrender of the Knights was unconditional. No member of the organization was rehired. Blacklisted on the railroads, many of the strikers faced a dark future.

The unremitting efforts of those who are preparing the workers for a general peaceful uprising, to bring about some essential reforms in working conditions, are revealed prematurely and inevitably by these great precursory movements that break out spontaneously wherever the abuses one is attempting to rectify are most intense, or wherever the mollifying influence of more prudent heads cannot be exerted as efficiently as in areas within easier reach.

A year ago on this very date there were only eighteen thousand workers rebelling; this year at the present moment, aside from the lesser strikes, there are over sixty thousand. The coal miners of Pennsylvania, Maryland, and Ohio have hardly a single miner at work; the Allegheny nail factories are deserted; strikers in the great foundries, textile mills, and shoe factories of Massachusetts number more than ten thousand.

With the exception of last year, the factories refusing to give their operators the wage and respect they consider fair are blockaded or boycotted,[4] and the union's "local chapter" censures those factories by publishing this news in its newspaper, so that the workers and their friends do not buy the factory's goods.

Boycotting is on the wane; but examining closely the upsetting and voluminous mass of news from areas in a state of revolt, one discerns less submission, more determination, and

4. Although boycotts were not mentioned in the Knights of Labor's constitution and were not employed during the first years of its existence, by 1885 the Knights had become the most successful boycotting agency in the history of the American labor movement. Boycotts were levied against newspapers, manufacturers and dealers in hats, cigars, clothing, carpets, dry goods, shoes, stoves, flour, beer, pianos, and organs. Owners of hotels and theaters, and of excursion steamers, builders, coal mining companies, and many others felt the pressure of the boycott. In practically every case, the boycott was also a secondary boycott, the person or firm disregarding the boycott being boycotted in turn.

greater unity than in former struggles. Workers have not waited so long to rebel. Their demands are made without arrogance but with more energy. And as soon as they do ask for something, in the East as well as in the West, one notices the same knack of determination and fighting spirit.

If at the same time one reads about manifestations in the most distant places, it is obvious that their language and intensity of purpose are just as strong.

The language constantly used by the common people to express their firm resolve is often infantile and terrible, or childishly rhetorical, but at times it has an apostolic eloquence.

If the Order counseling and directing these strikes were not seen to be emerging everywhere, successful in some places but inspiring respect in all of them; if it were not seen to be spreading, concentrating, finding new locations, giving its attention wisely and energetically to everything—here reprimanding, there inciting to action, on the one hand restraining fanatics, on the other yielding to those who treat them with contempt; if, through the force these strikes arouse, and the skill that has guided the Order up to the present, the strikes had not attracted the attention of the entire country, and even abroad where the Order is proclaimed "the most important trade union of them all," then it might be said, because of the general text of the language of its documents, that its seriousness is not yet as great as its enthusiasm.

But this is when one looks merely at the rhetoric, for the pith of the documents shows precisely all that exaltation and concentration, all that proud and boundless fire, all that inability to see beyond the cause to which one's soul is given— all that the reformers, convinced of their justice, angrily fling aside like the cape of a hobgoblin.

"We are idiots, for we can neither see nor read nor feel nor know what words mean. Month after month we have submitted patiently to this humiliation; month after month we have asked, waited, begged to be heard in a friendly atmosphere.

"Month after month we have deliberated, hoping to have the railroad heads finally agree with us.

"Useless! Every day the violations have been more severe. What can we do? What would you do? Acknowledge defeat? Human nature cannot bear that.

"Men who are worthy of the name do not submit. We will stop working and we will do so again and again should the same circumstances occur, even if misery does stare us in the face."

This is what one assembly says. Another, when it appeals to *order* and to the *country* about Jay Gould's intention of hailing the Knights of Labor into court as a conspiratorial association, states it as follows:

"It may well be that the stratagems of the law, controlled by him, may take root in the courts of justice, and that the judges may see nothing but the rights of wealth through the gold-rimmed spectacles which he knows how to put before their eyes. But we appeal to that superior and higher court whose verdict is definitive and supremely fair; to that court do we appeal: here is our case."

And it lists the company's abuses. Referring to those who, because of need or treachery, serve a railroad—and there are very few—the proclamation breaks forth in this manner: "Cowards behind, scoundrels to the enemy; men in the lead."

Traitors, or poor devils! Those of abject spirit who are born to cringe, or the weak-kneed whom rebellion and misery terrify!

Who has not known, on school benches as well as on the benches of life, those who pay court, like lovelorn hens, to masters, the rich, the powerful, and to the fainthearted who, although not wicked themselves, timidly follow where the wicked lead them?

And there is also the possibility—who knows?—that love for one's home, and the dread of scarcity, is what may have moved some of the railroad workers, fifty out of ten thousand, to continue to serve the company. But this fact has

given rise to a greater conflict; one which puts the Order of
the Knights of Labor in danger of losing much of the respectful fellow-feeling with which it is visibly greeted, perhaps
because it is rightly seen as resolving the labor problem rather
than causing the bloody convulsion others fear.

Not even the privileged have the right to violate the rights
of others for the purpose of keeping their own. And the
powerful man must not abuse his power. Use inspires respect;
abuse causes anger. Aside from the more selfish and ambitious, the country at large accompanied with its vote the
Order's local chapters that decided on the railroad strike, and
with obvious reason. The states suffering from the strike are
not themselves throwing this decision in the face of its insti-
gators. The state governors have acted as voluntary mediators
between the labor union's highest representatives, who have
recognized and taken charge of the strike, and the railroad
heads, who refuse to have anything to do with it.

But when, with the violence that the Order rejected, the
strikers prevent the company from moving its trains; when
they block the movement of locomotives and put out their
fires; when they forcibly return to the depot the trains that
had already begun to leave; when they run to attack the
repair shops with all the fury of a mob, which finally called a
stop of its own accord; when they take possession of a locomotive belonging to the company and drive it along tracks
which are not their own, to run an errand for themselves—
then not even the public supports them, nor does the press
commend them, nor can the militia relax.[5]

Today the governors declared their intention of making

5. After this dispatch was written, on April 9, 1886, during a battle
between strikers and police, militia, and deputy sheriffs in East St.
Louis, seven workers were killed. Strikers were arrested daily and put in
jail on charges of contempt of court and inciting to riot. There were
even indictments for communicating with individuals "requesting them
not to work."

people respect the company's right to run its trains if it has men to work for it.

Fortunately, the strikers convince the workers. And fortunately, whatever the results for the country, the workers refuse to work for lower wages and under worse conditions than they consider fair, and they are justified in taking that stand. But if they should attempt to interfere with the freedom and property of others, the state militia would deal with the disruptive elements.

Excitement runs high, yet one does not expect the workers to carry arms.

The city of St. Louis is in a festive mood and displays a revolutionary atmosphere everywhere—in the people on the streets, in discussion groups where there is animated conversation, in the women dressed in their Sunday best. Suddenly the streets empty; a train has started whistling as it goes past!

A man stands beside the tracks holding an American flag. The train approaches slowly and the man waves his flag. He has a wrinkled face, a beard, and hairy hands; he wears a flannel shirt, short, loose trousers, and boots.

"Are you going to run over this flag?" he shouts at the engineer, and lays the flag on the tracks.

The train runs over it and tears it.

The man picks it up and smooths it out again, and in the deep silence of the crowd says: "You are torn and drooping, but we still respect you. Yesterday they cut out your stars, today they'll cut out your stripes, but you're still a good flag!"

La Nación (Buenos Aires), May 9, 1886
Dated New York, March 25, 1886

The Labor Problem in the United States

In the United States this [labor] problem presents itself, as everything does here, suddenly and on a colossal scale. Here, when there is force, it is overpowering, when there is hunger, it is great. . . . It is a well-known fact that this motley population is only American in its more recent stratum, the last generation, and in some places not even that.[1]

Without the brakes of patriotism, therefore, which even among scoundrels has much strength, this medley of Irish, Scotch, Germans, Swedes—meat-eating, beer-drinking people, with shoulders and hands like Atlas'—rush quickly and unbridled, restrained only by fear or the instinct of self-preservation, to the conquest of what they consider theirs: their right to a larger part of the product of a wealth of which they consider themselves the main factor and of which they are not the main beneficiaries. This advancing mass might be held back, often justly held back. They might be made to understand that though they are an indispensable part in the production of wealth, on the other hand the accumulation of capital, against the hateful abuses of which they justly rebel, is just as important a part. They might be able to realize that it is not merely a question of mal-

1. The total number of immigrants arriving in the United States during the decade 1880-1890 was more than 5.5 million, 2.5 million more during the 1890s.

adjustment in the distribution of industrial products that often creates unemployment or underpayment of labor, but rather the enormous production due to the accelerated output of machines, the excess of production over needs, the competition of foreign countries—fatal to countries which, like the United States, charge high customs duties on their imports—and the errors of industry itself, which feeds the laboring masses and which, fearing to have its own domestic market invaded by the products of free trade countries, advocates the continuance of high import tariffs, thus making it impossible for industry to compete successfully in rival markets.

Now Uncle Sam is adjusting his suspenders, pulling at his beard, passing his top hat from hand to hand, wiping with his cotton handkerchief his sweaty brow, from which for the first time drops of blood begin to ooze, while he faces this formidable problem brought about by his having protected himself too much.

Uncle Sam provides himself with everything, he owns forests of factories of all kinds, but is himself obliged to buy all that he manufactures. But where will he put it all? What will he do with so much? Where will he get the money to go on feeding his factories? What will he do with his millions of workers, who do not stand by to look at the problem, but see that business is rich while they are poor, who want better wages, more security, more respect?

All this could be said to the laboring masses to hold them back or to postpone until a more propitious occasion their demands for industrial reorganization. But as they have already drawn up their bill of rights, well founded on reason; as they see that their ills sprang partly from organized capital's insolence and disdain, from its illegal practices, from a system of unfair distribution of profits which keeps the working man a perpetual pauper; as they do not feel it is just that railroad workers should earn barely enough for a morsel of food and a blanket in order that the companies' bosses and henchmen may share in Gargantuan dividends; that for every thousand dollars of actual investment in the business twenty thousand dollars' worth of shares is issued, so that, since profits are naturally proportionate to capital investment, there is never enough with the profit of a thousand to pay dividends on twenty thousand; furthermore, as the holy poison of human dignity has gotten into men's veins and is there to stay, swelling them, pushing them on, we have come to a state where, a justice done here, a violence there, workers are on their feet, having decided not to sit down except on a hand-in-hand basis with capital.

Then things get worse, unhappily. None feel the need of being masters more than slaves do, and as the working classes have had so much to suffer at the hands of the masters who employ them, they have developed a despotic inclination and are not content with becoming the equals of those who have made them suffer, but going beyond all reason would raise themselves above them, submit them to terms which would deprive their employers of the very dignity and human freedom which they claim for themselves.

There, in their own injustice, lies their weakness, and from this, at least this once, stems their defeat.

La Nación (Buenos Aires), June 4, 1886
Dated New York, April 27, 1886

Henry George and Land Monopoly

The oppressed workers are turning their eyes to the land against the day when universal production, piled up by machines, is stacked sky-high in the markets, with no buyers. Avaricious European firms and impudently rich and titled Englishmen must not come near the free man and appropriate his country's soil, later to live in unjust luxury from its enormous and capricious production!

As silently as octopuses the great companies of Europe have been spreading their tentacles over the most fertile lands of North America. Countries with vast areas of land must be extremely vigilant! The sooner they begin protecting them, the better; Europe has a large surplus of idle and restless money. A Netherlands company already possesses 4,500,000 acres of the most productive land in New Mexico. An English syndicate has 3,000,000 acres in Texas. A German firm owns 1,000,000. And one man, the Marquis of Tweeddale, is owner of 1,750,000 acres of the nation's rich farmland. They bought entire states: all of New Mexico and its rangelands, all of Mississippi and its rivers, all of Florida and its orange groves.[2] But the Senate has risen in protest, and without a

1. This selection is an extract from a more complete article by Martí. See above, pp. 200-6, for another part of the same article.
2. Although foreign syndicates gobbled up large tracts of land in the United States, they were not the only ones guilty of obtaining large

dissenting voice has passed a bill prohibiting future acquisitions of any land in the United States by foreigners, who do not buy this privilege with their declaration to obey the laws of the land they covet. None but the foreigner who declares his intention of accepting citizenship in the Republic will be able to obtain land in it, unless that land is inherited or given in payment of a debt.

No company with more than 20 percent foreign membership will be able to buy land. Not even national companies—whether formed for building railroads, highways, or canals—will be permitted to obtain more than 5,000 acres in the territories where Congress has full power, and this only if those acres are obviously used for the company's operation.

It is necessary to take a friendly stand against threatening armies. Labor met certain defeat in its ill-advised uprisings this spring. Much is still needed to enable labor to act with that unity of purpose which will sufficiently invigorate its attack upon the present social structure. In the convention held this month, it was seen that the isolated trade unions,

---

holdings, frequently through bribery and fraud. Railroads, cattle barons, lumber companies, corporations, well-financed syndicates all had a share in seizing, or often stealing, public lands. Compliant officers of the Interior Department, under pressure from companies, withdrew public land from would-be homesteaders and allowed it to be taken over by syndicates. The corporations selected the cream of these lands.

Another source of fraud lay in surveys of government land. It had become customary for Washington to allow the surveyor-generals of the various states and territories to let contracts for public land surveys to their deputies. By gaining control of all surveying contacts, the syndicates cheated the government out of valuable land rights. Still another practice was landgrabbing by false entries under which corporations obtained huge tracts for little or nothing. When the true homesteader arrived he found that the best areas had fallen into the hands of the syndicates. In 1887 the Land Commissioner reported that "bold, reckless, and gigantic schemes to rob the government of its lands" had been exposed in every state and territory.

each one working for the good of the members of a particular occupation, were unwilling to yield their sovereignty to the Knights of Labor, or to be subject to its skills, defeats, and assessments.[3] But the Knights of Labor is in the hands of dedicated followers, and at an opportune moment.

Others stave off the June heat by playing ball, laying wagers, imitating the calisthenics of English soldiers. But George A. Swinton, Post,[4] and Powderly,[5] given the glorious task of making the world of humans swing on better hinges without bloodshed, are going from nation to nation teaching a way of obtaining for the working man, by concise and intelligent action, a secure existence in which his food and shelter will not have to be a donation of charity. These new evangelists do not preach blindly. They have not memorized their texts for reform. Every wrong suggests its own cure.

3. A conflict existed in the Knights of Labor between the pro- and anti-trade union elements, and many unions complained that the anti-union elements in the Knights sought to destroy their organizations. The anti-union elements, on the other hand, insisted that by concentrating only on organizing skilled workers, the unions violated the principle of labor solidarity. Unwilling to surrender their sovereignty to the Knights of Labor, many of the national trade unions met and formed the Federation of Organized Trades and Labor Unions of the United States and Canada, which became the American Federation of Labor in 1886.

4. Louis F. Post (1849-1928), single-taxer who edited Henry George's campaign paper, *The Daily Leader*, in the mayoralty campaign of 1886, later edited the single-tax weekly published in Chicago, *The Public* (1898-1913), and was U.S. Assistant Secretary of Labor (1913-1921).

5. Terence V. Powderly (1849-1924), joined the Machinists' and Blacksmiths' Union in 1870; was Secretary of the District Assembly of the Knights of Labor and elected Grand Master Workman in 1879; served as Mayor of Scranton from 1878 to 1882; pursued conservative policies as head of the Knights of Labor in an effort to appease the Catholic Church and the commercial press; supported the Republican Party in 1897 and was appointed the United States Commissioner-General of Immigration.

They have formulated their original texts from original wrongs, and with the enthusiastic and contagious force of reality, they are accommodating their propaganda to the reforms they are attempting. These men are new saints who travel the world shutting doors upon hate. They can see the hurricane coming and they are guiding its course. As a method they use peace. Realizing that the land never denies a man what he needs, they want the land administered in such a manner that its produce will be divided equally among all. Previous ideas spring from this central idea, which will grow old and gray before it is put into effect but must triumph in the end.

It is the mismanagement of public lands, principal source of all property, that is responsible for those insolent accumulations of wealth so ruinous to futile competition among the aspiring poor. It is the abuse of public lands that gives rise to those monstrous corporations that shrivel or flood the national fortune with their thunderings and greed. It is those evil partnerships of capital that compel the laborer to perish from unemployment, or to work for a grain of rice. It is those huge companies that elect senators and representatives at their own expense, or buy them off after they have been elected, to be sure of their support for the laws that keep these companies happy in abusing them. And they distribute, with national consent, new tracts of public land from whose produce they continue amassing their tremendous power.

Those apostles believe, then, that there must be a stop to the illegal alliance between the companies and their representatives who, in the name of the nation, provide the corporations with the wealth of the land for the interest of that part of it which is to be returned to them in the form of shares or the like, in payment for their vote—for their plunder!

Those apostles—George, Swinton, Post, and Powderly—believe that the nation, which is only another name for the guardian of common property, cannot put under private control the land that belongs to all and is necessary to all, except in lease or loan and for national use only. Those apostles believe that, since the public domain must become the property of those who live upon it, the less of it that is given away, the less it will cost later on to take it back from the hands of men who, through cunning or bribery, were fraudulently declaring bankruptcy with its use.

This, then, is the main significance of the unanimous vote of the Senate, and the analogous bill in the House, which prohibits foreign ownership of the land. It was an opportune act and did not to any extent decrease respect for the power of labor, now moving quietly ahead.

The courts are punishing labor's illegal coalitions, its sieges of proprietors who resist the workers' demands, its threats or acts of violence.[6] The proprietor is free to employ, or refuse to employ, whatever worker he wishes; by the same token the worker is free to work, or refuse to work, for his employer. The worker who forces the proprietor to consent to his demands, by means of coalitions or sieges or threats of violence is, under laws now in force, guilty of conspiracy.[7] Day

6. The courts were punishing all of labor's acts, not merely those Martí describes. Numerous arrests were made for picketing and boycotting and for "unlawful assemblages and unlawful words." In one case in New York City, Judge Power warned: "I hold that any man who walks up and down in front of a man's place of business commits a species of assault. I intend to hold such men hereafter on bond to keep the peace." In two months in New York City, there was a "legal round-up" of some one hundred strikers and boycotters under the charge of "conspiracy." Men who distributed circulars advising the boycott of a bakery got ten days. For boycotting Cavanagh, Sandford and Co., forty-seven tailors were indicted. In the famous Theiss boycotters' case, five union members were sentenced to State Prison at hard labor—two for two years and ten months; two for one and one-half years, and one for three years and eight months. (Philip S. Foner, *History of the Labor Movement in the United States* [New York, 1955], Vol. II, pp. 117-19.)

7. Only two states, Maryland and Michigan, had by 1886 enacted laws authorizing the formation of trade unions. Thirty-six states, in 1886, failed to provide for the legal formation of labor organizations, and in thirty-five the activities of workers in combination were subject

after day this spring the agitators have been starting to serve their prison sentences. In Chicago a jury is already considering the murder charge against the anarchists who incited to slaughter and spread it with their own hands.[8] But the Knights of Labor, served by those steelwilled men of peace, is a strong organization precisely for this reason: it condemns the use of force.[9]

La Nación (Buenos Aires), August 15, 1886
Dated New York, July 2, 1886

---

to limitations imposed by conspiracy statutes, or, where these were lacking, by judicial application of the English common law governing combinations. Conspiracy laws usually prohibited any person from trying to prevent any other person by threat, intimidation, or "unlawful interference" from working at a lawful business or occupation on any terms he saw fit. They also prohibited "any two or more persons" from combining "for the purpose of depriving the owner or possessor of property of its lawful use and management, or of preventing by threats, suggestions of danger, or any unlawful means, any person from being employed by or obtaining employment from such owner or possessor of property, on such terms as the parties concerned may agree upon. . . ." Violation was usually punishable by fine up to $500 or six months' imprisonment.

The courts defined intimidation so loosely that even if no interference with the right to work had occurred, the mere inducing of workers to break their contract with an employer was considered a conspiracy. Indeed, the mere presence of a large number of strikers outside a mine or factory often resulted in convictions for conspiracy. In nearly every case where such convictions were appealed to the state Supreme Courts, the judgments of the lower courts were sustained.

8. Martí is here referring to the trial growing out of the Haymarket Affair which is discussed below. See p. 287.

9. Martí here is referring to frequent statements by Terence V. Powderly, Grand Master Workman of the Knights of Labor, condemning radicalism, the use of violence in labor disputes, and especially the anarchists involved in the Haymarket Affair in Chicago. However, he does not note that Powderly's views were often condemned by members of the Knights of Labor.

The Schism of the Catholics in New York

Nothing of what is happening in the United States today is comparable in transcendence and interest with the struggle between the authorities of the Catholic Church and the Catholic people of New York.[1] This has reached such a point that for the first time the loyal observer wonders in amazement if Catholic doctrine can truly belong in a free nation without being harmful to it, and if such is the virtue of

---

1. At the beginning of the campaign to elect Henry George mayor of New York on the United Labor ticket in 1886, many, if not a majority of the Catholic priests supported George. But as the campaign advanced, "at the suggestion" of the "higher Catholic powers" all Catholic priests except Father Edward McGlynn (1837-1900) withdrew from active participation on behalf of the Labor Party candidate and single-tax advocate. On September 29, 1886, Archbishop Michael Augustine Corrigan (1839-1902), a strong conservative, forbade Father McGlynn to speak at a scheduled public meeting on behalf of George. Father McGlynn disobeyed, informing the Archbishop of New York: "I, in view of my rights and duties as a citizen, which were not surrendered when I became a priest, am determined to do what I can to support Mr. George; and I am also stimulated by love for the poor and oppressed laboring classes, which seems to be particularly consonant with the charitable and philanthropic character of the priesthood, by virtue of which it has gained everywhere its greatest triumphs." McGlynn was thereupon suspended from exercise of his priestly functions for a period of two weeks.

freedom that it restores to its primitive condition of poetic teaching a church which has unfortunately become man's most efficient instrument of deprivation. Yes, this is so! Sudden clashes reveal the heart of the matter. From the heated controversy in New York the corrupt Church was left chastised unmercifully, and the Church of justice and compassion triumphant. It is obvious that the virtue and poetry of the Church can fit into the modern world, with no threat to freedom. One feels that Catholicism in itself has no degrading power, as might be thought in view of the fact that so much about it is debasing and enslaving. The degrading element in Catholicism is the extent to which the Church's hierarchy abuses its authority and its malicious counsels knowingly confuse its own interests with the simple injunctions of the faith. It is understandable that one can be a sincere Catholic and a zealous and loyal citizen of a republic. And as always, it is the humble, the shoeless, the needy, the fishermen who band together shoulder to shoulder to fight injustice and make the Gospel fly with its silver wings aflame! Truth is

---

As soon as the exciting mayoralty campaign of 1886 was over, the Archbishop decided to take more decisive action against the rebel priest. On January 14, 1887, he removed McGlynn from the pastorate of St. Stephens. McGlynn was then ordered by the Pope to come to Rome to hear why he should refrain from pursuing his activities on behalf of the labor and single-tax movements, and when he refused, he was excommunicated from the Catholic Church, the order to take effect July 4, 1887. Father McGlynn had strong supporters among the clergy and laity of New York City and a real split occurred in the Catholic Church over his excommunication. McGlynn himself continued to support social reform causes as president of the Anti-Poverty Society. He was reinstated to the ministry in December 1892. (See Foner, op. cit., pp. 126-27, 146-47; Stephen Bell, *Rebel, Priest and Prophet* [New York, 1937], pp. 34-62; *Irish World,* November 6, 1886, January-March 1887; *New York Times,* January 14-20, 1887.) For another article by Martí on the subject, see "La Excomunión del Padre McGlynn," *Obras Completas* [La Habana, 1946], Vol. I, pp. 1819-28.)

revealed more clearly to the poor and the sufferers! A piece
of bread and a glass of water never deceive!

I have just sat on their benches, have just seen them,
mingled with them, seen the souls of men shine in all their
splendor when I had thought that a despotic religion with
unlawful purposes had extinguished that splendor. Ah,
religion—as dogma always false in the light of a lofty wisdom,
as poetry eternally true! In a word, what are religious dogmas
but the beginnings of natural truths? Their very candor and
crudity inspire love, as in poetry. That is why, because these
dogmas are ineffable grains of certainty, they so gently capti-
vate the poetic spirits who do not willingly descend to the
concrete study of the true.

Oh, if they could but know how religions merge and are
weighed and measured there, and how Nature, crowned with
harmony and robed with song, emerges from among them
more beautiful than all! The strongest part of man's faith in
religions is his faith in himself and his proud resistance to
believing he is capable of being wrong. The most powerful
aspect of faith is affection for the tender years when it was
received, and for the adored hands that gave it to us. Why do
men quarrel about those things which can be analyzed without effort, known without pain, and which leave all of us
confused in an extraordinary and common poetry?

I have just seen them, sat beside them, smoothed the
wrinkles of their frowning souls which, stone upon stone and
thorn by thorn, their exile is causing. Another man would
have rejoiced in their protest; I rejoiced in their unity. Why
were those Catholics, those working people, those Irishmen
there? Why were those housewives there, worn out and
white-haired? Why were the good men of all creeds there if
not to honor the saintly priest, persecuted by the Archbishop
of their Church for having stood beside the poor?

It was at Cooper Union, in the free school's meeting hall—

Cooper Union, built by that grand old man Cooper[2] with his own earnings so that others could learn how to overcome the difficulties he had found in life. Although he was far from handsome, a handsomer man never lived! The meeting was held in Cooper Union's lower hall. It was raining outside and overflowing inside. Hardly an ignoble face was to be seen, not because there were none but because there seemed to be none. Six thousand people, six thousand Catholics, filled the seats, the halls, the doorways, the spacious corridors. Their "Sogarth Aroon," the "priest of the poor," had finally been thrown out of their church. For twenty-two years he had advised them without belittling them, had shared his inheritance and salary with the unfortunate, had not seduced their wives or led their daughters to a life of easy virtue. It was he who built in their own poor neighborhood a church whose doors were always open, he who never used the influence of faith to intimidate the people's spirit, or darken their thought, or reduce their free minds to the blind service of the worldly and impure interests of the Church—he, Father McGlynn! He has been thrown out of his house and his church; his own successor evicted him from his bedroom; his name was stricken from the confession box. Who will go to confession now with a soul full of hate? Because the Father has been saying what Jesus said, what the Church of Ireland says with the Pope's blessing, what Archbishop Meade preaches to his diocese, what that deepthinking Balmes lays at the feet of the Pontiff as ecclesiastical truth—because he

2. Peter Cooper (1791-1883), industrial pioneer and inventor, founder of Cooper Union in New York (1857-1859), which offered popular instruction in science and art. A social reformer as well as a wealthy capitalist, Cooper ran for president on the Greenback Party ticket in 1876, offering a program of currency reform for the solution of the economic crisis. He received 80,000 votes. Martí, who admired Cooper, wrote an appreciative essay on him. See *Obras Completas*, Vol. I., pp. 1072-80.

said that the land must belong to the nation, and that the nation must not distribute it among the few; because with his dignity and fame, his virtue and wisdom, his sermons and advice, he helped in the magnificent autumn elections those energetic workers and fine thinkers who look to the law for the solution to needless poverty—for all these things his Archbishop robs him of his parish, and the Pope orders him to Rome for discipline!

When from the political rostrum Father McGlynn defended Cleveland in the elections two years ago because he thought he was honest, the Archbishop was not displeased, for Cleveland was the candidate of the party with which the New York Church was negotiating—negotiating and scheming![3] But the same thing about Father McGlynn that seemed good to the Archbishop when the priest was defending the archiepiscopal candidate, that same expression of political preference on the part of a Catholic priest seemed bad now that Father McGlynn's defense could be alarming to those wealthy Protestants who entrench themselves in the Church and use it to stand against justice for the poor who built it!

The Catholic Church came to the United States on the shoulders of Irish immigrants whose religious faith, as with the Polish, has been strengthened by the fact that in times past their saints were the leaders of their independence, and by the fact that the Norman and English conquerors have always attacked their religion and their country at the same time. The Catholic religion has become the fatherland for the Irish, but not the Catholic religion that the servile and ungrateful secretary to Pope Pius VII established in agreement with the Protestant king of England George III when, on asking favors of this implacable enemy of the Irish Catholics, he made him observe that "the Protestant colonies in America have rebelled against your Gracious Majesty, while

3. Martí is referring to the Democratic Party, which Catholics traditionally supported.

the Catholic colony in Canada has remained loyal." For the Irish, it was that other religion of those bishops who were gentlemen and poets—those who, their banners emblazoned with a gold harp on a field as green as their own countryside, pushed aside the hungry clergy arrived from Rome sullied by iniquitous ostentation, by all the vices of an arrogant oligarchy, and by the immoral commitment of aiding the princes from whom they had received donations, a clergy using the influence of the faith to act against those princes' enemies and vassals. These merchants of divinity bit the dust before those simple Irish theologians who could always count on a meal at the tables of the poor, and who desired no more purple than that conferred upon them by the conqueror's sword as it stabbed them through, a hymn on their lips, among the hordes of faithful peasants who were fighting furiously for their freedom. The Irish curate was the soothing pillow, the medicine, the poem, the legend, the rage of Ireland. From generation to generation, spurred on by misfortune, this fondness for the priest has been accumulating in the Irishman, and he would sooner burn his own heart in his pipe than uproot his affection for his "Sogarth Aroon," his poetry and advice, his country in exile, the smell of his native countryside, his medicine and his soothing pillow!

Thus Catholicism grew rapidly in the United States, not by springing up spontaneously or from any real increase in members, but by a simple transplant, and there is no reason to wonder or marvel at this. There were as many more Catholics in the United States at the end of every year as there were Irish immigrants arriving during the year. With them came the priest who was their adviser and all they had left of their country. With the priest, the Church. With their children thus reared in Catholicism, the new generation of parishioners. With the noble tolerance of the United States, the facility of raising above the Protestant steeples the steeples built with Irish pennies. Those were the foundations of Catholicism in these States: men in work shirts and coarse jackets, poor women with swollen lips and scalded hands.

How is it that such fertile fields were not invaded by the bold and despotic souls whose lamentable and perennial predominance is the plague and ruin of the Church? Pomp and vanity continued the work begun by faith. Scorning the humble people to whom it owed its establishment and wealth, the Church raised money in the streets of the wealthy, and with its sumptuous regalia easily dazzled the vulgar appetite for ostentation, so common to people of sudden aggrandizement and little culture. It took advantage of the normal disturbances of public life, in an age of study and readjustment of social conditions, to appear before the apprehensive monied classes as the only force which, by means of its subtle influence over the soul, could check the dreaded march of the poor, keeping alive their faith in a world to come where their thirst for justice would be slaked, in order to dull their eagerness to slake it in the present world. So one can see how in this stronghold of Protestantism, the Protestants, still representing the wealthy and cultured class here, are the staunch and tacit friends, the grateful accomplices, of the religion that roasted them on the spit, one that today they cherish because it helps them safeguard their unjust accumulation of worldly possessions! Pharisees, all of them, and augurers!

Having acquired the desire for power, in a place where religious mystery and threatening times hold it in such high esteem, the Catholic Church cast its eyes on the origin of that power—here the ballot box—as in monarchies it casts them on the sovereigns. And it began trafficking in votes. When the Irish immigration increased in strength, the Democratic was the weaker party, and since liberal opinion always belongs to defeated parties, the immigrants were drawn to it as soon as they acquired citizenship. For this reason the Catholic element became a formidable factor in the Democratic Party, and that party achieved success in New York City and in other cities where the Irish congregated. Soon the Church, with its ability to influence votes, and the men who needed those votes to climb to where they could enjoy public office, weighed and measured and brought about changes in power. The Catholic Church began to have interested and compliant representatives in meeting halls and on town councils and governors' boards, and to sell its influence on the ballot box in exchange for donations of land and the passage of laws to its liking. Feeling capable of electing legislators, or of blocking their election, it tried to make laws for the exclusive benefit of the Church, and in the name of freedom it set about, little by little, proposing every means of replacing it.

The Church had courage for everything, since it felt strong among the masses because of their unquestioning faith, among the powerful because of the alliances it offered them for the protection of their worldly possessions, and among the politicians because of their need for the Catholic vote. Among the mansions in the wealthy section of the city it erected a marble cathedral surrounded by almshouses, so that everyone could see and admire them. How different from those Father McGlynn maintained in the slums, where people are acquainted with affliction! Miracles of ecclesiastical influence began to appear: mediocre lawyers with a sudden clientele; unctuous physicians who left the sick and discouraged women ready to be anointed; bankers trusted by their depositors for no visible reason; silk-robed, well-fed cardinals who came from England, smooth and fresh as new apples, to convert the wealthy families to faith in the Archbishop. There were dazzling hospitals and asylums. The more enterprising candidates solicited support from the Church's neutrality. Even the newspapers, which should be the bona fide priests, mitigated or concealed their beliefs, flirted with the archiepiscopal palace, and seemed to applaud its attacks on the people's freedom—some for fear of being abandoned by their Catholic readers, and others in their desire to strengthen a valued ally in the struggle to preserve their privileges! The affable influence of the "Sogarth Aroon" was employed to take the Irish vote wherever it suited archiepiscopal authority, conniving to profit by the laws which, like this authority, trafficked in votes. The power of the Church in the United

States thus grew to enormous proportions: because of the large number of European immigrants, the collusion and usefulness of political cliques, the timid hopes of the working masses, the disorganization and lukewarm character of the Protestant sects, the carelessness of the times in religious matters, the little that is known of the ambitions and methods of the Roman clergy, and the foolish vanity of the recently arrived immigrants so enamored of this new ostentation. But it owed its growth in power especially to that vile tendency—characteristically born on this altar of money—to consider the Church's hold over the common people as the firmest obstacle to their demands for betterment, and as the surest bulwark for the fortunes of the rich.

So it seems that all the problems that interest and confuse mankind are to take shape and be resolved in the United States, that the free exercise of reason is going to save men many years of doubt and misery, and that the end of the nineteenth century will leave in the zenith a sun that rose at the end of the eighteenth in rivers of blood, multitudes of words, and the sound of heads. Men seem determined to know and assert themselves, and lend strength to one another, with none but the bonds agreed upon for their mutual honor and security. They stagger, shake, and demolish, like all gigantic bodies when rising from the earth. Too much light misleads and usually blinds them. There is a great threshing of ideas, and all the chaff is carried away by the wind. Human majesty has grown enormously. False republics are becoming known; if sifted in a sieve, they would produce nothing but the souls of lackeys. Where freedom truly prevails, with nothing to hinder its rule but our own natures, there is no throne like the mind of a free man, no authority nobler than that of his thoughts! All that torments and belittles man is being called to trial and must surrender. Whatever is incompatible with human dignity will fall. Nobody will be able to clip the wings of the poetry of the soul, and there will always be that magnificent eagerness and that longing look toward the clouds. Whatever wishes to remain must become reconciled to the spirit of liberty or consider itself dead. Whatever lowers or reduces man's stature will be struck down.

With liberties, as with privileges, it follows that together they prosper or are endangered, and one of them cannot be sought or misused unless all of them feel the harm or the benefit. Therefore the Catholic Church in the United States, with both its impure and its virtuous elements, is being brought to judgment for enslaving and tyrannizing when the generous souls of a country decide to lead the downtrodden for purposes of helping them and mitigating the physical and spiritual servitude in which they live. All the pompous officialdom is aligned on one side and all the suffering on the other. There is the brotherhood of despotism and the brotherhood of affliction.

Still alive in memory, as if a legion of apostles were seen to pass by, is the admirable campaign for the election of the mayor of New York in the autumn of 1886. Evidenced there for the first time, and in full strength, was the spirit of reform that animates the working masses and the devoted men who suffer from their complaints. There are some passionate men in whom the human species is purified by all the tortures of the furnace. There are men ready to lend unselfishly, to suffer for others, to wear themselves out showing people the light! This campaign demonstrated the wonder of a new political party, a party able to count a mere three years of preparatory mistakes and dissension, struggling along without friends or money or servile, complacent officialdom, and without any corrupted accomplices. And it was on the point of winning, for not only was it inspired by the usual enthusiasm of political campaigns, but also by the impetus of redemption, something demanded in vain from parties that do nothing but talk and make promises.

The origins of this historical movement are already known. Henry George came from California and reissued his book, *Progress and Poverty,* and it spread through Christendom like a Bible.[4] In it is that same love expressed by the Nazarene, set down in the practical language of our days. The main thesis of the work, destined to have bearing on the causes of a poverty which grows in spite of human progress, is that the land must belong to the nation. From this essential premise, the book derives all the needed reforms. Let the man who works and improves the land possess it. Let him pay the state for it while he uses it. Let nobody have rights to land unless he pays the state for its use, and let him pay no more than its rental. Thus the weight of taxes to the nation will fall only upon those who receive from it a way of paying them, life without unjust taxes will be easy and inexpensive, and the poor will have homes, time for cultivating their minds, understanding their public obligations, and loving their children.

George's book was a revelation not merely to the working man, but to thinkers. Only Darwin[5] in the natural sciences has left on our times a mark comparable to that of George in the social sciences. Darwin's hand appears in politics, history, and poetry; wherever English is spoken, the cherished ideas of George are impressed on the mind with commanding force. He is a man born to be the father of men. When he sees an unhappy man, he feels a slap on his own cheek! The labor

---

4. In 1885 Professor Richard T. Ely wrote that "tens of thousands of laborers have read *Progress and Poverty*, who have never before looked between two covers of an economic book. . . ." In Ireland the book had a strong influence on the land reform movement. In England George Bernard Shaw and Charles Darwin commented favorably on the work, and Tolstoy read pages from *Progress and Poverty* to his peasants. However, Karl Marx wrote to John Swinton on June 2, 1881: "As to the book of Mr. Henry George, I consider it as a last attempt—to save the capitalistic regime." (*Karl Marx and Frederick Engels, Letters to Americans, 1848-1895* [New York, 1953], p. 127.)

For the details of the mayoralty campaign of 1886 in New York City, see Foner, op. cit., pp. 116-27.

5. Charles Robert Darwin (1809-1882), British naturalist, expounded the theory of evolution by natural selection in *On the Origin of Species* (1859), a major challenge to religious fundamentalism.

unions cluster around him; to succeed, he tells them, you must educate yourselves! In a nation where suffrage is the origin of law, revolution lives in suffrage. Right must be staunchly defended, but it is more useful to love than to hate. When the working people of New York began to feel their power, all of them—Catholics, Protestants, and Jews; Irishmen, Germans, and Hungarians; Republicans and Democrats—appointed George their candidate, to show signs of their power and resolve on the occasion of New York's mayoralty election.

It was not a party being formed, but a church in process of growth. Such fervor has never been seen outside of religious movements. Even in physical attributes those men seemed to be endowed with supernatural strength. They never became hoarse from talking. They needed no sleep. They forged ahead as if they had discovered in themselves a new being. They were as joyful as newlyweds. They improvised a treasury, election machinery, conferences, a newspaper. Great was the alarm of the political cliques, the leagues of ruffians and profiteers who live in luxury from the buying and selling of votes. Those hordes of voters were running away from them and beginning to see the light. "Look to the law for righting your wrongs!" said the political parties to the workers when censuring them for their attempts at violence or anarchy, but as soon as the workers organized themselves into a party to look to the law for help, they were called anarchists and revolutionaries. The press ignored them; the upper classes refused them aid; the Republicans, on the side of privilege, denounced them as enemies of the country; and the Democrats, threatened at close range in their occupations and influence, demanded assistance from the powers allied to them, in order to administer the law for the good of all. The entire Church fell upon the workers who built it. The Archbishop, after having deposed a priest for supporting the policies of the common people, ordered his priests, via a pastoral letter, to support the policies of the ruffians and profiteers determined to betray them. Only one parish priest, the most illus-

trious of them all, the only illustrious one, refused to abandon the common people—Father McGlynn!

So then, if the Archbishop, who should be an example to
priests, can favor a certain policy, how can it be considered a
crime for a priest to do what the Archbishop does? And who
are the holy ones—those who ally themselves with the powerful to stamp out the rights of the downtrodden, or those
who, defying the wrath of the powerful, and being above
them in virtue and intelligence, toss the purple aside and go
quietly to sit down among the sufferers?

There is said to be a saintliness equal to Father McGlynn's,
but none greater, and that there is so much meekness in his
lofty spirit that in all his wisdom he finds no obstacle to the
dogma of the descent of grace. They say he considers the
tallest man so enslaved by his body that he never quite understands why the man who achieves success because of his body
should be only a man. He is said to regard virtue as so desirable and beautiful that it is enough of a wife for him. They
say he lives to comfort the unhappy, to strengthen and
expand men's souls, and to lift them up, by means of the
hope and beauty of worship, to an ardent poetic state. And
they say that he creates at the heart of the Church the spirit
of universal charity which engendered its triumph over the
ambition, the selfishness, and the despotism that has dis-
figured it. And they also say that he has the indomitable
energy of one who, instead of serving men, serves mankind!

Whatever stifles or debilitates man, he considers a crime. It
cannot be that God supplies man with a mind, and that the
Archbishop, who is less than God, should keep him from
expressing it. And if from the pulpit some priests, by order of
the Archbishop, can intimidate their parishioners to vote for
the enemy of the poor, how is it that one particular priest, by
his rights as a free man, cannot help the poor away from the
altar, and even help them in nonreligious matters, without
resorting to his purely religious authority over their consciousness? Who is the sinner, he who from the holy pulpit

misuses his authority in the area of dogma to immorally favor those who sell the law in payment for the vote that puts them in a position to dictate it; or he who, knowing that on the side of the poor there is nothing but bitterness, comforts them from within the Church as a priest, and helps them outside of it as a citizen?

The parish priest, it is true, owes obedience to his archbishop in ecclesiastical matters; but in political opinions, in the realm of simple economy and social reform, in matters having nothing to do with the Church, how can the parish priest owe absolute obedience to his archbishop if those matters are not connected with the administrative affairs of the Church, or with the practice of worship, to which his authority over the priest is limited? How is it that nationalization of the land should be held as a harmful Catholic doctrine in New York, if at this very moment it is a doctrine promulgated by all the Catholic clergy in Ireland? Or must the parish priest be allowed no more plan of action than is ordered by his archbishop, who is not his authority in matters of politics, and become like a slave trembling at the wrath of his master, merely because the offending priest has the courage to tenderly intercede on behalf of the unfortunate? Or should the priest give up his country?

Inasmuch as the Archbishop, who had expressed in a pastoral letter an opinion on land ownership, wrongfully forbade Father McGlynn from attending an open meeting in which the land question was to be discussed, and inasmuch as the Father disregarded him in this matter concerning which as a priest he had the right to disregard him, and as a man had the duty to do so, the Archbishop suspended him from his parochial duties—suspended the one who had made his parish a community of love! Inasmuch as on a matter of material policy he disobeyed his ecclesiastical superior, the Pope ordered him—Father McGlynn, virtue incarnate—to Rome for discipline. And because, instead of going, he humbly explained to the Pope in a letter the mistake for which he was condemned, the Pope defrocked him—stripped Father McGlynn, the only saintly priest in the diocese, of his clerical vestments!

Here is where the handsome spectacle appeared. Obviously, power will never want for friends. Those who live from the Church's vote—the politicians who fear it, the men it supports or recommends, those who see it as a safeguard for their excessive wealth, and the press interested in preserving its alliance with it—are all contentedly fluttering in the shade of the Archbishop's palace. But the parish has deserted its pews en masse, has draped with immortelles the confessional box bare of its priest, and has indignantly thrown the new priest out of the sanctuary—the new priest who had the temerity to appear there to break up a meeting of parishioners gathered to express their affection for their much beloved "Sogarth Aroon." "Nobody will harm him, nor will he want for a thing on this earth!" "We built this church with our own money, so who will dare throw us out of it?"

"This saint who lives for the poor, whom could he have offended?" "Why do they mistreat him? Because he's against our having religious schools we don't need, when we have public schools for learning, and our homes and church for religion?" "He loves us Catholics but he also loves us men!" The women at the meeting were the most enthusiastic. A woman drew up the protest which those in charge of the session took to the Archbishop. Husky workmen sobbed, their faces in their hands. Father McGlynn, humble and sick, had not seen or talked with anybody and was suffering in the modest home of a sister.

But the New York Catholics rose in fury against the Archbishop and laid plans for huge meetings. They set the ineffable piety of the persecuted priest against the contemptible character of those vicars and bishops who are the pride of archbishops. With all the intensity of the Irish soul they succeeded in regaining their right to think freely about public issues, to denounce the Archbishop's immoral dealings with the mercenary politicians whose dictates he obeys, to proclaim that aside from the truths of God and the management of his own house, "the Archbishop of New York has no more authority over the political opinions of his flock than has the agent who goes looking for naturalists in deepest Africa." And they remember that there once was an archbishop in Ireland who died of shame and neglect for having condemned the just resistance of Irish Catholics to the crown of England. "It is on our conscience, God, but let nobody come to mow down our thinking, or rob us of our right to govern our Republic according to our own understanding!" "In matters of dogma, the Church is our mother, but outside of dogma, our country's Constitution is our Church."

"Hands off, Archbishop!"

Never, not even in George's autumn campaign, was there greater enthusiasm. The hall resounded with cheering when those prominent Catholics fervently justified the absolute freedom of their political opinions.

"So then, to our joy, he who was honor itself for his wise use of propaganda, and is famous in New York for his charity; this holy Father McGlynn, our joy and integrity, who has taught us by his loving word and example all the beauty and justice of faith; the one who poured his entire fortune into our hands and returned to us in alms the wages we paid him, and never wanted to forsake the slums of his poor—this man was evicted from the church built with his own hands, was denied for one more day the room where he prayed and suffered? And that other Bishop Ducey, who smuggled an embezzling banker to Canada under his robes, is enjoying the full trust of the Church? And so the Archbishop compels our Pope to deal unjustly with this glory of the Christian faith, and goes grieving to the funeral of that Catholic destroyer of freedom, that James McMaster[6] who shone like the eyes of a

---

6. James Alphonsus McMaster (1820-1886), Catholic journalist, publisher and editor of the *Freeman's Journal,* outstanding Catholic journal which was against the abolition of slavery and during the Civil

hyena, and spent his life vilifying free peoples and using his poisonous remarks to help rulers and slaveowners?" "Deliver us, Lord, from speaking out against our faith, from obeying the priests who work against our freedom as citizens, and from forsaking our 'Sogarth Aroon' by whose immense charity Catholicism has become the foundation of our souls!"

The schism of the Catholics remains in this state of upheaval. How many intrigues and collusions, how many dangers to the Republic it has brought to light! And so the Church buys influence and sells votes? And so it is angered by saintliness? And so it is an ally of the wealthy members of hostile sects? And so it forbids its priests to exercise their political rights unless they exercise them on behalf of the men who traffic in votes for the Church? And so it attempts to degrade and ruin those who offend its political authority and meekly follow what the sweet and gentle Jesus taught? And so one cannot be a man and a Catholic at the same time? We shall see how one can, as these new fishermen are teaching us! Oh Jesus, where could you have been in this struggle? On your way to Canada with the rich robber, or in the lowly cottage where Father McGlynn is waiting and suffering?

El Partido Liberal (Mexico);
La Nación (Buenos Aires), April 14, 1887
Dated New York, January 16, 1887

War was so hostile to the Lincoln administration that it was suppressed for a time and the publisher imprisoned.

A Terrible Drama: The Funeral
of the Haymarket Martyrs

Neither fear of social justice, nor blind sympathy on the part of those who initiate it, must guide nations in their crises, or the reporter of those crises. Freedom is well served only by the one who, at the risk of being taken for its enemy, is calmly preserving it from those whose mistakes are endangering it. He who excuses their wrongs and crimes because of an effeminate fear of appearing lukewarm in its defense does not deserve the title of defender of freedom. Nor should we pardon anyone who is incapable of controlling the hatred and antipathy that the crime inspires, or who passes judgment on social ills without knowing and weighing the historic causes from which they come, or the generous impulses they produce.

In a solemn procession of mourning followers, the flower-covered coffins containing the bodies of the four anarchists

---

1. The Haymarket Affair resulted from the explosion of a dynamite bomb in the midst of a squadron of police attempting to disperse a peaceful labor meeting protesting police brutality held in Chicago's Haymarket Square on May 4, 1886. While police brutality against workers was common in Chicago, the particular protest in this instance grew out of a police attack on strikers at the McCormick Harvester Machine Company on May 3 during which at least one striker was killed, five or six were seriously wounded, and an undetermined number were injured.

Chicago had sentenced to the gallows,[2] and the man who, because he preferred not to die that way, exploded a dynamite bomb concealed in the thick curls of his young head of chestnut hair,[3] have just been taken to their graves.

Accused of instigating or being a party to the frightful death of one of the policemen who suggested dispersing the group, these men were gathered to protest the death of six workers at the hands of the police, in an attack on the only factory to break the strike. Accused of having made and helped to throw—even if it were not thrown—the orange-sized bomb that knocked down the rear ranks of the police and left one dead, later caused the death of six more, and seriously wounded fifty others, the judge, in accord with the

---

The bomb explosion left policemen killed and some sixty wounded. The actual bombthrower was never found, but during a wave of hysteria, a number of anarchists, anarchosyndicalists, and alleged anarchists were rounded up by the police, and eight men were indicted and brought to trial. After a proceeding during which no sound evidence was presented to prove their connection with actual bombthrowing, they were sentenced to death or imprisonment. Four were hanged, one committed suicide, and three went to prison, later to be pardoned as having been, like the others, innocent. These men, who were punished for their opinions and not for any crimes, became known as the "Haymarket Martyrs."

For the Haymarket Affair, see Henry David, *The History of the Haymarket Affair* (New York, 1936); Philip S. Foner, *Autobiographies of the Haymarket Martyrs* (New York, 1970); Philip S. Foner, *History of the Labor Movement in the United States* (New York, 1955), Vol. II, pp. 105-15; Lucy Parsons, *Famous Speeches of the Haymarket Anarchists* (New York, 1969). For an earlier article by Martí, less sympathetic to the "Haymarket Martyrs," see "El proceso de los siete anarquistas de Chicago," *Obras Completas* (La Habana, 1946), Vol. I, pp. 1736-40.

2. Albert R. Parsons, August Spies, George Engel, and Adolph Fischer were the four men executed.

3. Louis Lingg committed suicide (or, as some charged, was murdered by police guards).

verdict of the jury, condemned one of the criminals to fifteen years in the penitentiary and seven others to death by hanging.[4]

Never since the War of the South, since the tragic days when John Brown died like a criminal for attempting single-handed at Harper's Ferry what the nation, inspired by his bravery, attempted later as a crown of glory—never was there such interest in or such a hue and cry about a hanging in the United States.

Furious as a wolf, the entire Republic engaged in the fight to prevent the efforts of a benevolent lawyer,[5] a girl in love with one of the prisoners,[6] and a Spanish-Indian halfbreed mother of another[7]—alone against an enraged country—from robbing the gallows of the seven human bodies it believed essential to the gallows' perpetuation.

The nation is terrified by the increased organization among the lower classes, by the sudden agreement among the working masses, who restrain themselves only in the presence of the rivalries of their employers. It is frightened of the impending separation of the country's population into the same two classes of privileged and discontented that cause so much ferment in European society. Therefore the Republic decided, by tacit agreement resembling complicity, to use a crime born of its own transgressions as much as of the fanaticism of the criminals in order to strike terror by holding them up as an example—not to the doleful rabble that will never triumph

---

4. Oscar Neebe was sentenced to fifteen years' imprisonment, and Samuel Fielden and Michael Schwab, originally sentenced to be executed, had their sentences commuted to life imprisonment by Governor Oglesby of Illinois.

5. The reference is to William Perkins Black, lawyer for the condemned men.

6. Nina Van Zandt, the girl referred to, was in love with August Spies.

7. The reference is to Lucy Parsons, the wife, not mother, of Albert R. Parsons.

in a country of reason, but to the tremendous emerging strata. The free man's natural aversion to crime, together with the harsh ill-will of the despotic Irishman who regards this country as his own and the German and Slav as the intruder, assumed on the part of the privileged sector—in this trial which has been a battle, an unfair hypocritical battle— the sympathies and almost inhuman aid of those who suffer from the same wrongs, the same desertion, the same bestial working conditions, the same heartbreaking misery whose constant spectacle fired the Chicago anarchists with such eagerness to right those wrongs that it dulled their judgment.

When the carpenters were already at work setting up the timbers for the scaffold, some who felt ashamed and others who dreaded a barbarous retribution went to plead for mercy to the governor, a feeble old man subservient to the supplications and flattery of the monied classes who were asking him, even at the risk of his life, to save the threatened society.

Until that time only three voices, not counting the professional defenders and natural friends of the victims, had dared to intercede for those unfortunate men who, on the pretext of a specific accusation that was never proved, and on the pretext of their having tried to establish a reign of terror, were dying as the prey of social terror. These voices belonged to Howells, the Boston novelist whose generosity caused him to sacrifice reputation and friends;[8] Adler, the strong but cautious thinker who discerns a new world in the travail of our century;[9] and Train, a monomaniac who spends all his

8. William Dean Howells (1837-1920), American novelist and "Dean of American Letters," who denounced the conviction of the eight men as judicial murder in a letter to the *New York Times,* November 4, 1886, and played an important role in the defense efforts on behalf of the condemned men. Martí uses the word "fame," but clearly it was Howells' reputation rather than his fame that was affected.

9. Felix Adler (1851-1933), German-born founder, in 1876, of the Society for Ethical Culture in New York City, who was active in the defense efforts.

time in the public square feeding the birds and talking with children.[10]

Finally, in a horrible dance of death, turning and twisting and crammed into their white tunics, the accused men died.

Finally, without having been able to put more fire into the stoves, more bread into the pantries, more social justice into the distribution of wealth; without having instituted more safeguards against hunger for the useful members of society; without having been able to secure more light and hope for the hovels of the poor, or more relief for all that seethes and suffers—the nearly disjointed body of the man who, believing he was giving men a sublime example of love, tossed away his life with the weapon he thought was revealed to redeem them, was placed in a wooden coffin. Because of its unconscionable cult of wealth, and lacking any of the shackles of tradition, this Republic has fallen into monarchical inequality, injustice, and violence.

The revolutionary theories of the European worker in the United States were like drops of blood carried away by the sea, whereas life in a spacious land and under a republican form of government enabled the recent arrival to earn his bread and lay aside a portion of his earnings for his old age, and in his own house.

But then came the corrupting war and the habit of authority and domination which is its bitter aftereffect. Then came the credit that stimulated the creation of colossal fortunes and the disorderly foreign influx. Then came the leisure of the war's unemployed, always ready, because of the need to maintain their well-being and because of the fatal inclination of those who have smelled blood, to serve the impure interests resulting from it.

10. George Francis Train (1829-1904), financier, speculator, eccentric radical, and supporter of women's rights, who was active in the defense movement, and charged that Lingg had not committed suicide but had been murdered by jail authorities.

The Republic changed from a wonderfully desirable village to a monarchy in disguise.

European immigrants denounced with renewed anger the wrongs they thought they had left behind in their own repressive countries.

The ill-will of the nation's workers, recognizing themselves to be the victims of the greed and inequality of a feudal people, exploded with a greater faith in the freedom they hoped to see succeed in the social realm as it was succeeding in the political.

Since the country's inhabitants are accustomed to winning without bloodshed through the power of the vote, and since they neither understand nor excuse those who were born in nations where suffrage is a tool of repression, they see nothing in the apathetic work of those of foreign birth but a new aspect of the old abuse that scourges their thinkers, challenges their heroes, and curses their poets. But, although the essential differences in political practices, and the disagreements and rivalries of the races already arguing about supremacy in this part of the continent, might have stood in the way of the immediate formation of a formidable labor party with identical methods and purposes, the common denominator of pain has accelerated the concerted action of all who suffer. A horrendous act was needed, no matter how much it might be a natural consequence of inflamed passions, so that those who hasten indomitably from the identical misfortune can interrupt their efforts to eradicate and repair, while their bloody recourses are condemned for being ineffective by men who, because of an insane love of justice, seize those who have lost their faith in freedom.

In the recently emerging West, where the commanding influence of an old society like that of the East, reflected in its literature and customs, puts fewer restrictions on the new elements; where a somewhat more rudimentary kind of life facilitates close relationships among men, more harassed and scattered in the larger and more cultured cities; where the same astounding rapidity of growth, accumulating mansions and factories on the one hand, and wretched masses of people on the other, clearly reveals the evils of a system that punishes the most industrious with hunger, the most generous with persecution, the useful father with the misery of his children—there the unhappy working man has been making his voice heard. In the West, where the impoverished day laborer is joined by wife and children in reading books that teach the causes of, and the cures for, their unhappiness; where the industrialists, justified in their own eyes by the success of their grand and glorious factories, are carrying to extremes, prejudiced by prosperity, the unjust methods and harsh treatment that keep them prosperous—there both the workers and their friends have been able to speak their minds. In the West, where German leaven coming out of the imperial country is keeping in ferment the harassed and intelligent laboring masses, putting upon the iniquitous land the three terrible curses of Heine; in the West, and especially in its major city Chicago, the discontented among the working masses, the ardent counsel of their friends, and the rage piled up by the effrontery and inclemency of their bosses, have found living expression.

Since everything tends toward the great and the small at the same time, just as water rises from the sea as mist and then condenses and returns to the sea again, so the human problem—condensed in Chicago because of its free institutions at the same time as it infused the Republic and the world with fear or hope, due to events in the city and the passions of its men—changed into a bitter and angry local problem.

Hatred for injustice changed into hatred for its representatives.

Secular fury, enfeebled by inheritance, eating away and consuming like lava, is inherited by men who, out of their deep compassion, see themselves as holy beings, and this fury is concentrated upon those who persist in the abuses provoking it. When the mind starts working, it never stops; when anguish reaches the boiling point, it explodes; when speech begins to become inflammatory, it bursts its bounds; when vanity starts boasting, it acts as a spur; when hope is put into action, it ends in either triumph or catastrophe. "For the revolutionary," said Saint-Just,[11] "the only rest is the grave!"

What man motivated by ideas fails to realize that the harmony of all harmonies, where love presides over passion, is scarcely revealed to those great thinkers who, seated on the crest of time and blocking out the sun with their hands, see the world at the boiling point? What man who deals with men is unaware that, since they are more flesh than enlightenment, they barely recognize what seems self-evident; scarcely discern the surface; are hardly aware of anything but their own desires or threats; can scarcely conceive of anything but a frontal attack from the wind, or the apparent and therefore not always real expedient that can stop people from shutting the door on their hatred, pride, or appetites? What man suffering from human wrongs, no matter how much he restrains his reason, fails to feel inflamed and misled by one of those social evils which might well keep in a state of constant madness those who watch their wives and children rotting in those social evils, especially when he examines them closely, as if they were slapping him in the face, burying him in the mud, and staining his hands with blood.

Once those wrongs are recognized, the generous soul goes out to seek a remedy. Once the peaceful means are exhausted, the liberal soul resorts to violence for that remedy. Another person's pain works in the generous soul the way a worm works in an open wound.

Was it not Desmoulins[12] who said: "As long as one em-

11. Louis Antoine Léon de Saint-Just (1767-1794), French revolutionist who was guillotined.

12. Camille Benoît Desmoulins (1760-1794), French revolutionary leader, known as the "tribune" of the French Revolution, who led the march on the Bastille and was guillotined. At his death he cried, "Citizens! My only crime is that I have shed tears."

braces freedom, what matter if it be upon heaps of corpses?"

Blinded by generosity, dazzled by vanity, drunk on popularity, demented by constant transgression, by their apparent impotence in the struggle for suffrage, by the hope of being able to establish in an emerging region their ideal nation, the diligent leaders of these angry masses—educated in lands where the vote has barely commenced—do not stray from the present, do not dare to appear weak in the eyes of their followers, do not see that in this free nation the only obstacle to sincerely desired social change lies in the lack of agreement on the part of those who seek that change. These diligent leaders, weary of suffering and with a vision of a universal phalanstery in their minds, do not believe that world justice can ever be brought about by peaceful means.

They pass judgment like cornered animals. All that is in process of growth they consider as growing against them. "My daughter slaves fifteen hours a day to earn fifteen cents." "I haven't had any work this winter because I belong to a labor union."

The judge sentences them.

The police, proud of the authority and uniforms that put fear into the hearts of the uncultured, manhandle and murder them.

The impoverished are cold and hungry, live in stinking houses.

America, then, is the same as Europe!

These wretched people fail to understand that they are merely cogs in the gears of society; if they are to change, all the gears must change. The hunted wild boar is deaf to the joyous music of the wind, to the song of the universe, and to the grandiose movement of the cosmos. The wild boar braces its rump against the trunk of an obscure tree, sinks its fangs into the belly of its pursuer, and turns its victim's entrails inside out.

Where will those tired masses, suffering more and more each day, find that divine state of greatness to which the thinker must ascend to control the rage their unnecessary misery causes? They have tried every conceivable recourse. It is that reign of terror depicted by Carlyle:[13] "Man's dismal and desperate battle against his condition and all that surrounds him."

And just as the life of man is concentrated in his spinal cord, and the life of the earth in its molten mass, there emerge from among those hordes of people swelling with pride and vomiting fire beings in whom all of life's horror, desperation, and sorrow seems to have been fused.

They come from hell; what language must they speak but the language of hell?

Their speeches, even when read, throw sparks, mouthfuls of smoke, food but half digested, reddish vapors.[14]

This is a horrible world; create another, as on Sinai amid the roar of thunder; as in '93, from a sea of blood! "Better to blow up ten men with dynamite than let ten men starve slowly, as they are doing in the factories!"

Montezuma's[15] pronouncement sounds again: "The gods are thirsty!"

A handsome youth, who has himself painted against a background of clouds, with the sun on his face, sits at a writing desk surrounded by bombs, crosses his legs, and lights a cigar. As one fits pieces of wood together to make a doll's house, he explains the world of justice that will flower over

---

13. Thomas Carlyle (1795-1881), Scottish-born writer whose *History of the French Revolution* (1837) which, though it saw the event as a grim result of a corrupt society, placed emphasis more on the terror than the changes for the better as a result of the uprisings. Carlyle, a conservative, made a fetish of the hero in history.

14. The speeches of the Haymarket defendants to the court before sentence was pronounced lasted three days, and are viewed as imperishable classics of proletarian literature. They reveal these highminded and courageous men as true heroes of the working class.

15. Montezuma II (1480? -1520), last Aztec emperor in Mexico, overthrown by Hernando Cortés.

the land when the impact of Chicago's social revolution, symbol of worldwide oppression, bursts forth.

But everything was words, meetings in corners, gun drills in one or another cellar, three rival newspapers circulating among two thousand desperate readers, and dissemination of the most recent methods of killing. The guiltiest are those who, through the vainglory of freedom, permitted men to exercise it by means of the violence of their generosity!

When the workers showed a stronger will to better their condition, their employers showed an even stronger determination to resist them.

The worker believes he has a right to a certain security for the future, a certain amount of comfort and cleanliness for his house, a right to feed without worry the children he begets, a fairer share in the products of the work of which he is an indispensable factor, some time in the sun for helping his wife plant a rosebush in his yard, some corner in which to live that is not a stinking hole one cannot enter without nausea, as in the city of New York. And every time the Chicago workers asked for this in some way, the capitalists banded together and punished them by denying them the work that means their meat, their heat, and their light. The bosses set the police on them, the police who are always eager to let their nightsticks fall upon the heads of the shoddily clothed. At times a policeman would kill some daring soul who resisted with stones, or some child. The workers were finally starved into returning to their jobs, spirits grim, misery further irritated, decency offended, meditating vengeance.[16]

16. The Chicago police had the worst reputation in the country for their wanton savagery against labor. "The police of Chicago reflected the hostility of the employing class, regarding strikes *per se* as evidence that the men had placed themselves in opposition to law and order . . . it had become a pastime for a squad of mounted police, or a detachment in close formation, to disperse with the billy any gathering of

Heard only by their few partisans, the anarchists have been meeting year after year, organized into groups each of which kept a section under arms.[17] In their three quite distinct newspapers they publicly preached social revolution, declaring in the name of humanity a war on existing society.[18] They decided that a radical conversion could not be brought about by peaceful means, and recommended the use of dyna-

---

workingmen. The billy was an impartial instrument; men, women, children, and shopkeeping bystanders alike composed its harvest. It was the police, aided by the 'Pinkertons,' who added the great leaven of bitterness to the contest. To the workingmen they furnished concrete and hateful examples of the autocracy against which they protested." (E. L. Bogart and C. M. Thompson, *The Industrial State, 1870-1893,* Vol. IV of *The Centennial History of Illinois* [Springfield, Ill., 1920], pp. 167-68.)

17. As far back as 1875, a small group of German socialists in Chicago had formed an armed club to protect workers against military and police assaults. This club came to be known as the "Lehr und Wehr Verein." In 1878 all members of the Socialist Labor Party were ordered to leave these clubs, but this order was resented and, together with other issues, led to a split in the party in 1880. The group that seceded from the SLP formed an organization known as the Social Revolutionary Club. Soon Social Revolutionary clubs sprang up in a number of cities. The Chicago club, the most important in the movement, was led by Albert R. Parsons and August Spies. A national conference of Social Revolutionary clubs was held in Chicago in 1881, and the following year, under the leadership of Johann Most, the International Working People's Association was formed in Pittsburgh as the unifying center for American anarchists. The Chicago section, led by Parsons, Spies, Schwab, Fielden, and others, penetrated deeply into the trade union movement, and soon had 5,000-6,000 members.

18. The papers published by the Social Revolutionaries in Chicago were: the *Alarm* in English, a fortnightly edited by Parsons with an edition of 2,000-3,000; in German, the daily *Arbeiter-Zeitung*, edited by Spies, with an edition of 3,600; and the *Verbote*, a weekly in German, and a daily in Bohemian.

mite as the holy weapon of the disinherited as well as methods of preparing it.[19]

It was not in the treacherous shadows but in a direct confrontation with those whom they considered their enemies that they proclaimed themselves free and rebellious in order to emancipate mankind. They recognized that they were in a state of war, gave their blessings to the discovery of a substance which through its unique power was to equalize forces and save bloodshed, and strongly encouraged the study and manufacture of the new weapon with the same cool horror and diabolical calm as if they were writing a regulation treatise on ballistics. Reading these instructions, one sees bone-white circles in a sea of smoke; into the darkened room comes a ghost, gnawing on a human rib and sharpening its nails. To measure the entire depths of man's desperation, one must see if the horror that generally makes preparations calmly is getting the upper hand over that against which it is rebelling with a centuries-old fury; one must live in exile from one's homeland or from humanity.

Parsons,[20] the American once proposed for the presidency

19. The manifesto of the International Working People's Association, drawn up mainly by Most, made no reference either to political action or to immediate demands. It emphasized the "destruction of the existing class rule, by all means, that is, by energetic, relentless, revolutionary, and international action," and "the establishment of a free society based upon cooperative organization of production." The manifesto ended with an appeal to one remedy for the evils of capitalism—*force!* However, the Chicago anarchists did support immediate demands and became an important force in the movement for the eight-hour day in the Windy City.

20. Albert R. Parsons (1848-1887), a self-taught intellectual who came from a notable family in New England, and won distinction after the Civil War for his defense of Negro rights in Texas; he became a member of the Typographical Union in Chicago, was active in the Socialist Labor Party until he became convinced that force, not political action, was the route to socialism, and then turned to anarchism

of the Republic by his socialist friends,[21] and one who believed in humanity as much as in his one God, used to gather his followers together on Sundays to raise their spirits to the point where they could defend themselves. He spoke in a bounding, whiplashing, incisive style; his fiery message carried far.

Parsons' halfbreed wife, whose heart the grief of the working people stabbed like a dagger, would break out into stirring speeches after her husband had surrendered the floor. Such was the impact of her rugged and flaming attack that the anguish of the downtrodden was said never to have been depicted so eloquently. Her eyes flashed lightning, her words shot bullets, she clenched her fists; but when speaking of the sorrows of an impoverished mother, her voice took on an immense softness and the tears flowed.

Spies,[22] head of the *Arbeiter-Zeitung*, wrote with a certain chill of the grave, as if from the chamber of death. He argued for anarchy, picturing it as the desirable gateway to the truly

---

and the editing of the *Alarm*. Parsons spoke at the meeting in Haymarket Square where the bomb was exploded, but had already left when the event took place.

21. Martí's reference to Parsons' having been nominated for President of the United States is explained by Parsons himself in his autobiography: "In 1879 I was a delegate to the national convention held in Allegheny City, Pa., of the Socialist Labor party, and was there nominated as the Labor candidate for President of the United States. I declined the honor, not being of constitutional age—35 years." This was the first nomination of a workingman by workingmen for that office in the United States. See Philip S. Foner, *The Autobiographies of the Haymarket Martyrs*, p. 35.

22. August Spies (1855-1887), born in central Germany of a family of moderate means, was forced by the death of his father when he was seventeen to leave for the United States. He settled in Chicago and joined the SLP in 1877, became a member of the "Lehr und Wehr Verein," left the SLP for the anarchist movement, and in 1880 assumed the editorship of the *Arbeiter-Zeitung*.

free life. For seven years he explained its fundamentals in his daily newspaper, and then the need for revolution, and finally, like Parsons in the *Alarm,* the methods of organizing to insure its success.

Reading him is like stepping off into space. What is happening to this turning world?

Spies went blithely on where the firmest wisdom feels insecure. He pared his style as if he were cutting a diamond. A mournful Narcissus, he was astonished and pleased with his greatness. The next day a poor young girl would give him her life; she clung to the bars of his prison cell the way the Christian martyr clung to the cross, and he barely parted with a few cold words, recalling that Jesus, occupied with man's redemption, did not love the Magdalene.

When Spies harangued the workers, laying his becoming Prince Albert aside, it was not a man talking but a whistling gale, distant and lugubrious. He was word stripped of flesh. He leaned toward his listeners like a tree bent by the hurricane, and it truly did seem as if a freezing wind were coming out of the branches and blowing over the heads of men.

His hands dug into those restless hairy chests, then wrung out, passed before their eyes, and let them smell their own entrails. Right after the police had put a striker to death in a scuffle, Spies would climb into the wagon—rickety rostrum of revolutions—livid with rage, and with horrendous impetus his spare and unvarnished words soon glistened and warmed like a quiver of fire. Then he would walk through the gloomy streets alone.

Jealous of Spies, Engel[23] strove to put anarchism on a war footing, himself at the head of the company, where one

23. George Engel (1836-1887), born in Germany, came to the United States in 1873 after a year's stay in England. He lived in Philadelphia for a year and then went on to Chicago where he joined the SLP and finally left for the International Working People's Association.

learned how to load a rifle or aim it straight at the heart, in the cellar on nights of military training "for when the great hour arrives"; he with his *Anarchist* and his conversations, accusing Spies of a lukewarm attitude because he was jealous of his mind. Engel alone was the pure, the stainless, the man worth hearing. Anarchy, which without further waiting leaves men in control of everything equally, is the only philosophy to follow: the world a teetotum, and he—the handle. The world would spin happily, like the ball of the teetotum, "when the workers developed some shame!"

He used to go from group to group, and was present at the Anarchist General Committee composed of delegates from the several groups. He accused the committee of baseness and treachery because "with us, those eighty of us alone," it did not resolve to support the true revolution desired by Parsons, the man who calls dynamite "a sublime substance," and who tells the workers to "go and take whatever you need from the stores; the stores and everything in them are yours." Engel is a member of the "Lehr und Wehr Verein," [24] of which Spies has also been a member ever since a brutal police attack that left many workers dead provoked the group to carry guns, to arm for defense and to change, as brutal attacks always do, the *Anarchist*'s stand by means of the Springfield rifle. Engel was the sun, like his own rotund body: the "great rebel," the "autonomous one."

And Lingg? [25] He never wasted his manly beauty on those

24. The "Lehr und Wehr Verein," an armed club formed by social-ists in Chicago in 1875, was considered as the workingman's answer to the militia created by the employer class to be used against workers. It grew during the labor disturbances of the great railroad strike of 1877 but was mainly influential among the immigrant radicals, especially the Germans.

25. Louis Lingg (1864-1887), youngest of the eight prisoners, was born in Mannheim Baden, where he was apprenticed to a carpenter and joined a Workingmen's Education Society; he became an anarchist in Switzerland, and came to America in the summer of 1885 to escape military service in Germany, to which he would have been deported by

intense and enervating love affairs that generally sap the strength of a man in the glorious years of his youth. Raised in a German city by a sickly father and an avaricious mother, he knew the kind of life a liberal justly detests. His father was a porter, his mother a washerwoman, and he as handsome as Tannhäuser or Lohengrin—well-made body, seductive eyes, a head of thick, curly, chestnut hair. For what purpose all this beauty in such a horrible world? He found his own history in that of the working class, and the first down on his chin found him learning how to make bombs. Since infamy is reaching the heart of the globe, the explosion must reach the heavens!

At the age of twenty-two he had just arrived from Germany. What in other men was mere words, in him was action. He, he alone, was making bombs because, except in men of blinding energy, to be a prime mover a man finds it natural to kill, if only to release that energy.

And while Schwab,[26] nourished on reading poetry, helped Spies to write; while Fielden[27] of the silver tongue went from

---

the Swiss under an arrangement with the German government. (Martí is in error when he states that Lingg arrived in the United States from Germany.) Lingg immediately settled in Chicago and became a leading figure in trade union circles, helping to organize the International Carpenters' and Joiners' Union in addition to working in the anarchist cause. He believed that the sooner the workers understood the inadequacies of trade unionism in solving their problems, the sooner they would become revolutionists.

26. Michael Schwab (1853–), born in Bavaria, Germany, came to the United States in 1878, settled in Chicago in 1879, became active in the socialist movement in that city and in Milwaukee, moved over to the anarchists, and joined the editorial staff of the *Arbeiter-Zeitung* in 1882.

27. Samuel Fielden (1826–), born in Lancashire, England; with Albert R. Parsons, he was the only one of the eight men of neither German birth nor descent. A workingman all his life, he came to the United States in 1868, was drawn into the radical movement, and became successively a socialist and anarchist.

town to town lifting souls to the knowledge of future reform; while Fischer[28] encouraged and Neebe[29] organized, Lingg, in a hidden room with his four companions, one of whom was to betray him, made bombs as he was ordered to do by Johann Most in his *Science of Revolutionary War.* With his lips sealed, as Spies advised in the *Alarm,* he filled the deadly sphere with dynamite and plugged the hole through which the wick runs to the explosive material within. Arms crossed, he awaited the hour.

And so Chicago's anarchist forces were moving forward with such sluggishness, envy, and internal disorder, with such diversity of opinion about the proper time for the armed revolt, with such a meager supply of the frightful materials of war and of the cruel craftsmen ready to fashion them, that the only certain power of anarchy—disheveled mistress of a few ardent spirits—was the fury that at some extreme moment might produce social scorn in the masses rejecting it. The worker, who is a man with aspirations, resists with the wisdom of Nature the idea of a world where man is annihilated. But when, shot down in wholesale numbers for demanding one free hour to see his children by daylight, he rises out of the mortal mudpuddle, drawing aside the strands of blood on his forehead as if they were a pair of red curtains, then the death dream of a tragic group of men—crazed by pity, unfurling their steaming wings, hovering above the sinister mob, the clamorous corpse in their hands, spreading

28. Adolph Fischer (1856-1887), born in Bremen, Germany, left for the United States when he was fifteen, already a socialist, moved to Chicago where he worked as a compositor for the *Arbeiter-Zeitung.* Believing the views of Parsons and Spies to be too mild, he had aided Engel in founding the *Anarchist* to provide a more revolutionary organ.

29. Oscar Neebe (1850—), of German descent though born in New York City, by trade a tinsmith, had developed a fairly successful yeast business by 1886, and while active in the labor and radical movement, actually knew little of anarchism or socialism.

over grim hearts the brightness of an infernal dawn—can envelop desperate souls like a turbid cloud of smoke. Were they not protected by law? And the press, exasperating them with its hatred instead of allaying their fears with justice, was it not popularizing their cause? Their newspapers, growing in indignation, disdain and boldness, did they not circulate freely? Well, what did they want (since it was clear to their eyes that a man lives under abject despotism) other than to fulfill the obligations counseled by the Declaration of Independence in overthrowing that despotism and substituting for it a free association of communities that exchange among themselves their products of equal value, governing themselves by mutual agreement and without war, and educating themselves in accord with knowledge having no distinctions of race, creed, or sex? Was the nation not rebelling, like a herd of elephants sleeping in the grass, with their self-same outcries and afflictions? Is it not likely that the threat of resorting to force, a probable but dangerous means, will be used to obtain by intimidation what cannot be obtained by law? Those ideas of theirs, which the privileged were toning down with their cordiality, just as they were changing them into rifles and dynamite with their defiance—did they not stem from the purest sense of compassion exalted to the point of folly by the spectacle of irreparable misery, and anointed by the hope of just and lofty times? Had not Parsons, evangelist of universal rejoicing, been proposed for the presidency of the Republic? Had not Spies, as a candidate for a seat in Congress, struggled with those plans of theirs in the elections? Were the political parties not soliciting votes for them, offering to respect the propaganda of their doctrines? How were the criminals to believe the words and acts permitted them by law? And was it not the blood feasts of the police that put guns into the hands of the fiercest? The police are drunk on the wine of the executioner, like all the common people when clothed with authority.

The newly arrived Lingg hated Spies with the obstinacy of the novice—Spies, the man of ideas, irresolute and morose,

philosopher of the system, who dominated Lingg because of
his superior understanding. But the art and greatness required
by culture, even in the work of destruction, aroused the ill-
will of the scanty group of irreconcilables who looked upon
Engel, beloved of Lingg, as their leader. Engel was glad to be
at war with the universe, and measured his worth by his
adversary.

Because Parsons was jealous of Engel, whose nature he
passionately emulated, he joined Spies as hero of the work
and friend of literature. Fielden, seeing popular anger increasing in his London, and loyal to the country whose egotistical
love forbids his system, thought he would help the hard-won
success of the disinherited English by promoting anarchy in
America. Engel—"The time has come"; Spies—"Can this terrible hour have come?"; Lingg, busily involved with a sharp
wooden point, some clay, and nitroglycerin—"You'll see,
when I finish my bombs, if the time has come!" Fielden, who
saw the bruised and fearful working class in the United States
rebelling from coast to coast, determined to demand, as
proof of its power, that the working day be shortened to
eight hours.[30] He gathered together the various groups—until
then united only by their hatred of industrial oppression and
the policy of hunting down and killing their oppressors—and
repeated: "Yes, my friends; if we're not allowed to see our
children by daylight, the time has come."

Then came springtime, friend of the poor. And without
fear of the cold, equipped with light-giving strength, hopeful
of using the winter's savings to cope with the first hunger
pangs, a million workers scattered throughout the Republic
decided to demand the factories give them a working day not
to exceed the legal eight hours, in compliance with the violated law. Whoever wants to know if their demand was just,

30. As Martí notes, the Chicago anarchists were active in the movement for the eight-hour day.

let him come here. Let him watch the men returning to their indecent living quarters in the dark of night, like cowed oxen; let him watch them going to work from their distant hovels, the men shivering, the women livid and unkempt, when the sun itself has not yet broken from its sleep!

Pained and angry, sure of the resistance their bravado provoked, their riot guns ready for action, the Chicago police invited the workers to battle—not with the calm of the law, but with the haste of abhorrence.

Determined to defend their rights through the legal recourse of the strike, the workers had been turning their backs on the dismal preachers of anarchism and on those who, mauled by the nightstick or shot by the police bullet, were resolved, while clutching their wounds, to meet the next attack face to face and gun to gun.

March arrived. The factories threw out the workers who approached them with their demands, as if they were kicking a mangy dog into the street. As the Knights of Labor commanded, the workers abandoned the factories in a body. Porkers rotted without packers to wrap them; bewildered cattle lowed unattended in the corrals; the mute grain elevators rose in the terrible silence, giant sentinels keeping watch over the rivers. But in that muffled calm, like the victory flag of the industrial power that wins every battle in the end, there came from the McCormick reaper plant—manned by workers whom poverty had forced to serve as instruments against their brothers—a wisp of smoke rising skyward like a black snake, twisting and turning and crouching on the blue sky.

After three days of rage the Black Road, as the road to the McCormick plant was called, filled with angered workers one cloudy afternoon; they were wearing their overcoats and shaking their clenched fists at the column of smoke. By some mysterious decree, is not man always bound for where he expects danger, and where he seems to enjoy exacerbating his own misery? "There was the defiant factory, employing, in order to subdue the workers fighting against cold and hunger, the very victims of that cold and hunger, the starving victims themselves! Will there be no end, then, to this struggle for bread and coal in which, through the forces of evil itself, the workers' own brothers are rising against them? Well, is this not a worldwide battle in which the world-builders must defeat their exploiters? We surely want to see on what side those traitors are raising their heads!" Almost eight thousand were arriving, well into the afternoon. They sat down in groups on the bare rocks, walked in columns along the winding road, angrily pointed out the wretched hovels so conspicuous on the harsh landscape, like the spots on a leper.

The speakers used rocks as a platform, and their invective shook that gathering in which eyes flashed and chins trembled. The speaker was a carter, a smelter, a mason. The smoke from the McCormick plant wound above it. Time to stop working for the day. "Let's see what side those traitors are on!" "Down, down with that speaker; he's a socialist!"

And the man on the improvised platform, arousing as if with his own hands the most hidden afflictions of those enraged hearts, stirring up those anxious parents to resist to the point of victory, even if their children have to ask them for bread in vain, for the sake of the children's lasting welfare—that speaker was Spies. First they abandoned him, then they surrounded him, then they looked at one another, recognized one another in that implacable portrayal, approved and applauded him. "That fellow surely knows how to talk; let him speak for us in the factories!" But the workers in the plant had already heard the bell for leaving time; who cared what Spies was saying? They picked up stones from the road, stormed the factory, and shattered all the windows! Urged on by the crowds, the police outside took a stand against them! "Those are the ones, there they are, pale as death, the ones who for a day's pay help trample on their own brothers!" Stones! Some of the workers climbed up to the factory's tower, terrified and looking like ghosts. Belching fire, a police patrol wagon came up the road under a furious hail of stones, one man on the footboard brandishing his revolver, another on the coach box. The policemen crouching inside made their way through the crowd by shooting, the horses knocking people down and trampling them. The police leaped out of the wagon, fell into battle formation, and fired on the crowds, who shot wildly and threw stones to defend themselves. When the mobs, surrounded by patrols from the entire city, went back to their own neighborhoods, where the women were as furious as the men, they took refuge, not to go to sleep, but to secretly bury six bodies; they did not want their enemy to win again.[31]

Did all those hearts not reach the boiling point? Did the anarchists not join forces? Did Spies not write an impassioned letter in his *Arbeiter-Zeitung?* Did not Engel again state that the hour had finally come, and Lingg, who some months back had been beaten over the head by the patrol, did he not pack his live bombs into a leather trunk? Did not the hatred aroused by police brutality and its blind attacks mount in intensity? "Workers, to arms!" said Spies in a fiery circular which everyone read shuddering. "To arms against those who murder you for exercising your rights as men!"[32]

31. The workers at the McCormick Harvester factory, members of the Knights of Labor, were on strike for the eight-hour day and a $2.00 daily wage, for an end to wagecutting and the piecework system. On May 3, 1886, 300 scabs, guarded by 350 to 500 police, had been put to work in an effort to break the strike. When the strikers, aided by several hundred striking lumber-shovers, demonstrated against the scabs, the police fired without warning into the crowd of unarmed workers. At least four were killed and many wounded. The Chicago *Daily News* reported six dead.

32. Spies had been at the Black Road massacre of workers and had seen the workers scattering before the charge of armed police. Furious at the brutality of the police, he wrote an account of the episode for the columns of the *Arbeiter-Zeitung,* including an indignant, bitter circular which came to be known as the "Revenge Circular" because of the heading which read, "Revenge! Workingmen! To Arms!" It opened: "Your masters sent out their bloodhounds—the police—they killed six

"We will meet tomorrow," agreed the anarchists, "in a way and in a place where it will cost them dearly if they attack us!" "Put *ruhe* in your *Arbeiter,* Spies: *ruhe* means we must all be armed." And from the *Arbeiter* press came a circular inviting the workers, with the mayor's permission, to meet in Haymarket Square to protest the murders by the police.

They did meet, fifty thousand strong, with wives and children, to hear the men who offered to give voice to their anguish. This time, however, the platform was not out in the open, as usual, but in a corner of the square near some dark alleys. Spies, who had crossed the words "Workers, to arms" out of the printed invitation, talks about the affliction with caustic eloquence—not so that his hearers miss the import of his message, but to attempt, with singular modesty, to fortify their spirits for the necessary reforms. "Is this Germany or Russia or Spain?" Spies asks. At the very moment of the mayor's arrival,[33] although he does not interrupt the meeting, Parsons, aware of the gravity of the occasion and of the vast number of people present, is declaiming one of Spies's editorials, published a hundred times with impunity. And just when Fielden in a wild outburst is asking whether, being prepared to die, it is not the same thing to die defending oneself from the enemy as to die from bestial work, a crowd begins to form. The police, one hundred and eighty of them, come up the street, revolvers in hand. They arrive at the speaker's stand and suggest that the crowds disperse. The workers do not pull back quickly enough. "What have we

---

of your brothers at McCormick's this afternoon." It ended: "To arms, we call you, to arms." It was signed, "Your Brothers." The circular appeared both in English and German. Spies later disclaimed authorship of the heading, insisting that the word "Revenge" had been inserted without his knowledge.

33. Carter H. Harrison, mayor of Chicago, attended the meeting and left before the bomb incident, convinced that all was peaceful and did not justify police interference. Unfortunately, after he left, the police tried to disperse the meeting.

done against the peace?" asks Fielden, and the police open fire.

Then a thin red line is seen threading its twisting way through the air and down upon their heads. The ground trembles; the projectile sinks four feet below the surface; the howling policemen in the two front ranks fall, one on top of the other; the cries of a dying man rend the air. The other police respond with superhuman courage, leaping over their companions in a hail of bullets to fight the resisting workers. "We left without firing a shot!" say some; "we hardly tried to resist," say others; "they met us with bullets," say the police. A few minutes later there is nothing in that dismal corner of the square but stretchers, gunpowder, and smoke. Again the workers hide their dead in entryways and cellars. One policeman dies in the square, his entire hand plunged into his wound. He pulls it out to send his last breath to his wife. Another, still standing, is full of holes from head to foot, for when the bomb fragments struck his flesh, they sliced it like chisels.

How to picture Chicago's terror and the Republic's? Spies reminds the people of Robespierre,[34] Engel of Marat,[35] Parsons of Danton.[36] How to picture it? Why, these men are ferocious beasts—Tinvilles, Henriots, Chaumettes, men who want to pour the old world away through a gutter of blood and fertilize the world with living flesh! Chase them through the streets with a lasso the way they wanted to chase a policeman yesterday! Greet them with bullets wherever they

34. Maximilien Marie Isidore Robespierre (1758-1794), Jacobin leader of the French Revolution, leader in the movement to execute Louis XVI, and symbol of terror—an incorruptible but righteously bigoted revolutionary. He died on the guillotine.

35. Jean-Paul Marat (1743-1793), Swiss-born French revolutionary leader and journalist who was assassinated. He is viewed as a representative of the moderate wing of revolutionists.

36. Georges Jacques Danton (1759-1794), popular but moderate French revolutionary leader; guillotined.

appear the way their wives greeted the "traitors" with rotten eggs yesterday! Is it not said, although it is a lie, that their cellars are stocked with bombs? Is it not said, although this too is a lie, that their wives, real Furies, are melting lead like those women of Paris who scraped the walls to give their husbands lime for making gunpowder? We want this worm that is eating us! There they are, as in the uprisings of the Terror, breaking into an apothecary shop whose proprietor told the police where they were holding their meetings, smashing his bottles and jars, dying in the streets like dogs, poisoned with colchicum wine![37] Off with the heads of all who have appeared! To the gallows with the speechmakers and their ideas!

Spies, Schwab, and Fischer are taken prisoner at the printing office where the police find a letter from Johann Most, a letter from an abject and driveling toad who treats Spies as an intimate friend and talks to him about his bombs, about "the medicine," about a rival of his, and about Paulus the Great "who goes to wallow in the bogs of Shevitsch's dog of a newspaper."[38] The wounded Fielden is taken out of his house. So with Engel and Neebe. And Lingg is taken out of his cellar. He sees a policeman come in, puts a revolver to his chest, the policeman grabs him, the two roll on the floor fighting, get up, fall down again and into the wretched little room full of nuts and bolts, chisels and bombs, Lingg swearing and cursing the while. Tables are left standing without legs, chairs without their backs. Lingg has almost choked his adversary when another policeman attacks and almost chokes Lingg. That youth so eager to deflate English law cannot even speak English! Three hundred prisoners in one day. The country is frightened, the jails full.

The trial? Everything said can be proved, except that the eight anarchists accused of killing the policeman Degan had

37. Wine made from a poisonous root.
38. Schevitsch was the editor of the *New Yorker Volkszeitung,* the leading German-language organ of the Socialist Labor Party.

prepared, or even covered up, a plot to end in his death.[39] The witnesses are the police themselves and four bought anarchists, one of them an admitted perjurer. According to evidence brought out in the trial, Lingg himself, whose bombs were similar to the Haymarket kind, as was evident from the cap, was far away from the catastrophe. Parsons, pleased with his speech, was watching the crowd from a nearby house. The perjurer was the man who said, and later denied, that he saw Spies strike the match to light the fuse of the bomb, saw Lingg and another man carry the leather trunk to a nearby corner of the square. He said that on the night when the six were killed at the plant, the anarchists agreed, at Engel's behest, to carry guns in order to stave off further attacks, and to use the word "ruhe" in the *Arbeiter*. He claimed that Spies was for a moment in the place where this decision was taken, that there were bombs in his office, and heaps of "manuals on revolutionary warfare" in several houses. What indeed was fully proved beyond doubt was that, all adverse testimony notwithstanding, the bomb-thrower was a stranger. What did happen was that Parsons, a well-loved brother of a noble Southern general, spontaneously appeared in court one day to share the luck of his friends.[40] What indeed makes one tremble is the unhappiness of the loyal Nina Van Zandt.[41] Captivated by the arrogant handsomeness and the humanitarian doctrines of Spies, she offered to marry him on the threshold of his death, and, on the arm of her mother, who came from a distinguished

39. The eight men on trial were accused of being "accessories before the fact to the murder of Officer Joseph M. Degan," who was one of the policemen killed in the bomb explosion.

40. Parsons had left Chicago on May 4 for Geneva, Wisconsin, and could have disappeared, but he decided to appear in court and stand trial with his comrades.

41. Nina Van Zandt, a handsome daughter of a well-to-do family, had fallen in love with Spies during the trial, and married him by proxy while he was in jail. Although Martí treats her sympathetically, she was the object of coarse and brutal attacks in the press for her act.

family, she married the convict with a brother as proxy. Day after day she brought to the bars of Spies's cell flowers, books, and the consolation of her love. She used her savings to publish a short but proud autobiography of her husband to obtain money for his defense. She went to the governor and fell on her knees before him. What was truly startling was the tempestuous eloquence of the halfbreed Lucy Parsons, who traveled over the United States—rejected here, hooted there, thrown into prison elsewhere; today followed by weeping laborers, tomorrow by farmers who turned her out as if she were a witch, later by cruel gangs of small boys—for the sole purpose of "picturing to the world the horrible conditions endured by the luckless members of society, a thousand times worse than the means proposed for putting an end to their sufferings." The trial? The seven were condemned to death by hanging, and Neebe to the penitentiary by virtue of a special charge of conspiring to homicide, a charge in no way proved true, for explaining in the press and on the rostrum the doctrines whose dissemination the law allows. In New York they were punished with twelve months in jail and a two-hundred-dollar fine for directly inciting to revolt!

What man whose duty it is to punish crimes, even proved crimes, fails to take into account the circumstances that cause them, the passions that justify them, and the reasons for committing them? Nations, like physicians, must prefer to foresee the disease, or cure it in its incipient stages, rather than allow it to get the upper hand so they are forced to combat, with desperate and bloody measures, the wrongs they themselves have brought about.

But those seven must not die. The year passes. The Supreme Court, in a decision unworthy of the affair, confirms the death sentence.[42] What happens, then, to lead Chicago to

---

42. On September 14, 1887, the Supreme Court of Illinois sustained both the rulings and verdict of the lower court. The Supreme Court of the United States refused to review the case.

ask for clemency as ardently now as it asked for punishment before? What made the labor unions of the Republic finally send their representatives to Chicago to intercede for those guilty of having espoused the cause of labor too fervently?[43] What made the clamor of the nation's hatred equal the impulse to mercy of those who were there after the cruelty that provoked the crime?

The entire press from New York to San Francisco falsifies the trial, pictures the seven convicts as harmful beasts, puts images of policemen blown apart by the bomb on everyone's breakfast table, describes their deserted homes, their golden-haired children, their desperate widows. What about that aged governor who refuses to confirm the sentence? Who will defend us tomorrow when the monstrous working man rebels, if the police see that forgiving their enemies encourages them to repeat the crime? What ingratitude to the police not to put those men to death! "No!" cries a police chief to Nina Van Zandt, who goes with her mother to ask for a writ of clemency and is unable to talk because of her tears; not one hand reaches out to take from the poor, deathly pale creature the petition she is presenting to them one by one!

Can the supplications of Felix Adler, the recommendations of the state judges, the masterly summary in which Trumbull[44] shows the cruelty and stupidity of the trial, be futile?

43. The United Trades of New York passed a resolution urging organized labor all over the country to hold protest meetings. The powerful Central Labor Union of New York endorsed a similar appeal, signed by fourteen well-known labor leaders, including Samuel Gompers, president of the American Federation of Labor, and Frank Ferrell, Negro leader of the Knights of Labor. The AFL at its convention passed a resolution pleading for clemency, but while many locals of the Knights of Labor supported the defense movement, the national leadership, especially Terence V. Powderly, took no part in the movement, and actually threatened to suspend or even expel a district assembly taking action.

44. Lyman Trumbull (1813-1896), U.S. Senator from Illinois, sympathetic to labor, criticized the trial and claimed that in view of the

The prison is like a public festival: trains filled with people enter and leave the city; Spies, Fielden, and Schwab, at the insistence of their lawyer, have signed a letter to the governor in which they swear they have never resorted to force. Not the others: they write bold letters that say: "Either liberty or the death we do not fear!" Will the cynical Spies, the implacable Engel, the diabolical Parsons be able to save themselves? Fielden and Schwab perhaps can be saved because the trial brings out little about them, and, aged as they are, the governor takes pity on them, for he too is well along in years.

The lawyers for the defense, deputies from the labor unions, mothers, wives, and sisters of the condemned, go on a pilgrimage to the governor to implore him to spare the lives of those they love, their reception frequently interrupted by sobbing. There at the moment of truth one can see the emptiness of rhetorical eloquence! Trite phrases in the face of death! "Sir," asks a laborer, "will you condemn seven anarchists to death because one anarchist threw a bomb at the police, when the courts refused to condemn Pinkerton's police[45] when one of them killed a child worker without provocation?" Yes, the governor will condemn them; the entire Republic demands he do so as an example. Who put the four bombs discovered by the turnkeys in Lingg's cell yesterday? So that ferocious soul wants to die in the ruins of the prison, symbol in his eyes of the world's wickedness! Whose lives will Governor Oglesby finally save?

Surely not the life of Lingg from whose cell, shaken by a sudden explosion, comes a thread of blue smoke as if from a

---

nationwide hysteria it was "about impossible that they should have a fair and impartial trial."

45. Pinkerton's police were men employed by Allan Pinkerton (1819-1884), who operated an antilabor, anti-trade union employment agency which supplied employers with detectives and strikebreakers. He also furnished employers with undercover agents who often committed acts of violence and then blamed militant trade unionists for these acts.

cigar! There lies Lingg, stretched out alive, torn to bits, his face a pool of blood, his two eyes staring out of a mass of red. He had placed between his teeth a capsule of dynamite he kept hidden in his bushy hair, had lighted the fuse with a candle, and had brought the capsule up to his chin. He is brutally carried off and dropped onto the bathroom floor. When the blood is washed away the ruptured larynx shows between the shreds of torn flesh, and streams of blood like water from a spring run along the curls of his hair. And in this condition he wrote! He begged them to sit him up! And he died six hours later, when Fielden and Schwab had already been pardoned, when the women—those sublime women, now convinced of their men's misfortune and pale as ashes— were knocking for the last time on those barbarous doors, no longer bearing flowers and fruit as in the days of hope!

The first is Fischer's wife, who recognizes death on his white lips. She waits for him dry-eyed, but will she leave that frightful embrace alive? Thus, thus is the soul wrenched from the body! With loving words he pours honey into her ears, lifts her up and clasps her to his breast, kisses her lips, her neck, her back, pushes her from him. "Goodbye!" Then he moves away with a firm step, head lowered and arms crossed.

And Engel, how does he receive the last visit of his daughter? They surely must love one another, for neither he nor she is dead. Oh, he must love her dearly, for those who led Engel away tremble when they recall the tearful light of his final glance, like the glance of a man suddenly grown tall in his bonds.

"Goodbye, my son!" says Spies's mother, struggling to embrace him as they forcibly drag her from her choking son. "Oh, Nina, Nina!" cries Spies, as he clutches to his breast for the first and last time the widow who was never his wife. And on the brink of his death she is seen to open like a flower, to tremble like a flower, and like a flower wither and shed her petals in the terrible happiness of that adored kiss.

Lucy Parsons certainly cannot be called fainthearted, but

at that moment, aware of the force of life and the beauty of death, like Ophelia returned to reason, she walks among the wardens like a flashing zircon, and although they respectfully offer her their arms, they refuse to allow her to bid her husband goodbye simply because, holding her children in a close embrace, she   pleads for their permission with the ardor and fury of flames.

So night has come, and all is dark in the greenish, calcimined prison halls. Above the footsteps of the armed guards; above the laughter and shouting of the jailers and members of the press, interspersed from time to time with the ringing of keys; above the incessant clatter of the telegraph (the apparatus was installed there by the *New York Sun*) that clicks and scolds and curses and rattles on in imitation of the inflections of the human voice, like teeth in a skull; above the silence surrounding all these sounds one can hear the last nails being driven into the scaffold. It stands at the end of the corridor, and the carpenters are giving it the finishing touch. "The ropes are fine; they've just been tested by the warden!" "The executioner will find the rope securing the trap door latch hidden in the box at the bottom." "The trap door is solid, ten feet above the floor." "No, the scaffold isn't made of new lumber; the planks have been repainted a yellowish tan to make them look nice on this occasion. Everything must be made decent, very decent." "Yes, the militia is on hand, and nobody will be permitted near the prison." "Lingg surely is handsome!" Laughter, tobacco, brandy, smoke that chokes the wakeful convicts in their cells. Electric lights sputter, balking and obstructing in the heavy humid air. A cat sits motionless on the railing of the cellblocks, watching the scaffold . . . when suddenly a melodious voice, filled with strength and feeling, rings out in Engel's cell. It is the voice of one of those men supposed to be human beasts—tremulous at first, then vibrant, then pure and serene as from one who now feels free of dust and shackles. Transported by ecstasy, his arms held high as if offering his spirit to heaven, Engel is reciting Heinrich Heine's "The Silesian Weavers."[46]

> From the sad eyes there flow no tears;
> They sit before their looms gnashing their teeth.
> "We weave your ancient shroud, oh Germany;
> Three curses we weave into the cloth."
> Weave on, weave on, oh weavers!
>
> "A curse of vengeance on the God
> To whom we prayed in winter's cold and hunger;
> In vain we hoped and waited,
> But He despised and mocked and fooled us."
> Weave on, weave on, oh weavers!
>
> "A curse on the king of the rich
> Whose haughty breast our mortal anguish failed to move;
> He wrested from us our final penny
> And had us shot like dogs."
> Weave on, weave on, oh weavers!
>
> "A curse on the false fatherland
> Whcrc nothing flourishcs but shamc and deep rejection;
> Where every flower is plucked in early bloom
> And worms refresh themselves on rot and putrefaction."
> Weave on, weave on, oh weavers!
>
> "The shuttle flies, the loom is creaking,
> We diligently weave both night and day.
> Old Germany, we weave your winding sheet
> And into it the threefold curse."
> Weave on, weave on, oh weavers!

46. Heinrich Heine (1797-1856), German-Jewish poet, wit, and radical, whose poem "The Weavers" offered revolutionary inspiration, and gave title to Gerhart Hauptmann's play *The Weavers*. In Martí's article, the poem appears in Spanish. The translation here is from the German original.

The three curses of Iteine referred to above are here set forth.

Bursting into sobs, Engel drops to his cot, sitting there with his aged face in his hands. The entire prison has listened to him silently, some as if in prayer, the inmates appearing at the bars of their cells, the reporters and jailers trembling with emotion, the telegraph still, Spies half seated, Parsons standing in his cell with arms outspread as if he were about to take flight.

Daylight finds Engel talking with his guards about the curious incidents in his life as a conspirator, at the rapid rate of a man condemned to death; finds Spies strengthened by a long sleep; finds Fischer leisurely dressing in the same clothes he took off the night before to rest more comfortably; finds Parsons, whose lips move constantly, stamping on his clothes after a short and hysterical sleep.

"Oh, Fischer, how can you be so calm when the warden who has to give the signal for your death is pacing his office like a wild animal, his face red to hold back the tears?" "Because," replied Fischer, clapping a hand on the trembling arm of the guard and looking straight into his eyes, "I believe that my death will help the cause I've been wedded to all my life, and love better than my own life—the cause of the worker—and because my sentence is biased, illegal, and unjust!" "Now that it's eight in the morning, Engel, only two hours before your death, and you can read in the kindly expressions on people's faces, and in the way they walk and talk, and in the cat's mournful miaowing, that they think your blood's freezing up in your veins—how is it you're not shaking with fear?" "Shaking with fear because I've been defeated by the ones I wanted to defeat? I don't think this is a just world, and I've been fighting—I'm fighting now with my death—to create a world of justice. What do I care if my death is a judicial murder? Can a man who has embraced a cause as glorious as ours desire to live when he can die for it? No, warden, I don't want any drugs; I want some port wine!" And he drinks three glasses, one after another. Spies, his legs crossed as when he was describing for the *Arbeiter-Zeitung,* in tones of flame and bone-white, the happy universe to follow this civilization of bailiffs and mastiffs, is writing long letters, calmly rereading them, slowly putting them into their envelopes, and occasionally letting his pen rest as he leans back in his chair to puff mouthfuls of smoke rings into the air like a German student. Oh, fatherland, origin of life, you come like light and air to bring comfort in a thousand subtle ways even to those who deny you because of a greater love for humanity! "Yes, warden," says Spies, "I'll drink a glass of Rhine wine. . . ." When the silence begins to fill with anguish, just at the moment when everyone stops talking at once, as if before a solemn apparition—at executions as well as at banquets—Fischer, the German Fischer, his face lighted by a happy smile and turned skyward, bursts forth into the strains of the "Marseillaise." Parsons is measuring his cell with great strides: an enormous audience stands before him, an audience of angels emerging in splendor out of the mists, and so that he may cross over the world like a purifying star, the angels offer him the fiery cape of the prophet Elijah. Reaching out to receive the gift, he turns and faces the bars, as if to show the murderers his triumph. He gesticulates, argues, shakes his raised fist, and when the impassioned words reach his lips, they die away like waves that become confused and perish on the shifting sands.

The sun fills the cells of the three condemned men with fire. Surrounded by these dismal walls, they seem in a biblical way alive in the midst of flames, when sudden sounds, rapid footsteps, and ominous whisperings begin to be heard. In an atmosphere turned the color of blood for no apparent reason, the warden and jailers appear at the iron bars to tell them that the hour has come, and they listen without losing their calm.

The men leave their cells by a narrow passageway. "All right?" "All right!" They hold hands, smile, grow in stature. "Let's go!" The doctor has given them stimulants; Spies and Fischer are brought new clothes; Engel refuses to take off his worsted slippers. Each is read the sentence in his cell; their hands are secured behind their backs with leather thongs; a white, shroudlike garment similar to that worn by catechumen Christians is slipped over their heads. Below are the spectators, sitting in rows of chairs before the gallows as if in a theater! Now the convicts are coming through the cell-block, at the end of which stands the scaffold. The livid warden walks ahead; beside each of the condemned men walks a constable. Spies's steps are slow and heavy; his blue eyes heartrending; his well-brushed hair, white as his own winding sheet, combed back from his noble forehead. Fischer follows him, robust and powerful, the veins of his neck showing his vigorous blood, his husky limbs standing out prominently through the shroud. Engel walks behind as if he were going to pay a call at the home of a friend, jerking the uncomfortable robe with his heels. Parsons, as if he were afraid of not dying, fierce, determined, concludes the procession at a lively pace. The hallway ends and they step onto the trap: ropes hanging, hair bristling, four shrouds.

Spies's face is prayerful, Fischer's firm and set, Parsons' radiantly proud. Engel's head is sunk into his shoulders as he makes his constable laugh with a joke. One after another their feet are tied with cords. Like snuffers over a candle flame the four hoods are thrown over their heads—Spies first, then Fischer, Engel, and Parsons. And while his friends' heads are being covered, Spies cries out, in tones that pierce the flesh of his hearers: "The voice you are about to silence will be more powerful in the future than all the words I could say right now!" While the constable is attending to Engel, Fischer says: "This is the greatest moment of my life!" "Hurrah for anarchy!" says Engel, who has been moving his manacled hands under his tunic, to the warden. "Men and women of my beloved America . . . ," Parsons begins to say.[47] A signal, a

47. There are various versions of just what were the condemned men's exact words as the nooses were placed around their necks. But it is generally believed that Spies said, "There will come a time when our silence will be more powerful than the voices you strangle today!" Fischer, "Hurrah for anarchy"; Engle, "This is the happiest moment of my life!" Parsons, "Will I be allowed to speak, O men of America? Let me speak, Sheriff Matson! Let the voice of the people be heard!" (David, op. cit., p. 463.)

sound, the trap springs, and all four bodies fall at once, spinning and colliding. Parsons dies in falling; there is a quick turn and he stops. Fischer swings, shudders, tries to work free of the noose, stretches his neck, draws up his legs, and dies. Engel swings back and forth in his floating tunic, raises and lowers his chest in a tidelike motion, and strangles. In a frightful dance Spies spins round like a hanging sack of beans, bends his body, heaves sideways, draws his knees up to his forehead, lifts one leg, stretches both, shakes his arms, shudders, and finally expires, his neck broken. He seems to be bowing his head to the spectators.

Two days later—two days of terrible scenes in the homes, constant processions of tearful friends in front of the livid bodies, signs of grief hanging on thousands of doors below a red silk flower, crowds respectfully gathered to place roses and floral wreaths on the caskets—stunned Chicago saw Spies's flower-covered casket pass by behind a band playing dirges, preceded by a crazy soldier waving an American flag as a challenge. Then came Parsons' black casket, followed by fourteen craftsmen carrying symbolic gifts of flowers; Fischer's decorated with a colossal wreath of lilies and carnations; and those of Engel and Lingg draped with red flags. Next came the carriages of their widows who were veiled from head to foot in deep mourning, and the various societies: trade unions, *vereins,* choral groups, deputations, three hundred women in a body wearing black armbands, six thousand bereaved, bareheaded workers wearing red roses on their breasts.

And then, surrounded by twenty-five thousand congenial souls[48] under the sunless sky that covered those bare plains, Captain Black, the pale, black-garbed counsel for the defense,

48. According to Henry David, "probably a quarter of a million lined the route taken by the funeral cortège," while there were perhaps "as many as fifteen thousand" at Waldheim "who observed the simple burial exercises." (Op. cit., p. 465.)

holds his hand over the coffins. "What is truth?" he asks in a silence so deep that one can clearly hear the moaning of the grieving women and the crowd. "Since Jesus of Nazareth brought it to the world, what is the truth that man cannot know until he lifts it with his arms and pays for it with his death? These men are not despised felons, thirsty for disorder, blood, and violence, but men who have tried to bring peace. These are hearts filled with tenderness, beloved by all who knew them and were intimately acquainted with the power and glory of their lives. Their anarchy was government by order and not by force, their dream a new world without misery or slavery, their sorrow the belief that selfishness will never give way to justice by peaceful means, oh cross of Nazareth which for these bodies was a gallows!"

From the enveloping gloom, and as the five hanged men are being lowered from the pine-board platform into their graves, a voice rings out that seems to have come from a heavy beard and a serious and bitter heart: "I have not come to accuse that executioner they call a warden, or the nation that has been thanking God in its churches today for these men's death on the gallows, but I have come to accuse the workers of Chicago who have permitted five of their noblest friends to be executed!" Night and the defense lawyer's hand laid on that restless shoulder disperse the audience and their hurrahs; flowers, flags, the dead, and the grieving disappeared into the same black gloom. The throngs returning to their homes sound like the distant waves of the sea. And the evening edition of the *Arbeiter-Zeitung* reports that when the eager multitudes enter the city, they are greeted with: "We have lost a battle, unhappy friends, but we will finally see a world ordered according to justice; let us be wise as serpents, and gentle as doves!"

La Nación (Buenos Aires), January 1, 1888
Dated New York, November 13, 1887

VII
The Menace of United States Imperialism

The United States View of Mexico

... It was at night, as is usual in these cases, when in a conference room in one of New York's leading hotels the directors of the American Annexation League[1] and the delegates from its many branches met in solemn conclave to make an inventory of their forces and show their power to the mysterious representatives sent to the League by the annexationist territories of Canada. They were also there to honor the president of the Company for the Occupation and Development of Northern Mexico, a Colonel Cutting.[2] Presiding was Colonel Gibbons,[3] a well-known lawyer. Many Canadians were present, in addition to the delegates of the

1. The American Annexation League was organized by American businessmen and political leaders in 1878 to acquire new markets for expanding American manufacturing and for the investment of capital through the annexation of territories adjacent to the United States, particularly in Latin America and Canada.
2. Colonel Francis Cutting (1828-1892) had been an advocate of the annexation of all of Mexico before the Civil War, and was one of the founders of the American Annexation League. For Martí's other reference to Cutting, see p. 35.
3. Colonel George Gibbons (1842-1904) was an agent for a number of American corporations in Latin America and one of the founders of the American Annexation League.

League—whose immediate objective is "to take advantage of any civil strife in Mexico, Honduras, or Cuba in order to act quickly and assemble an army." But no one was there from Honduras, Cuba, or Mexico. "The occasion may soon come," said the president, "it is certain to come at any moment." "Honduras too?" asked a novice. "Oh yes; look at Byrne's map. Honduras has a lot of mines." "Don't let them underestimate us," said a speaker, "we know what we have behind us; Walker started with less thirty years ago! All we must do is be careful not to end the way he did."

The Annexation League was established nine years ago, and today, with branches in several states of the Republic, it numbers over ten thousand members ready to "march to the colors." "Good people," says one of the reports, "and hard to restrain, but the times are not yet ripe for an isolated and independent attack." Delegates from each of the American Annexation League's numerous branches read this report, and these documents, together with the delegates' verbal comments, give the League confidence in that heavy-shouldered cur who is so impatient for war and plunder. There is always such a man springing up in strong and densely populated nations, just as poisonous mushrooms spring up in the choicest trees. The people feel duty bound to run to the first powerful voice. Far from lacking members, the League's branches have too many, it is said, and they are organized like a reserve army.

Special delegates have come for this important gathering from all of southern and eastern Canada—delegates of no little note, since two of them are deputies in the Dominion's parliament. And how can one take the League's endeavors entirely lightly, at least in regard to what it is doing in Canada, when at the same time as a special convention is being held to declare its relations to the neighboring country, and to confer with its representatives, the Democratic newspapers the *Sun* and the *World* are asking the party to add to its platform the League's plans for annexing Canada to the

United States?[4] And the other newspapers are not even raising their eyebrows. In New Brunswick not a single citizen
wants to be English, according to one of the deputies, and all
of Manitoba is annexation-minded.

"Why not Mexico," another newspaper inquired of the
Sun, "since it is so close and just as necessary to us as the
Dominion of Canada?"

"We must not covet Mexico," the *Sun* responded, "for its
annexation would be violent, immaterial, and contemptible.
Furthermore, we would find it cumbersome because Mexico's
institutions, language, and race are not ours, and there would
be no way of arriving at a beneficial assimilation. In Canada,
on the other hand, the people come from the English, like
ourselves; they speak English, like ourselves, and the country
desires fusion with our Republic, as do we with it." That very
statement was made by the Canadians at the meeting—the
Canadians, who are known by number instead of name so
their native government will not accuse them of treason.

But regardless of the importance of this matter, the conference considered it less so than the presence of Colonel
Cutting. "He is coming," it was whispered, "to unite the
forces of the Annexation League with those of the Company
for the Occupation and Development of Northern Mexico."
"Yes, that's why; he's working hard on the project. The two
associations are going to hold one meeting." "Where?" "In
Niagara Falls." "Oh, on the Canadian border?" "Then what is
the first thing on the agenda, Canada or Mexico?"

And in the midst of these comments, all true and to the
point, and after Cutting had tried to stir up hatred with the
perfidious picture he painted of his imprisonment in Mexico
—which hardly managed to give the invading company a good
pretext—he began explaining to the meeting how the "com-

4. Martí is referring to editorials in the *New York Sun* of June 5,
1887, and the *New York World* of June 7, 1887, advocating the annexation of Canada and urging the Democratic Party to make this demand
a key feature in its platform during the presidential campaign of 1888.

pany's forces" were organized. The meeting lent him a responsive ear. His statements should be repeated, and all the newspapers are printing them. He said that the company's soldiers belong to different states, but that more of them come from the South because it is nearer to them; that fifteen thousand of them are now mobilized; that the company's objective is to dispossess Mexico of its northern states, especially Sonora, California, Chihuahua, and Coahuila; that "its people" are tried and true, strong and fearless, adventurous and already embarked on such undertakings. In short, he said what cannot be so, that Nuevo León and Tamaulipas —like a son who has just killed his mother because she insisted upon making him go of his own free will—are prepared to be taken over by the United States. And he made the idiotic statement that if the government were overthrown, many Mexicans would lend their support to the invasion in spite of their hatred for the North. He is about to call a general preparatory meeting in New Orleans.

A Niagara Falls hotel has already been selected for the general meeting. Cutting looks out for his personal comfort. Now he insists on publicizing and disseminating everything favorable to Mexico, so that when these bandits raise their heads in either place, people will be neither indifferent nor inclined in his favor, but will feel that his restraint comes from his conscience; all of which cannot succeed without quickly seizing every occasion to inspire respect in anyone who, with his efforts or his purse or his indifference, can be antagonistic. Are not Lincoln's historians this very minute recounting how turbulent spirits from the frontier have been stirring up the fire year after year, making scattered forays, and how they have finally brought about the war between South and North, of which they were the whip and the vanguard? Poisoned arrows are only arrows, but they can kill. And it is good to recognize them and take precautions against their use. . . .

El Partido Liberal (Mexico City)
Dated New York, June 23, 1887

The Argentine Republic as Viewed from the United States

For the past two years here the U.S. newspapers have shown a marked desire to know the countries and resources of our America, for they consider it a necessary if not an obligatory field for the surplus products of North American industries—provided that these investigations of wealth and customs are not swayed by the cordial enthusiasm which inspires love for our courteous and gentlemanly countries, and induces us to make sacrifices to pay the proper interest for it. On the contrary, they study and chronicle us with merely a hasty glance and with obvious ill-humor, like an impoverished nobleman in the predicament of asking a favor of someone he does not regard as his equal. That is why, since most of our American countries are truly admirable for having climbed from the most obscure and adverse origins in the face of obstacles deadly to their present condition, not a day passes when these ignorant and scornful newspapers do not treat us like trivial little nations lacking in transcendence, as farcical nations, as petty republics without knowledge or ability, as "nations with unsteady legs," to quote Charles Dudley Warner[1] when he spoke of Mexico yesterday—"The

1. Charles Dudley Warner (1829-1900), essayist, editor, and novelist, editor of the *Hartford Courant.* Warner returned from a visit to Mexico in 1887 and in speeches and in articles in *Harper's Monthly Magazine* denigrated the Mexican people. (See *Harper's Monthly Magazine,* LXXV [June-July 1887], pp. 23, 283.)

dregs of a degenerate civilization with neither virility nor purpose!"

This Warner deserves to have someone pull out the hairs of his beard, as in the days of the Cid![2] It is a pity, because to tell the truth he writes with a certain warmth, precision, and vivacity, rare everywhere!

Civilization in Mexico, as everywhere in our America, is not decaying; it is beginning. It will have the character of our nature, the character of the pampas and the *ombú* tree. Civilization in our America has been built upon a basket of poisonous snakes, with a strength which will shine in the future like columns of light, with a handful of glorious men, martial apostles, encyclopedic minds, and liberated university graduates.

What has Mexican civilization become but the heroic struggle of a few anointed ones against the inert millions, against the privileged able to protect themselves from treason and from selling their republic to the foreigner? What civilization did Mexico inherit—did our entire America inherit—when she already had courage of her own to declare herself free? Our lands have done more to climb to where they are than did the United States when she continued falling, perhaps in essentials, from the wonder of her origins.

Dudley Warner sees the details clearly, but of what use is it if he fails to see things affectionately? What he loves he depicts well—celestial lakes, magnificent cultivated fields, choruses of mountains wrapped in misty veils like virgins; but merit does not reside in that, since to be fair he needs only to overcome his antipathy, if he has any, and to faithfully describe, as if he wanted to, what by his nature he dislikes. Not that all is good, or that the evil which one sees should be dissembled, for nations are not created with cosmetics, nor do they take pleasure in contemplating their beauty in the quiet waters of a fountain; but all must be treated impartially, and along with the real one must see the justification and study things in their origins and meanings, not in their

2. A figure in Spanish history and literature famed for his strength and manliness.

mere appearances. What if this country here were to be judged by its outer shell, and its mistakes not regarded with the compassion and reason needed to forgive them! Warner understands Nature; in spite of his form, however, he is a narrowminded writer who does not know how to put himself into the shoes of another race, like the man in the Indian story who, because he was held down by the foot of an elephant, maintained that everything was an elephant foot. Over and above the question of races, which influence nothing but character, lies the essential human spirit which dominates and unifies them. Their emperors, looking down like Emerson from an eminence and seeing the entire panorama, possess the ideas, and their second lieutenants, mindful of the small matters of their squad, want everything modeled after that panorama.

Unsteady legs indeed! Davids have done more than Goliaths. San Martín is not known for having weighed as much as a mountain. Bolívar was hardly any heavier than his sword. The priest Hidalgo[3] reached some hundred and thirty pounds. Unsteady legs indeed! Precisely thus was the guide who took a certain traveler from Acapulco to Mexico City, the guide who ended his trek with the large sum of money still safe in the pouch hung from his belt. That guide was of tender years and sparse flesh, very lean and longlegged. But since a corpulent Frenchman who joined the caravan had persisted in punching him and making fun of him when he arrived, and flourishing his saber and challenging his bravery because he

3. Simón Bolívar (1783-1830), called "the Liberator," the great Venezuelan leader in the Latin American struggle for independence from Spain.

José de San Martín (1778-1850), the soldier, statesman, and national hero of Argentina who, with Simón Bolívar, led the Latin American independence movement. (Martí's essays on Bolívar and San Martín appear in the second volume of this collection.)

Miguel Hidalgo (1753-1811), Mexican village priest who was the first leader of the Mexican revolution against Spain. He called for the revolt at his church in Dolores, Guanajuato, September 16, 1810, and it is therefore known as "Grito de Dolores."

thought him weak, the boy leaped from his team of horses with such a bound that everyone considered him a giant, especially the Frenchman, who put up his saber as soon as he saw the boy's eyes—so fiery that there was no way to make him continue his journey until the Frenchman dismounted and accepted his challenge to a duel. That boy's legs did not seem "unsteady" to the Frenchman!

Almost always preceded by a reputation for the country's natural wealth, myopic articles about Guatemala have appeared in monthly magazines especially; for with reproachable politics Guatemala is now offering her alliance to the United States in exchange for the latter's misuse of its fearful influence upon Mexico in order that the Mexican government permit the Guatemalan government to act as a major and absolute power among the Central American countries which Guatemala regards as her natural spoils. These countries are Costa Rica, an extremely industrious beehive inspiring affection for the friendliness of her inhabitants, the *hermaniticos* as they are called in Central America, and respect for her industry and diligence; Honduras, raising her wise and meaningful younger generation in the gold and silver mines which are cropping up everywhere on the surface of the earth the way hot ashes make kernels of corn burst open into snowy flowers; Colombia, mounted upon gold, her ample bosom confined by a corselet of emeralds, her mind, unfortunately filled with jargon, fanned by the broad wings of Muzo's blue butterflies;[4] Chile, "the country of the South American Yankee" where Eleroy Curtis, secretary of the flying North American commission which traveled through our countries two years ago, saw "St. Lucia Drive, the most beautiful place I have ever visited," a country whose people he considered "the most active, enterprising and ingenious of Spanish Americans—yet aggressive, bold, arrogant, wise, rancorous, naturally ferocious, and coldblooded," mixing his virtues and defects in this account and in what is not discussed here, in such a way that the latter traits outnumber the former.

And *Harper's Magazine,* which among the illustrated periodicals justly claims the position of stubborn representative of the eaglelike spirit of North America, has this very day published a respectful study of "the other end of the hemisphere," of Argentina and Uruguay where a poorly controlled astonishment leaves the writer—Eleroy Curtis himself—no space for censure.

When the commissioners disembarked in Buenos Aires, he foretold the stupor with which they saw that unexpected and now dreaded greatness appear "upon the shoulders of a tempestuous Italian." And the superficial writer, who conveyed such an impression of all other American countries that even the most prosperous among them turned out to be half barbaric and deformed, sees nothing in Buenos Aires but the gaucho expiring upon his multicolored poncho in the service of a magical and powerful nation.[5]

The study contains little literature; but its very nakedness enhances its effect and is his best choice, since from the abruptness of the opening passages he reveals the fear and imposes the respect which in his judgment Argentina deserves from a country which "disregards her disgracefully." With present-day costs of production and transportation in the

4. Muzo is a village in Central Colombia famous for its emerald mines.

5. The reference is to the article, "The Other End of the Hemisphere" by William Eleroy Curtis in *Harper's Monthly Magainze*, LXXV (October 1887), pp. 893-909. In the article, Curtis called for American economic penetration of Latin America and called prospects for U.S. business enterprise in Argentina especially attractive. All this, he noted, called for greater knowledge of Latin America on the part of the American people. "For a people so boastful of our enterprise and intelligence, we are shamefully ignorant of what is going on at the other end of the hemisphere, although transactions there are of much greater concern to us than the struggle for home rule in Ireland or the invasion of Afghanistan." (P. 893.)

United States, however, "the Argentinians will end by throwing us out of the grain and provender markets."

And there is something of the prize fighter's swinging of arms in that avalanche of statistical contrasts. The author is no longer concerned, as he was in the rest of the countries he visited, "whether the Costa Rican goes barefoot," true only of some luckless peasant; or if in Santiago de Chile people are left to die of cold in their houses, huddled in their animal skins around a consumptive brazier. What ought to concern you, imbeciles, is that "it costs us fifty dollars to put a Chicago-cured steer in London, and it costs them twenty-five; that they began exporting grain five years ago and soon are going to take away the Brazilian grain market, just as Chile has taken the Pacific market from us. Your concern should be that with their almost totally arable land, deep rivers, and impatient railroads, the nations of the Plata have advantages greater than those of any other nation on the globe!"

And with Cato's astonishment at the end of his speech, with a continuous and almost angry praise which is gradually arousing the attention of his proud but lethargic compatriots,[6] instead of entertaining himself by describing statues and buildings, instead of attempting to write unfortunate rudimentary sketches of the merely political history of our sublime struggle to reach an agreement (with a generosity and enthusiasm difficult for other races to understand) between our superstitious and primitive population and our magnificent and virtuous ideals; instead of loudly ridiculing the laughable customs which we may be preserving only because of that tender respect of a loyal grandchild for the dotage of his kindly old people—this is what Curtis tells the North Americans: "Do not trust that uninhabitable Patagonia, for it

6. Marcus Porcius Cato (234 B.C.-149 B.C.), Roman statesman who for years closed every speech in the Roman Senate with the words, "Furthermore, I am of the opinion that Carthage ought to be destroyed."

is as barren as our great desert. Our population is increasing by 79 percent and theirs by 154. You believe that our Minneapolis is the most rapidly growing city in the world, but Buenos Aires is growing much more rapidly than Minneapolis. Wheelwright from Pennsylvania founded their first railroad, Halsey from New Jersey their first cattle ranch, Hale from Boston the first commission house to open the doors to foreign trade."[7] But they are of such fiber that not only do they imitate our methods but improve upon them, and we are of such fiber that while England sends three hundred and nine steam vessels down there in a single year, the United States, enticed by an annual subsidy of one hundred thousand dollars, which we did not decide to match, sent not a one. The refrigerated meat company of London and the Plata is now becoming an enormous commercial octopus which will monopolize the meat business the way our Standard Oil Co. is monopolizing the petroleum business.[8] And when that nation which is a century ahead of any other Spanish American country, whose cities have more telephones and electric

7. Martí is paraphrasing William Eleroy Curtis, even though he uses quotation marks. Curtis wrote (op. cit., pp. 893-95): "The pampas are similar to the prairies of our own West; the 'bleak and uninhabitable wastes' of Patagonia have developed into the richest of pastures, like the 'Great American Desert' which used to lie between the Missouri River and the mountains. . . .

"During the last twenty-five years the population of the United States has increased but 79 per cent, and the city of Buenos Ayres is growing faster than Minneapolis or Denver. . . .

". . . William Wheelwright of Pennsylvania . . . constructed the first railway in South America from Quilmar to Buenos Ayres. . . . Thomas Lloyd Halsey, of New Jersey, . . . introduced improved stock from the United States, and commenced the business of raising them. . . . Samuel B. Hale, who went down from Boston in 1828, . . . established the first commission-house in the republic. . . ." (Op. cit., pp. 893-95.)

8. The Standard Oil Company, created mainly by John D. Rockefeller, was a major example of monopoly capitalism in the United States, and the symbol of the Trust.

lights than ours (and we invented them), whose intelligent zeal is adopting every useful idea or method, whose schools outnumber ours, whose animal wealth and relative wealth is greater than our own, whose tentacles of luxurious railroads reach so successfully across the entire continent that we here might well be envious; when Patagonia—from where the Indian has fled like the ostrich—is populated by the herds of cattle now overrunning it; when trade and traffic and the Pacific mines are being brought down to Patagonia via the northern railroad—then Buenos Aires will be a London and New York combined. Then the constancy of that Latin nation will have erected, against Nature herself, a populous emporium, a new sister marvel, on the river banks which its founder Mendoza[9] selected for the site of the city with more haste than wisdom, thinking about war rather than work. That country is no longer the "Argentine Confederacy," as our geography textbooks persist in stupidly calling it, but a Nation—Nation with a capital N like our own: "One and indivisible," and "United we stand, divided we fall," and everything else we are pleased to call ourselves. The Argentine Republic is all of this; referring to it in any other manner is to hurt the patriots who have made it what it is with their blood, and to make a mockery of our own intelligence.

Just as the stark account of Darwin's voyage on the frigate *Beagle*[10] is sometimes, through the influence of the sincere author's American charm, as epic as our resplendent native, as bright as a fresh, shining, and almost fragrant Negro—so, by its effect upon this cold and uneven narrator, by the order

9. Mendoza was a city in Argentina, capital of Mendoza Province, founded by Antonio de Mendoza (1485-1552), first Spanish viceroy of New Spain.

10. The *Beagle* circumnavigated the world from December 27, 1831, to October 2, 1836, carrying as one of its passengers Charles Darwin, who obtained important scientific information from the voyage for his work on evolution.

and poetry infusing it, by the antiquated style of beauty it acquired with its descriptive language, the primitive elements —picturesque like everything grandiose—with which that new nation has been built, are indicated more successfully than by rhetorical eagerness or mercenary ecstasy. At times he depicts the pastoral, in the tireless yet tender gaucho "devouring space, half savage and half gentleman," protecting as if she were a wife the widow of the man who paid with his life for the crime of defeating him in the pampas festivities. At other times one is shown the present-day enthusiasm which, with no more historical assistance than native incentive, bridles rivers, builds cities where grass grew, causes envy for nations so virtuously that it hides their vices from the hostile foreigner, and covers the marvelous plains with a people worthy of them.

The pleasing peculiarities most attractive to him as a traveler embellish his article, in which locomotives are bargained for, loaded ships come and go, and the last band of Indians is locked up with Homeric simplicity. And even in this we notice how the observer is dominated by the amazement of finding even in the lowly and popular aspect of the Argentinian the only condition inspiring the North American with respect: opulence. "What family do you come from?" is the first question a Philadelphian asks of anyone seeking lodgings in the city. In Boston they ask: "What do you know?" New Yorkers ask: "How much money have you?" New York has now absorbed the entire nation, and in every corner of it there is but one question: "How much money have you?" Eleroy Curtis is not attracted to the works of art adorning the public squares, but to the spurs and stirrups of heavy silver, to the silver slipper where the Argentine Amazon nestles her short foot, to the feather tunics plucked from ostriches, "now disappearing, like our buffalo," to the vicuña poncho "as costly as a camel hair shawl." "The Argentine poncho is a magnificent thing," he says, "and I hope some New York dandy will set the fashion by wearing one, for never was there a better or more graceful wrap!"

"The farmer goes to his ranch in a Pullman car instead of on a horse weighed down with silver-studded trappings, and talks to his head overseer by telephone, and slaughters his cattle by electric light." "A theater seat costs six pesos." "In Buenos Aires there are banks clearing more money than almost any others on earth, and they occupy palaces of iron, glass, and marble." "Their credit is good and their bonds are above par." He praises, admires, and treats everything with great respect, although at the pace of a traveler; and expressing his unexpected impressions in concrete terms and with obvious concentration, he puts aside the presumption which makes the man from North America stand out as unique among people, and predicts that the coming generation—trained as in the United States to give the country useful men and women—will erase the last remains of Spanish domination. And after loyally summarizing the liberal and sensible laws of the Republic, he declares that although Brazil, built upon diamonds, takes precedence over it in effeminate and uncultured inhabitants, and although Chile "is becoming vain due to the devastation of Peru," Argentina is "the most prosperous of all, the nation whose religious and civil liberties are best established, and the one which is building the foundations of national greatness most carefully and successfully."

La Nación (Buenos Aires), December 4, 1887
Dated New York, October 22, 1887

The Washington Pan-American Congress

1

"Pan-Americans," says one newspaper; "Clay's dream,"[1] says another; a third, "The right influence"; a fourth, "Not yet"; a fifth, "Steamers to South America"; a sixth, "Manifest destiny";[2] a seventh, "The Gulf is ours." And still others: "That Congress!," "The subsidy hunters," "Actions against the candidates," "Blaine's Congress,"[3] "The bread parade,"

1. As early as 1820 Henry Clay advocated "a human freedom league in America" to embrace "all nations from Hudson's Bay to Cape Horn." However, while Clay was an ardent supporter of the independence of Latin American states, he opposed the independence of Cuba while Secretary of State (1825-1829) and used his power to prevent its realization. (See Philip S. Foner, *History of Cuba and Its Relations with the United States* [New York, 1962], Vol. 1, pp. 156-69.)

2. "Manifest Destiny" was an expression first used by John L. O'Sullivan in 1845, and meant that God had manifestly intended Americans to spread over the continent. It was used by expansionists and imperialists after the Civil War to justify American expansionism.

3. As Secretary of State under President Garfield, Blaine issued an invitation on November 29, 1881, to all the Latin American countries to meet in Washington on November 22, 1882. But after President Garfield was assassinated, President Arthur revoked the invitation, frustrating Blaine's plan.

"Blaine's myth." The parade of delegates is ending and the sessions of the Pan-American Congress are about to begin.[4] Never in America, from its independence to the present, has there been a matter requiring more good judgment or more vigilance, or demanding a clearer and more thorough examination, than the invitation which the powerful United States (glutted with unsaleable merchandise and determined to extend its dominions in America) is sending to the less powerful American nations (bound by free and useful commerce to the European nations) for purposes of arranging an alliance against Europe and cutting off transactions with the rest of the world. Spanish America learned how to save itself from the tyranny of Spain; and now, after viewing with judicial eyes the antecedents, motives, and ingredients of the invitation, it is essential to say, for it is true, that the time has come for Spanish America to declare its second independence.

In matters of such great interest, a false alarm would be as culpable as dissimulation. One must neither exaggerate nor distort what is seen, nor must one remain silent on the subject. Dangers must not be recognized only when they are upon us, but when they can be avoided. In politics the main thing is to clarify and foresee. Only a virile and unanimous response, for which there is still time without risk, can free all the Spanish American nations at one time from the anxiety and agitation—fatal in a country's hour of development—in which the secular and admittedly predominant policy of a powerful and ambitious neighbor, with the possible connivance of the weak or venal republics, would forever hold them. This powerful neighbor has never desired to incite them, nor has it exerted control over them except to prevent

4. The Pan-American Congress began in Philadelphia on October 2, 1889, and reassembled in Washington on November 19, 1889, deliberating until April 19, 1890. Seventeen states were represented in the Congress, Santo Domingo being the only one to decline the invitation from Secretary of State Thomas Francis Bayard (1885-1889).

their expansion, as in Panama; or to take possession of their territory, as in Mexico, Nicaragua, Santo Domingo, Haiti, and Cuba; or to cut off their trade with the rest of the world, as in Colombia; or to oblige them to buy what it cannot sell, as it is now doing, and to form a confederacy for purposes of controlling them.

Nations must be considered in depth, for they bury their roots far below the surface. They must be examined in their entirety so that we do not marvel at these apparently sudden changes and this cohabitation of lofty virtues and rapacious talents. That humanistic and communicative freedom which can move peoples across snow-covered mountains to rescue a sister nation, or can induce them to die in a body, smiling under the saber, until the species may be led along the paths of redemption by the light of the hecatomb, was never a characteristic of North America, not even in the generous carelessness of its youth. The Dutch trader, the egotistical German, and the overbearing Englishman, together with the leaven of a municipal government of the nobility, formed the dough of the nation that saw no crime in leaving a mass of men, on the pretext of the ignorance in which they were kept, in slavery to those who opposed being slaves themselves.

The French horse at Yorktown had barely stopped frothing at the mouth when, with excuses of continental neutrality, the nation which in a later and more equitable century disputed with its former allies (because of its geographical superiority) the right to protect a neutral work of human betterment on the continent of freedom—that nation refused to help them fight their oppressors.[5] Offering no assistance

5. Martí is referring to the fact that the United States refused to recognize the independent republics of Spanish America for a number of years. In 1818 a resolution introduced in Congress calling upon the President to take the initial step in recognizing the independence of La Plata was defeated, 115 to 45.

except when it was no longer needed, it saw at its gates an epic race fighting a stirring war for the principles of decency and freedom which the North raised as a banner against the English, while the hand of the man who wrote those principles was still alive. And when the South, separately free, invited the North to the table of friendship, the North raised none of the objections it might have raised, but with the lips that had just proclaimed that no European monarch could have slaves in America, demanded that the armies of the South abandon their plans to redeem the American islands in the Gulf from the slavery of a European monarchy. The thirteen Northern states had just united, with no less difficulty than the hybrid colonies of the South, and were now preventing the possible union of objective and spirit—so necessary to the Southern peoples—from being strengthened (as it had been, and can still be) by granting independence to the islands placed by Nature to guard their doorstep. And when the Union did appear—out of the reality of life, with the candor of the forests and the strength and sagacity of creatures who wanted more territory for slaves—it fought a war for a neighboring country and cut a coveted region out of living flesh, taking advantage of upheaval in the friendly country, which was held by a cohort of evangelists struggling to impose upon a poisoned remnant of the European colony the dogmas of freedom of the neighbors who were attacking them. And when, with the candor of the forests and the strength and sagacity of the creatures inhabiting them, there appeared out of the reality of poverty and at a time of national readjustment a sad and kindly leader, the woodcutter Lincoln, the North could calmly hear a demagogue advising him to purchase, as a dumping ground for the armed Negroes who had helped him preserve the Union,[6] the nation of fer-

6. Lincoln was an ardent advocate of Negro colonization. A feature of his recommendations for the emancipation of slaves in the District of Columbia in the spring of 1862 was the provision of $100,000 for the voluntary emigration of freedmen to Haiti and Liberia. Largely at Lincoln's suggestion, the State Department made inquiries of South

vent children and enthusiastic virgins who in their passion for freedom were shortly thereafter to go into mourning for Lincoln, without fear of the deputies from Madrid. It could hear and provide safe conduct for the mediator about to propose to the South that it turn its guns upon Mexico, where the French were a menace,[7] and then come back to the Republic laden with laurels and the spoils of all the land from the Rio Grande to the Isthmus. The North had been dreaming about these dominions from the cradle, with Jefferson's "Nothing would be more appropriate"; with Adams' "The thirteen destined states"; with Clay's "Prophetic vision"; with Webster's "Great light of the North"; with Sumner's "The purpose is certain, and commerce contributary"; with Sewall's statement on everyone's lips, "The entire continent is yours, without limits"; with Everett's "Continental unification"; with Douglas' "Trade alliance"; with Ingalls' "From the Isthmus to the pole, the inevitable result"; with Blaine's "Necessity to stamp out the causes of yellow fever in Cuba."[8]

American governments concerning the possibility of colonizing American Negroes, and it was proposed that Negro colonies be established in Panama and the Île-à-Vache, an island in the Caribbean.

7. During the Civil War, taking advantage of the United States' involvement, France sought to establish a Catholic monarchy in Mexico. Maximilian of Austria was placed at the head of Mexico's government soon after French army units had taken over Mexico City in June 1863. It was suggested in the United States that the Union and Confederate armies cooperate in ousting Maximilian and taking possession of Mexico. However, nothing came of the proposal and Maximilian was captured and executed by the Mexicans in June 1867.

8. Martí is referring to Thomas Jefferson's desire for the United States to acquire Cuba and the oratory by men like John Quincy Adams, Henry Clay, Daniel Webster, Charles Sumner, William H. Seward. Harold M. Sewall, Stephen A. Douglas, Edward Everett, John James Ingalls, and James G. Blaine emphasizing that the manifest destiny of the United States might not be considered attained until our possessions extended to the Isthmus of Panama and our dictates to the Straits of Magellan.

And when a thoroughly rapacious nation, reared in the hope and certainty of possessing a continent, reaches this state of mind—spurred on by its jealousy of Europe, by universal ambition, by a need for guarantees essential to its future power and a sole and obligatory market for the false production it believes must be maintained (and even increased) to keep its influence and high standard of living—then it is urgent to put as many restraints on it as can be concocted with the circumspection of ideas, the rapid and skillful increase of opposing interests, the frank and prompt agreement of all who have similar reasons for fear, and the declaration of the truth. Good will toward free nations endures until they betray freedom and endanger that of our own country.

But if these conclusions have been reached in spite of individual events and fortunate episodes, after studying the relationship between America's two nationalities in terms of their history and their present elements, and of both the constant and the renewed character of the United States, it must not therefore be assumed that the United States holds nothing but aggressive and dreadful opinions upon these matters. The concrete case of the Congress, in which contradictory forces are present, should not be seen as an embodiment and proof of these opinions, but rather as a result of the joint action of related domestic factors, public and private. And these in turn should be influenced by the Spanish American elements of nationality and interest, either resisting or submitting to them, and by the local rights and opinions of the press according to its declarations or needs. The press is either bold in its desires or feline and cautious, either servile and unquestioning or censorious and derisive. Was it not at Blaine's inauguration that someone said, with the decorum befitting a foreigner, that his speech was like an imperial broth made out of bits and pieces of the harangues of the Marquess of Lansdowne and Henry Clay? Once this breach of courtesy had been surmounted, however, the press showed its healthy broadmindedness, and one discovers that the resistance imposed by seemliness and influence, in the face of extemporaneous and violent attempts at coalition, has as natural allies the rights of those local industries vulnerable to coalition, the less hidebound newspapers, and the opinions of the country. Thus anyone who talks honestly about this or that idea in the United States, when speaking about the Congress, is completely mistaken, for in the United States the idea of the continent is prevalent, particularly among the men at the helm today. But this idea cannot flourish without the continuous flogging of those who, from their seats in the wings, see in the Congress the marked pressure brought to bear by the companies that solicit subsidies for their ships, or by the agents used by the skilled politicians, who know who their supporters are, to defeat their rivals. This they do by giving double attention to the wealthy industries (offering them the markets they desire while dispensing with the slow work of commercial preparation) and to the national concern that looks upon England as its inherent enemy and rejoices in everything that pleases the Irish masses who wield such power at the ballot box. One ought to take into consideration, then, how the Congress originated, into what hands it has fallen, what its present relations with the rest of the country are, and what it can eventually become by virtue of these factors and the men who influence and administer it.

It all started in the sorry days when Secretary Blaine's policy in Chile and Peru was censured from the bench of the accused, where Belmont placed it.[9] It was patently proved

9. Martí is referring to the Landreau claim against Peru involving a contract for the exploitation of the guano beds. (Guano is the dried excrement left on their breeding grounds by millions of guano birds— mainly penguins, cormorants, and gannets—which provided the base for the mass fertilizer manufacture for nineteenth-century agriculture.) As Secretary of State in 1881 Blaine insisted upon the recognition of the Landreau claim upon any of the guano territory ceded to Chile by Peru, thereby involving the United States in the relations between the two republics and endangering the prospects of peace between them. Perry

that Blaine had haggled with Chile over the affairs of Peru, whose free efforts he blocked by offering something which honor and good judgment decided should be rejected. These were foreign affairs, always more fearful than domestic quarrels, and the Republican Blaine, finding himself a spokesman in the other fellow's house, had ordered something done, "without right and unwisely," based upon the personal business interests of Landreau, for whom the United States cabinet minister confessed to be acting as agent. In the judgment of the Republican Frelinghuysen,[10] this affair was thoroughly discredited. Blaine had confused and weakened the defeated with promises he was never to keep, or his promises brought the poison of ambition. He gave the victors the right to disregard an intervention lacking in defenses of its own, and to the charge of being an invader of American rights he added the charge of being mercenary. Conscientious politicians live on the continuous reputation of their integrity and utility, which exempts them from dazzling maneuvers or unnecessary acts of daring. But those who do not have this excellence and authority in the eyes of their country, resort for their luster and influence to hidden intrigue with the powerful and to bold and flattering innovations. This wooing of the masses must be watched, for the actions of these politicians reveal their desires. The industries were already protected in their

---

Belmont, a young New York Democrat who was a member of the House of Representatives Committee on Foreign Affairs, portrayed Blaine as having brought the United States to the verge of war with Chile over the Landreau claim, and the Democrats charged in the presidential campaign of 1884 that Blaine, the Republican candidate, had "meddled and muddled" in South America. Since J. C. Landreau only claimed American citizenship and was never clearly a citizen, it was even charged that Blaine was using him in an effort "to put the guano beds of Peru into his pocket."

10. Frederick Theodore Frelinghuysen (1817-1885), U.S. senator from New Jersey who succeeded Blaine as Secretary of State under President Arthur. Although a Republican, Frelinghuysen echoed Democrat Perry Belmont's criticism of Blaine's role in the Landreau claim.

difficulties with overproduction, and were demanding a policy to help them sell, and ships to carry their merchandise, to be subsidized by the nation. The steamship lines, on condition that they be reimbursed, advanced substantial sums to the parties in their time of need; sure of their prey they demanded the subsidies promised to them in private. The Panama Canal gave those who had not been able to open it the chance to prevent "a decrepit Europe" from opening it, or a chance to imitate the policy of "a decrepit Europe" in the Suez and wait for others to finish it so they could encircle it. The men involved with Landreau's guano interests saw the possibility of converting the nation's office of Secretary of State into their private agency. The personal and political interests of a discerning candidate, the exacting need of a party's providers, the tradition of continental dominion perpetuated in the Republic, and the case of putting it to the test in a weak and restless country, were all working together.

The plan for the American Congress came out of Secretary Blaine's office with the repute of legend, the hidden inducement of special interests, and the magic which to the common man always spells novelty and daring.

So clear were its sole purposes that the country, which should have been grateful to it, accused it of unnecessary and unlawful intent. Because of Guiteau,[11] Blaine renounced his cabinet post. His own party, far from repudiating his intervention in Peru, and not until three years had passed, named a nonpolitical peace commission to go and study for America the causes of the trade imbalance and the halfhearted friendship between the continent's two nationalities. On the way, its members discussed the Congress, and recommended it to both House and Senate when they returned.

According to the commission's findings, the causes of the cool friendship were the ignorance and arrogance of the

11. Charles J. Guiteau assassinated President Garfield, and Blaine resigned as Secretary of State soon after Chester A. Arthur assumed the presidency.

Northern industrialists, who neither studied nor pleased the markets of the South, the scant trust they placed in Europe's liberal credit, Europe's imitation of United States' brands, the lack of banks and a common system of weights and measures, the "enormous duties" which "could be removed with reciprocal concessions," the many fines and other difficulties of customs regulations, and "above all, the lack of communication via steamship."

These were the causes, no others. When the commission returned, the Democrats were in power, the party that was hard pressed to maintain, in opposition to most of its adherents and thanks to the courage of its chief, the tendency to stimulate trade by the natural means of lowering the costs of production. One must believe—as everyone convinced of this said at the time, and is writing now—that the Democrats were not responsible for this plan of the Congress. They never viewed it very favorably because, using national reductions in the cost of living and of manufactured products, they had in mind a frank and legitimate manner of cementing friendship with the free peoples of America. But a political party cannot with impunity object to plans which, as far as can be seen, tend to strengthen the country's influence and trade. Nor would the Democrats have preferred the culpable interests that originated the project, because within their own ranks—already quite troubled by divided economic opinions— the industrialists in need of consumers and the shipping lines that contribute generous sums to their benefactors in one party or another, were finding decisive support. The growing authority of Cleveland, leader of the reforms, consolidated the alliance of protectionists from both parties, and prepared the formidable coalition of interests which in one last effort defeated his candidacy. The anguish of the industrialists had increased so much since 1881, when the idea of the Congress was accused of being reprehensibly audacious, that in 1888 when both Houses approved the Congress, it was welcomed because of the great need for selling, more natural and profitable than before. In this way the project, originating in the conjunction of protectionist interests and the political needs of an astute candidate, came to appear unanimous and put forth with mature deliberation by both of the country's factions. Now that these two elements have been cleared of the candidate's political interest and of the monetary interests of the enterprises maintaining him, it is well to ask if a new interest might not have arisen. This could have occurred because of events favorable to the broadening of the plan, and favorable to an extreme policy in which, with the zeal of an unexpected candidacy, the legends of expansion and supremacy that have begun to be given the force and body of a political plan by the civil war of a rudimentary people—and by the jealousies of republics which should have known how to guard against anyone showing the intention and ability to profiteer from them—are reaching a peak.

The protectionist funds threw Cleveland out of the presidency.[12] The Republican magnates have an admitted part in the industries assisted by protectionism. The wool growers contributed enormous sums to the election because the Republicans decided not to lower duties on wool. The lead mining industry bribed the Republicans to close the borders to Mexican lead. And the sugar interests. And the copper. And the leather industry that offered to create an import tax. The Congress was far away. The industrialists were promised the Americas as a market; there was guarded conversation about mysterious taxes and "inevitable results"; the growers and mining interests were promised that domestic markets

12. Cleveland was defeated when he ran for reelection in 1888. As president he had attacked high tariffs and, in a message to Congress in December 1887, he had made a sweeping arraignment of high protective tariffs as imposing the heaviest burden on poor workers and farmers. During the presidential campaign of 1888, industrialists throughout the country who favored high tariffs put pressure on their workers to vote against Cleveland, warning that they would close their plants if he were reelected, and also threw money into the campaign chest of Benjamin Harrison, the Republican candidate.

would be closed to foreign products. Nobody mentioned that the purchase of manufactured goods by the Spanish nations would have to be paid for by buying raw materials from the factories of the North, or that there would be another way of making them buy them. "The inevitable result," "Clay's dream," "Manifest destiny." Sewall's lines ran from newspaper to newspaper like a slogan for the Nicaraguan Canal: "Either for Panama or Nicaragua or both, because both will be ours"; "The Môle St. Nicolas Peninsula in Haiti, key to the Gulf, is ours already." The party, promising to unite one with the other, won with the hidden force of the slogan, reinforced by the immediate need for power.

With the Congress a reality, and with the interests of the manufacturers clashing with those of agriculture and the mining companies, one can see how impossible it would be to assure a market to the protectionist manufacturer without in return closing the nation's markets, through the free admission of raw materials, to the protectionist growers and miners. The necessity of escaping from the dilemma of losing power in the coming elections through lack of protectionist support, or of keeping its support by means of the prestige of artificial agreements obtained by coercion, is beginning, by uniting the party's general interests, to join the constant and growing interests of the candidate who seeks a program in the chance for exceptional influence. This would offer the nation what it has been expecting and preparing for ever since its birth, a period of change for the weakest and most unfortunate nations of America—some because of the desperation of their slavery, and others because of the pressures of life. Aside from Mexico, a land of inherent strength, these are the nations closest to the United States. Thus, what started by being a premature maneuver of a skillful aspirant becomes—because of the urgent needs of the protectionists, and the interests of an agile candidate who makes use of slogans, and through the conjunction of changes and the hopes of a good life for the people of the Gulf—the frank and forthright achievement of an era of United States dominion over the nations of America.

It is quite right to affirm this, despite the apparent mildness of the invitation to the Congress, because the Congress itself, in its relations between the United States and the other American nations, cannot be seen apart from the relations, attempts, and confessed violations of the United States in the rest of America at the very moment when its nations are in conference, for future relations will be understood by what these present ones are, and for what purpose. And after bringing to light the nature and objectives of projected friendships, a study will have to be made to see which of the two Americas they suit, and if they are absolutely necessary to their peace and life in common, or if the two will be better off as natural friends based upon freedom than as a unanimous assembly of people bound to a nation of differing interests, hybrid composition, and frightful problems, a nation resolved, before putting its own house in order, to engage in an arrogant and perhaps childish rivalry with the world. It will have to be determined whether nations that have learned how to establish themselves independently—and the farther away, the more efficiently—should surrender their sovereignty to the nation which, although under greater obligation to help them, never once came to their aid, or whether it is right to set forth in full view of the world the determination to live in the health of truth, without unnecessary ties to an aggressive nation of another composition and purpose, before the demand for a forced alliance can rankle and bow to vanity and a national point of honor. What must be studied are the elements of the Congress, both intrinsically and as outside influences, in order to predict whether or not there are greater probabilities that the titles of patronage and prominence are being recognized on the continent, even if for merit, by a nation beginning to regard freedom—the perennial and universal hope of mankind—as its right, and to invoke it for purposes of depriving other nations of it. In this first attempt at control, declared in its improperly excessive pretensions and in the contemporary work of territorial expansion and unconscionable influence, we will have to discover whether there are more nations (if not all, as it should be) which with the integrity of reason and the security they still possess, will decisively refuse to accept a master or more which will submit to the passing of the contemptible juggernaut. These latter nations, fearing that a cause will appear only when they have begun to comply and the control is recognized, will bow down to the juggernaut that presses forward in triumph among the hired censer-bearers from the invading country, crushing the heads of slaves.

Yesterday's edition of the *New York Sun* said: "Whoever does not want the juggernaut to crush him, let him climb into its car!" It would probably be better to block its path.

This is what genius is for: to overcome force with ability. The Texans did climb into the car, and like rabid foxes, the conflagration behind them, or with their dead slung over their horses' backs, they had to leave their land of Texas, barefoot and hungry.

2

At a cursory glance there would be no reason for these precautions, for out of the Congress's eight proposals the first and last cover all that is of general benefit to the peoples of America.[13] Each of our nations has sought these things inde-

13. The Congress proposed the negotiation of separate reciprocity treaties; an international American bank; the construction of a Pan-American railroad to run from the Mexican border to the southern end of Chile; the improvement of lines of trade between the ports of the Atlantic and the Pacific and the Gulf of Mexico; a sanitary code for the protection of the public health; conventions to regulate trademarks, patents, and copyrights; the establishment of a common monetary unit;

pendently, as soon as we brushed off the dust from the ruins out of which our nations came into the world. Of the six remaining proposals, one concerns shipbuilding, and for this our America did not need a brood of congresses, because Venezuela paid for ships from the United States when it placed its order, and Central America, still in diapers, did likewise. And Mexico, with its halfbreed pesos, has equipped itself with two fairskinned steamship lines when fairskinned superiority was taking no notice of its impoverished progeny. There is obviously no reason for a nation to do under the guide of another what that nation has already taught the guide. Another proposal should be recommended, for among simple friendly nations there must be no prolix or diverse

---

and the adoption of the metric system of weights and measures by all the American republics. The political proposals included the recommendation of a treaty for the extradition of criminals and the project for a commission to prepare a common code of civil and commercial law.

Two proposals by the United States were rejected by the Congress. One was the project for an American customs union which failed to win the support of the majority of the committee to which it was referred. (Instead, they recommended the negotiation of separate reciprocity treaties.) The other was Blaine's pet proposal, calling for the obligatory arbitration of all questions of diplomatic privileges, territorial limits, indemnification, rights of navigation, interpretation and implementation of treaties, and all other disputes of whatever nature, except only such matters as, in the exclusive judgment of any one of the nations involved, should compromise its independence. The chief opposition came from the delegates from Chile who saw in the proposal the aim of establishing a permanent court of arbitration dominated by the United States and opening the door for future actions such as Blaine's in the Landreau claim in 1881. Although Blaine pleaded for the adoption of his plan, calling it based on the "principle of American international law," it won the support of only seven of the seventeen republics—the United States, Argentina, Bolivia, Guatemala, Venezuela, Colombia, and Brazil—who signed the arbitration pact on April 9, 1890. But the majority of the states refused to adopt Blaine's "new Magna Carta."

another—that everything in North America must be its, and that this imperial right must be acknowledged from the Isthmus all the way south. On the other hand, there are the nations of diverse origins and purposes, busier and less distrustful every day, whose only real enemy is their own ambition and that of their neighbor inviting them to spare it the trouble of forcibly taking away from them tomorrow what they can willingly give it today. Must the nations of America place their affairs in the hands of their only enemy, to gain time for it and population and unification for themselves, and definitely deserve the respect and reputation of nations, before their submission can dare to be demanded by that neighbor whose will may be softened or whose political morale may be educated (by lessons from within or without) before it decides to incur the risk and opprobrium of falling upon decent, capable, just, and—like itself—free and prosperous peoples, simply because it happens to be on the same continent?

The customs union proposal that would permit free entrance of the products of every nation to all the countries of the union should be no cause for alarm; merely announcing it would make the proposal collapse, since it would be tantamount to quickly setting out to reshape fifteen nations to seek an adjustment to the surpluses of a friendly nation that has felt the pressures of need and wants its neighbors, for its own benefit, to deprive themselves of all, or almost all, of the manufactured articles which have been stored up through the years to meet national expenses. Taking United States products duty free—because its cosmopolitan factories produce all that is known or can be suggested by the entire world—would be like tossing the principal customs revenues into the sea, while the United States would continue collecting little less than all its own revenues, since what it receives from the American nations in valuable taxed articles entering the country amounts to no more than a hill of beans. And furthermore, it would be immoral and thankless, if it were possible because of previous commitments, to deprive it of the right to sell its inexpensive goods to the nations which advance funds and extend credit to it without demanding political allegiance, in order to make it possible for it to sell its expensive and inferior goods to a nation which neither advances funds nor extends credit (except where there are open mines and visible profits), and in addition does demand allegiance.

Why go as allies, at the height of youth, into the battle the United States is about to launch upon the rest of the world? Why must it fight its battles with Europe in the American republics, and rehearse its system of colonization on the territory of the free nations? Why such eagerness to enter the other fellow's house while the ones it wants to evict are entering its own? Why in the halls of this Congress arrange projects of reciprocity with all the American nations when one such project, that of Mexico, agreed upon by both governments to their mutual advantage, has for years been waiting in vain for congressional sanction, because the special interests affected by that project, to the detriment of national interests, oppose it?

In 1883, when the commission was going to invite the Pan-American Congress, were the doors not shut to South American wool to please the native sheep ranchers? On this very day, in the face of the Pan-American Congress, does the Senate not wish to increase the duties on carpet wool imported from the nations it is inviting to receive duty free, and preferentially, the products from a country that refuses to receive their products? Has not the Secretary of the Treasury, while the Pan-Americans are enjoying themselves in Kentucky, just confirmed a prohibitive duty on Mexican lead, when Mexico is the country he is inviting to discuss free entry of products from the north into the Mexican republic? Free entry has already been agreed upon, and is merely waiting for United States congressional permission. Are not the ranchers in the West protesting against the steamship companies that wish to avail themselves of the party those ranchers helped defeat, so they can import from South

America, for sale in the East with national funds, less costly beef on the hoof and fresh meat products than the nation's ranches can send from the West by rail? And why invite Chile, an exporter of copper, if United States copper, so helpful to the Republicans, demands that the doors be closed to copper? And the sugar growers, for what reason did they bring the Republicans to power except to have them close the doors to sugar?

Either the Republican government is being deprived of the support of the protectionists who elected it so it would maintain their profits—a useless sacrifice, since the United States Congress, on the side of industry, would disapprove of their deserting the government. Or, in the vague hope of regaining the concessions that would influence them in times to come, it is knowingly offering its services to the American nations, by formulating treaties to be broken in advance by the powers entrusted with implementing them, and by the interests that extolled them to the government. Or, by means of political artifice and compromises with the timid and bewildered nations, the Republican government is waiting to reduce the Pan-American Congress to making recommendations that will establish the lofty rights which the United States is assuming over America. Or it is gently and discreetly using these nations, hoping for more propitious times, so that its general agreements and polite admissions may be viewed by the eager protectionists, and by a country imbued with expansionist ideas, as a reward for the major influence of its decisive authority over America. And this must not be accomplished by the magic statesman from his prison in the Secretary's office, but under the power and authority of the presidency.

The *Herald* puts it this way: "It surely seems to us that this Congress is turning out to be nothing more than a political game, a pyrotechnical exhibition of magnetic politicians, a brilliant movement of anticipatory strategy for the coming presidential election!" "The steamship companies that helped put Blaine where he is are the ones Blaine wants to please," says the *Evening Post.* "If that Congress recalls any vague recommendations about the desirability of subsidizing steamship companies, and joins its corresponding quality of moonlight to the brotherhood of nations and the beauties of arbitrage, then the Congress can go to the devil, for it has played directly into the hands of the companies." "Apparently this Congress is going to end by being a great hunt for ship subsidies," says the *Times.* This whole pompous structure built by the United States is an extremely amusing national paradox. "Does it not endanger our reputation for being an intelligent and sensible nation?" asks the *Philadelphia Herald.* And the *New York Herald* makes this comment: "A magnificent advertisement for Blaine!"

But the Congress probably understands the propriety of dissolving as soon as possible. Meanwhile, the government in Washington is preparing to declare its possession of the Môle St. Nicolas peninsula, and perhaps, if Minister Douglass negotiates successfully, its protectorate over Haiti.[15] According to an undenied rumor, Douglass is in charge of seeing how Santo Domingo feels about the protectorate.[16] In Madrid, Minister

15. The desire of the Harrison Administration to get the Môle St. Nicolas as a naval base and a coaling station had much to do with the appointment of Frederick Douglass as minister to Haiti. With the control of this port in northwest Haiti, an important obstacle to American business penetration and naval expansion in the Caribbean would be removed. With Douglass conducting the negotiations, Haiti's fear of domination by American interests might easily by allayed. Certainly Haiti could trust the outstanding American Negro to safeguard its interests? But when Douglass refused to put pressure on the Haitian government to cede the Môle, American business interests put pressure on Blaine to take the matter out of his hands, and Blaine empowered Admiral Bancroft Gherardi, commander of the North Atlantic fleet, to manage the affair. In the end, however, Haiti formally refused the U.S. request for the lease of the Môle.

16. Douglass was originally appointed minister to Haiti in July 1889, and late in September, President Harrison added the post of chargé d'affaires to Santo Domingo.

Palmer is quietly negotiating for the acquisition of Cuba. Minister Mizner, to Mexico's consternation, is stirring up Costa Rica against Mexico on the one hand, and Colombia on the other.[17] Some North American companies have taken possession of Honduras; one wonders if the Hondurans have more of a stake in their country's wealth than is needed to protect their friends, and if it is good to have a recognized annexationist at the head of a government newspaper. Because of profits from the Canal, and visions of progress, Nicaragua and Costa Rica are in Washington full force. In Costa Rica against Mexico on the one hand, and Colombia on annexation with the United States to union with Central America. There is no more ostensible fondness for the Congress and its plans than that of the president of Colombia. Venezuela is enthusiastically waiting for Washington to dislodge England from Guiana, since Washington cannot be dislodged from Canada. It is waiting for a territory to be voluntarily confirmed by an American nation, the country which at this very instant is launching a war to rob it of the jewel of its territory, and to rob another American nation of the key to the Gulf of Mexico—the country that bursts into applause in the House of Representatives when a certain Chipman declares that the time is ripe for the starspangled banner to wave over Nicaragua as another state for the North.

The *Sun* states it this way: "We will purchase Alaska; make no mistake about it! We tell the world that we are determined to form a union of the entire North American continent, with the star-spangled banner waving from the icy regions of the North to the Isthmus, and from ocean to ocean." And the *Herald* says: "The vision of a protectorate over the republics of the South will become Henry Clay's constant rallying cry." The *Mail and Express,* intimate friends of Harrison for one reason, and of Blaine for another, calls

17. Mizner, U.S. minister to Central America, was also urging Blaine to send war vessels to Central American waters to protect American interests.

Blaine "the successor to Henry Clay, the great champion of American ideas." "All we want to do is to contribute to the prosperity of those nations," says the *Tribune*. And in another section of the newspaper, on the subject of another desire, it says: "Those nations can be the definitive and far-flung results of the general policy deliberately adopted by both parties in Congress." "We are not yet ready for that movement," the *Herald* declares; "Blaine is about fifty years ahead of his time." Let us grow, then, nations of America, before the fifty years have passed!

Looking below the surface, let us observe in a written opinion one such tactical and commanding idea which is visible in the very solicitude that most fairminded men put into not making a direct attack on the rash attempt to spread a railroad civilization over America in modern times the way Pizarro spread the faith of the cross. Nobody is being accused of immorality or of robber tactics, even if they had occurred. Censure consists largely in not discussing actions to come, inasmuch as in the factual part of Haiti's case the Democrats, despite their moderation, initiated the same policy of conquest as did the Republicans; it was actually the Democrats who, with the Louisiana Purchase,[18] inaugurated that policy under Jefferson. The press lives by what it hears, and by catering to opinion rather than guiding it, so that it dares not condemn the allegations from which the country might benefit, even if once they are made there may be no lack of people calling them criminal, regardless of how much better it would have been to stop the allegations before they were made than to bemoan them later. An example of this is the Texan allegation which Dana and Janvier and the Lincoln

18. The purchase from France in 1803 of the area between the Mississippi Valley and the Rocky Mountains and between Canada and the Gulf of Mexico for $15 million. It occurred during the first administration of President Thomas Jefferson.

biographers refer to purely and simply as a crime.[19] But it must be observed, for it is a fact, that the most estimable aspect of the press makes it clear that the Congress cannot possibly reach any real trade objectives, because each country's sovereignty opposes the surrender that the Congress demands, and because the policy of reciprocal concessions that the Congress suggests opposes resistance to reciprocity,[20] to which those responsible for gathering the American nations together are wholly committed in order to pretend, by means of the electoral apparatus or some hidden purpose, that they are violating it. The *Times, Post, Luck, Harper's, Advertiser,* and *Herald* have printed glorified and ridiculous accounts of the congress of nations assembled to enter an alliance against the world to please a party that cannot enter the alliance it invites or, short of dying out, do what it urges its associates to do.

Blaine himself knows that if the myth is to succeed in the elections, it is enough that a semblance of success, excused for being no greater because it stands at the beginning of the efforts, nourishes Adams'[21] faith in Cutting, and he feels that with the very existence of the Congress, because of the power of light on weak eyes, those efforts will be truly favored. But

19. Martí is referring to the seizure of Texas by Americans and its separation from Mexico in the 1830s and 1840s, an action condemned by Charles A. Dana of the *New York Tribune* and *New York Sun,* and by Abraham Lincoln.

20. The Pan-American Congress had rejected the customs union of American states and recommended the idea of partial reciprocity as a more realistic substitute. The task of removing at least some of the tariff barriers thus fell to the political and diplomatic skills of the various foreign ministers. But in Washington the Republican Party controlled every branch of government in 1890, and many of its spokesmen, conditioned by years of high protective tariffs, opposed reciprocity.

21. Henry Adams (1838-1918), son of Charles Francis Adams, noted historian and biographer.

he is afraid that, due to the great need of the various industries, more may be expected of the Congress than it will give.
He is afraid that nothing can come out of this matter of
commerce built upon present-day protectionist bases, and
that this will be made known in time, by a son today and a
newspaper tomorrow. All he expects from the meeting, as far
as can be seen, are some preliminaries of the fusion to come,
and more resistance than close friendships or even preparatory friendships. Therefore, the policy of dignity has as
valued and voluntary allies, within a single hostile country,
those men who because of an innate dignity in themselves
cannot conceive of a lack of it in those in whom it is attacked. Nor would anyone benefiting from the lack of dignity dare hope for that lack.

It is generally agreed that the Congress will be nothing but
a worthless meeting, or a presidential campaign banner, or a
pretext for a subsidy hunt. Those who know the benefits of
independence, and who cannot conceive of dispensing with it
unless absolutely necessary, are expecting all this from the
independent nations of America. Will the Gulf islands be
admitted to the presence of the new master on their knees?
Will Central America consent to divide in half, the Canal
blade slicing through its heart, or to unite on behalf of the
South as Mexico's oppressor? Mexico is a nation with the
same interests, the same destiny, and the same racial background as Central America. Will Colombia pawn or sell its
sovereignty? Will the free nations sweep the Isthmus clear of
obstacles to the juggernaut—those free nations that dwell
there and will climb into its car as did the Mexicans in Texas?
Through hopes of support against the European alien, because of an illusion of progress that is excusable only in a
provincial mentality, will Venezuela, being nearer and more
ambitious, stand up for the dominance of an even more
dreadful foreigner who announces that its eyes must be, and
are, fixed upon the entire American family of nations? Or
must admiration for the United States go so far as to lend a

hand to the exhausted young bull, like the peasant woman in *La Terre*? [22]

This blind admiration, because of the novice's enthusiasm or lack of study, is the main force in America upon which the policy of control depends in this matter. It is a policy invoking a dogma that needs no foreign supplication in the American republics, for centuries ago, even before entering the innocence of childhood, these republics learned how to bravely repulse the most stubborn and powerful nation on earth. And with no assistance from outside sources, they obliged it to respect their natural strength and the evidence of their abilities. What is the use of invoking the doctrine that originated as much with Monroe as with Canning,[23] to extend its dominion in America in order to prevent foreign domination there and assure a continent of its freedom? Or must the dogma be invoked against one foreign nation only to

22. *La Terre*, novel published by Emile Zola in 1887 about the land-hungry peasant class in France.

23. In the summer of 1823, George Canning, the British foreign minister, made his famous proposal to the American minister in London, Richard Rush, which eventually resulted in the enunciation of the Monroe Doctrine. Canning, in a confidential letter, suggested a joint Anglo-American declaration to the effect that the recovery of the Latin American colonies by Spain was hopeless, that neither England nor America aimed at the possession of any of them for herself; and they would not view the transfer of any portion of them to any other power with indifference. However, the United States informed Canning that, since both countries understood the necessity of a declaration against the interference by force of the European powers in Latin America, it would be better for them to act separately. Hence in his message to Congress on December 2, 1823, Monroe enunciated the doctrine that now bears his name. While stating that the United States would not meddle with European affairs, it declared that any attempt by the European powers "to extend their system to any portion of this hemisphere" would be viewed by the United States "as dangerous to our peace and safety." Thus the Monroe Doctrine was announced unilaterally by the United States.

bring in another? Or does one shake off foreign domination—which has a very different character, different interests, and different purposes—by putting on the appearance of freedom and surrendering it in action? Is it because the poison of loans, canals, and railroads comes with the foreigner? Or does the doctrine have to be crammed down the throats of the weaker nations of America by the nation that has Canada to the north, the Guianas and Belize to the south, and sees to it that Spain is supported? Indeed, it itself supported Spain, and permitted that country to return, at its very gates, to the American nation which Spain had already left.

Why pretend to be afraid of Spain? Although it may be exterminating its sons in the Antilles, it is well outside of America and cannot regain its spirit, for the daughter has progressed beyond the mother, keeping pace with the new world. And it cannot be regained in the realm of commerce, for America does not live on raisins and olives, and Spain has no more influence on the American nations than that which fear or antipathy or North American aggression might again give to it because of race or sentiment. Would the principal nations of America, who are willing and able to resist North American aggression, be abandoned and compromised by their sister republics when all of them should band together, with the strength of a unified spirit, to stop the common adversary, thus showing their passion for freedom by helping Cuba gain it from Spain, instead of opposing freedom by helping Spain? For Spain mishandled American ships, and appraised at two hundred dollars each the heads it shot from the bodies of America's sons. Or are the American nations merely blind statues and prodigies of filth?

A just admiration for the prosperity of all free and energetic peoples united to enjoy their freedom in a secure, varied, and virgin expanse—an ambition throughout the world—must never reach the point of excusing the crimes against freedom attempted by the nation that uses its power and reputation to create a new form of despotism. Nor do nations living under worse conditions need to act as its lackeys, for they have learned how to equal and even surpass it. The free nations of America have no reason to expect that the nation whose influence threw the French out of Mexico will rid them of the troublesome foreigner, brought there perhaps because of a desire to raise a barrier against Saxon power in the world's imbalance, when the French in Mexico were threatening it in the South with an alliance of rebel states, still Latin at heart—the nation that selfishly threw the European out of the free republic from which it wrested in a criminal war a piece of territory it has never returned. Walker went to Nicaragua[24] for the United States; for the United States López went to Cuba.[25] And now when slavery is no longer an excuse, the annexation alliance is afoot.[26] Allen is talking about helping that of Cuba; Douglass is going to obtain that of Haiti and Santo Domingo. In Madrid Palmer is gauging Spain's feelings about the sale of Cuba; in the

24. William Walker, the "gray-eyed man of destiny," and darling of the Southern slaveholding expansionists of the 1850s, invaded Nicaragua in 1855, installed a Nicaraguan puppet as president, with himself as effective head of the state, reestablished slavery, and was immediately recognized by the Pierce Administration. In 1860, upon invading Honduras, Walker was captured by the British who turned him over to the Hondurans; he was executed on September 12, 1860.

25. The reference is to Narciso López, the filibuster, who led an expedition ostensibly to end Spanish rule over Cuba in 1850, but as Martí indicates, actually to unite the island with the United States as a slave state or states. The expedition failed and López was executed by the Spaniards. For a discussion of the López filibustering expedition, see Philip S. Foner, *A History of Cuba and Its Relations with the United States* (New York, 1963), Vol. II, pp. 41-65.

26. Before the Civil War, annexation of Cuba by the United States was advocated, first, to add to the territory for slavery and second, to prevent the abolition of slavery in Cuba which would have had a detrimental influence on slavery in the United States. Cuban slaveholders favored annexation whenever it seemed likely that Spain would take steps to abolish slavery in the island in deed as well as word. (See ibid., pp. 9-19, 75-95.)

Antilles the bribed Central American newspapers are stirring up interest in the Washington-based annexation plans; in the Lesser Antilles the Northern newspapers are constantly giving reports on the progress of annexationist ideas. Washington persists in compelling Colombia to acknowledge its dictatorial rights over the Isthmus, and in depriving it of the authority to discuss its territory with other nations. And the United States, by virtue of the civil war it instigated, is acquiring the Môle St. Nicolas peninsula in Haiti. Some people consider "Clay's dream" an accomplished fact. Others consider it advisable to wait another half-century. Still others, born in Spanish America, believe they ought to help further the cause.

The Pan-American Congress will be an illustrious inventory showing in a dignified and energetic way which countries are defending the independence of Spanish America, the fulcrum of the world's balance of power. Or it may show whether or not any nations on a continent occupied by two peoples of different character and objectives can, through fear or confusion of ingrained slavery or by being induced to consent, decrease by their own desertion the indispensable and already too meager forces by which the family of a single nationality will be able to contain, with the respect it imposes and the wisdom it displays, attempts at domination by a nation reared in the hope of ruling the continent. Present-day events are proof of these attempts at dominance, and this at a time when the eagerness for markets on the part of its inflated industries, the opportunity to impose the predicted protectorate upon both the distant nations and the weak ones nearby, the material strength needed for the assault, and the ambitions of a bold and rapacious politician, are described as reaching a peak.

La Nación (Buenos Aires), December 19-20, 1889
Dated New York, November 2, 1889

The Monetary Congress
of the American Republics

On May 24, 1888, the President of the United States invited the American nations and the Kingdom of Hawaii to a Pan-American Congress in Washington, summoned by the Senate and the House of Representatives for the purpose of studying, among other things, "the adoption by each government of a common silver coinage system to be put into compulsory use by the citizens of every American nation in their reciprocal commercial transactions."

On April 7, 1890, the Pan-American Congress, of which the United States was a part, recommended the establishment of a Pan-American Monetary Alliance with the minting of one or more Pan-American coins, uniform in weight and legality, as a basis of this alliance, these to be used by all the countries

1. The International Monetary Commission, called by Secretary of State James G. Blaine, met in Washington, D.C., from January 7 to April 3, 1891. Martí, appointed Uruguay's delegate to the Commission, wrote this study of the origin and purpose of the conference to alert Latin American countries to the danger they faced. As the largest silver producer in the world, the United States sought to persuade the Latin American republics to adopt bimetallism and the equalization of gold and silver. This would help it in getting all other nations to adopt the same policy. But as Martí points out, the great majority of the Latin American countries, lacking silver, had little to gain from the proposed plan.

368

represented at this Congress. It also proposed that a commission meet in Washington to study the quantity, current rate, value, and relationship of the metals from which the Pan-American coins would be minted.

On March 23, 1891, after a month's delay requested by the Pan-American Commission meeting in Washington at the instigation of the U.S. delegation, "to have time to become acquainted with the opinion pending in the House of Representatives regarding the independent minting of silver," the U.S. delegation declared to the Congress that the creation of a common silver coinage system for obligatory use in all the American nations was a fascinating dream that could not be attempted without the agreement of the other world powers. The delegation recommended the use of gold and silver in a fixed relationship. Its desire was to invite all the powers to a World Monetary Congress, and have the American nations and the Kingdom of Hawaii seated there.

What is the lesson to be learned by America from the Pan-American Monetary Commission, convoked in 1888 by the United States, with the approval of Congress, to discuss the adoption of a common silver coinage system which in 1891 the United States claims to be a fascinating dream?

What will come to pass has no bearing on the form of things, but on their spirit. What matters is the real, not the apparent. In politics the real is what cannot be seen. Politics is the art of combining, for an increasing inner well-being, a

---

Martí's report was adopted unanimously and thus frustrated the efforts of the American silver interests, backed by the State Department, to ride roughshod over the welfare of the Latin American countries. (*Minutes of the International Monetary Commission, January 7–April 3, 1891* [Washington, D.C., 1891], pp. 47-78.) In the article printed here, Martí summarizes the significance of the Monetary Commission, indicating that it should serve as a warning signal for Latin American countries to guard against encroachment upon their destiny, and that economic domination would inevitably lead to political domination by the United States.

country's diverse or opposing factors, and of saving the country from the open hostility or the covetous friendship of other nations. In every invitation among nations one must look for hidden reasons. No nation does anything contrary to its own interests, from which it can be deduced that what a nation does is to its own advantage. If two nations do not share common interests, they cannot become allies. Should they do so, they would clash. Lesser nations still in the throes of gestation cannot safely join forces with nations seeking help for the excess production of a compact and aggressive population, and seeking an outlet for their own uneasy masses. The political acts of true republics turn out to be composed of such elements as national character, economic needs, party needs, and the needs of the politicians at the helm. When one nation is invited to join another, ignorant and bewildered politicians will be able to do so quickly, young people entranced with beautiful ideas will be able to celebrate the alliance unjudiciously, and venal or demented politicians will be able to receive it as a favor and glorify it with obsequious words. But he who feels in his heart the anguish of his country, he who is foresighted and vigilant, must make inquiries and be capable of telling what elements compose the national character of the host nation and the guest nation, and if they are predisposed to the common effort because of common antecedents and customs, and whether or not it is probable that the dreaded elements of the host country could develop in the attempted union at some risk to the guest country. He must make inquiries into the political forces of the country extending the invitation, the interests of its parties, and the interests of its men at the moment the invitation is extended. Whoever reaches a decision without prior investigation, or desires the union without acquainting himself with it, or recommends it merely because of some enticing phrase and the dazzling impression it makes, or defends it because of his puny provincial soul, will damage America. At what precise moment was the Pan-American Monetary Commission called and subsequently assembled? Is this Commission responsible for Pan-American policy being a banner of local politics and an instrument of party ambition, or is it not? Has the United States itself given this lesson to Spanish America, or has it not? Should Spanish America ignore it or profit from it?

A nation grows and influences other nations according to the elements composing it. The action of one country in an alliance of countries will conform to its salient elements, and not differ from them. If a lush and fragrant pasture is made available to a hungry horse, the horse will rush in, bury itself in the grass up to the withers, and angrily nip at anyone who bothers it.

Two condors or two lambs come together without as much danger as a condor and lamb. The same young condors, happily engaged in the spirited games and boastful squabbles of fledglings, would be unable to defend, or would not arrive in time and together to defend, the prey the mature bird snatched from them. To see ahead is one essential quality in the building and governing of nations. Governing is nothing more than foreseeing. Before joining another nation, it must be seen what harm or what benefit can accrue naturally out of the elements composing that nation.

It is not necessary merely to ascertain whether the nations are as great as they appear, and whether the same accumulation of power that dazzles the impatient and incapable has not come about at the cost of higher qualities, and by virtue of qualities which threaten those who admire that power. But rather, even when the greatness is genuine and profound, durable, just, useful, and cordial, it is quite possibly of another kind and the result of other methods than the greatness that can be aspired to unaided, and reached of its own accord through proper methods—the only viable ones—by a nation with a different concept of life and living in a different atmosphere and in a different way. When life is shared, ideas and customs must be shared. For those who must live together, it is not enough for their objectives in life to be the

372 The Menace of United States Imperialism

same, but their way of living as well. Either they fight or scorn each other, or they hate each other for their differences in manner as they did for those of their objectives. Countries without common methods, even when their goals are identical, cannot unite to achieve their common purposes with identical means.

And he who knows and sees cannot honestly say—for this can be said only by the one who does not know or see or who because of his own interests is unwilling to know or see—that even in the United States of today there may be a prevalence of this most human and virile (although always egotistical and victorious) element of the rebellious colonists, who are sometimes the younger sons of the nobility and sometimes of the Puritan bourgeoisie. But this element— which consumed the native race, fomented and lived from the slavery of another race, and reduced or robbed the neighboring countries—has been sharpened instead of softened by the continuous grafting of the European hordes, a tyrannical breeding of political and religious despotism whose only common quality is the appetite accumulated by exercising over the rest the authority that was exercised over themselves. They believe in need, in the barbarous right as the only right: "This will be ours because we need it." They believe in the invincible superiority of "the Anglo-Saxon race over the Latin." They believe in the inferiority of the Negroes whom they enslaved yesterday and are criticizing today, and of the Indians whom they are exterminating. They believe that the Spanish American nations are formed principally of Indians and Negroes. As long as the United States knows no more about Spanish America, and respects it no more, although with the numerous incessant, urgent, and wise explanations of our people and resources it could come to respect us—can this country invite Spanish America to an alliance that would be honest and useful to our Spanish American nations?

Whoever says economic union says political union. The nation that buys, commands. The nation that sells, serves.

Commerce must be balanced to assure freedom. The nation eager to die sells to a single nation, and the one eager to save itself sells to more than one. A country's excessive influence over the commerce of another becomes political influence. Politics is the work of men who surrender their feelings to an interest. When a strong nation supplies another with food, the strong nation becomes useful to it. When a strong nation wants to engage another in battle, it demands allegiance and service from those nations dependent upon it. The first thing a nation does to gain dominion over another is to separate it from other nations. Let the country desiring freedom be free in business affairs. Let it distribute its commerce among countries as strong as itself. If it must prefer one, let it prefer the one that needs it least and scorns it least. Let there be no alliances against Europe, nor with Europe against an American nation. The geographical fact of living together in America does not oblige political union, except in the mind of some candidate or some college graduate. Business interests follow the slopes of land and water, and stay close on the heels of whoever can offer something in exchange, be it monarchy or republic. Union with the world, and not with a part of it; not with one part against another. If the family of American republics has one mission in life, it is not that of having one of them ride roughshod over future republics.

Nor in agreements on a coinage system, which is an instrument of trade, can a healthy nation—out of reverence for a country that never came to its assistance, or did so because of emulation and fear of another—dispense with those nations that advance to it the funds needed for its enterprises, owe it their faith and affection, espouse its cause in its crises and offer it a means of escape from them, treat it as an equal without showing arrogant disdain, and buy its products. All legal tender in the world should be standardized. It shall be. Everything primitive, such as coinage differences, will disappear when there are no longer any primitive nations. And improved and equalized peace should populate the earth so that it may prevail in politics as well as in commerce. A

uniform coinage system must be attempted. All that prepares
for it must be done. The legal use of essential metals must be
recognized. A fixed relationship between gold and silver must
be established. All that brings man closer together and makes
life more moral and tolerable must be desired and helped to
become a reality. All that brings nations together must be
realized. But the way to bring them together is not by causing some to rise up against others, nor can the groundwork
for world peace be laid by arming a continent against the
nations that have given life to most of its countries, and are
maintaining them with their purchasing power. And the way
to bring them together is not by inviting the American nations, in debt to Europe, to unify—with the nation that never
extended them credit—behind a coinage system whose purpose is to compel their European creditors, who do extend
them credit, to accept a coinage system the Europeans reject.

The coins of commerce must be acceptable to the countries engaged in commerce. Any changes must be effected at
least in accord with those countries engaged in the greatest
amount of commerce. The seller cannot afford to offend his
best customer, and either extends credit to please the small
buyer, or refuses to buy from him and denies him credit. A
needy debtor must not offend or even alarm his creditors. A
coinage system upsetting to countries engaged in extensive
trade must not be introduced into countries little involved in
trade, or ceasing to trade or failing to trade for reasons of
coinage. When the greatest obstacle to the recognition and
standardization of silver coins is the fear of their overproduction in the United States, and of the spurious value
the United States can place upon them by means of its legislation, then everything that increases this fear is harmful to
silver. The future of silver coins lies in the moderation of
their producers. To force them is to devalue them. Spanish
American silver will rise or fall with the world's silver. If
Spanish American countries sell their products principally if
not exclusively in Europe, and receive loans and credit from
Europe, what good can result from adopting, through a

system wishing to do violence to the European, a coinage system that would not be received in Europe, or would be received there devalued? If the greatest obstacle to the elevation of silver and its fixed relation to gold is the fear of its fictitious value and overproduction in the United States, what benefit can accrue—either for the Spanish American countries producing silver or for the United States itself— from a coinage system that would insure a greater dominion and circulation for United States silver?

But the Pan-American Congress, able to see what it did not always see, failed to free the American republics from the future compromises from which it should have freed them; it should have studied the proposals of the convocation in the light of its political antecedents—the large surplus of manufactured goods brought about by a disorganized protectionism, the Republican Party's need to cajole its protectionist supporters, the frivolity with which a prestidigitator could paint an imperialistic idea with political colors and at the same time flatter (like a candidate's banner) the interests of the industrialists eager to sell and the latent and slightly immature tendency to subjugation in the national blood—this Pan-American Congress, postponing what it did not wish to resolve because of an unwise spirit of needless concession, or could not resolve because of devious pledges or too little time, recommended the creation of a Pan-American Monetary Alliance, the establishment of one or more international coins, and the meeting of a commission to decide upon their type and rules. The American republics paid polite attention to the recommendation. Delegates from most of them met in Washington. Mexico and Nicaragua, Brazil and Peru, Chile and Argentina delegated missions in residence. The minister from Argentina resigned his post, later to be filled by another delegate. The other republics sent special delegates. Paraguay had no representation. Neither did Central America, with the exception of Nicaragua and Honduras, whose delegate, a North American admiral's son, was unable to speak Spanish.

By unanimous agreement the minister from Mexico presided. There were sessions on protocol, rules and regulations, previous committees. The common topic here was not coinage revision, but doubt, or certainty, that an agreement could be reached. And there were heated exchanges in the debates. One delegate spoke about "true commerce," another prematurely declared himself hostile to "that impossible idea." A United States delegate demanded a long delay "to have time to become acquainted with the opinion pending in the House of Representatives on the free minting of silver." And still another, having brought the overpresumption of the United States delegate within the legal bounds of courtesy, established that "it might be understood that the delay was to enable the delegation from the host country to complete its preparatory studies, since by no means would it be assumed that the opinion of the House of Representatives had necessarily altered the opinions of the Commission."

Once the delay was arranged, and the House had disbanded without voting the law of free silver, the various delegations again occupied their places at the Commission table. Perhaps some of them had heard what the country's notables were saying without reservations. Perhaps they had heard that those who passed for friends of the government majority did not regard the Commission favorably; that the government was displeased by the minority's interest in maintaining a continental policy of those who are accused of artifice; and that this dangerous display of a continent-wide policy did not even proceed from a minority but from one man; that this empty-headed Commission should disband so that it would not serve as a political excuse for a candidate who does not stop halfway, and knows how to rob the ants of their anthills; that the simple discussion of a common silver coinage system both alarmed and offended the supporters of gold, whose opinions prevail on the present advisory committees of the Republican Party; that the Spanish-American countries would undoubtedly see for themselves, if they still have eyes, the danger of laying themselves open, through their idea of courtesy or their impatience for false progress, to a policy which draws them—through the flattery of words and the threads of intrigue—into an alliance forged by those who propose it with a concept different from that of those who accept it. A U.S. delegate stood up before the Commission, convoked by the United States to adopt a universal coinage system, and proposed, in the face of a firm exposition of monetary facts—in which it termed an international coinage system a "fascinating dream"—that the Commission declare inopportune the creation of one or more common silver coins. This delegate asked the Commission to judge that the establishment of the double standard of silver and gold, with a universally respected relationship, would facilitate the minting of those coins, and to recommend that the republics represented at the Congress, through the mediation of their respective governments, should send invitations to an International Monetary Congress to discuss the establishment of a uniform and appropriate monetary system based upon gold and silver. "There is another and far more extensive world across the ocean," said the delegate, "and that world's insistence on not elevating silver to the dignity of gold is the great and insuperable obstacle to the international adoption of silver that is now being presented." The United States, then, pointed out to a complacent America the risk the latter might have run in acceding too hastily to the United States' suggestions!

The Commission gave the assignment of studying the U.S. proposals to five countries: Chile, Argentina, Brazil, Colombia, and Uruguay, and the Commission unanimously agreed to recommend acceptance of the North American proposals. "The Commission could not find it surprising that the U.S. delegates should recognize the truths which the Pan-American Commission has found itself obliged to recognize on its own account." "Since it is elementary justice to do so, the Commission respected the principle of submitting to every nation on earth the proposal to standardize the metals and their proportions in the coins which must be used by every nation in their commercial transactions." "It would be a dream, unbefitting the greatness and generosity to which the republics are obliged, to refuse directly or indirectly—violating natural interests and human duties—to discuss this most freely with the other nations of the globe." But the Commission did not propose, as did the United States, that "all the world powers" be invited, "to avoid running the risk, with an invitation not sufficiently justified, of instilling fear—no less real for being unfounded—in the powers that would consider their summoning as a determination (no matter how skilled and dissembled) to hurry them into a solution they would surely have reached by themselves if they had so desired. For their suspicions are indeed aroused, or their punctilio is wounded by insisting that they would have no reason to ascribe to the monetary problem a single new factor of importance, or a single unknown fact." "Silver must gradually move closer to gold." "Overproduction moves silver away from gold." "Silver coins cannot, must not, be made to disappear." "A uniform coinage system must be established, but with the honest and trusting agreement of all the working people on earth to assure it a durable base, and not by any violent and crafty recourses taken to the economy—recourses that foment ill-will and provoke retribution and therefore cannot last." "But the invitation as a whole is not recommended." And when upon reviewing the monetary details it was the Commission's turn to note the spirit in which Spanish America understood them, and now understands whatever concerns the individual and independent life of its people, it noted it thus:

"The countries represented at this Congress did not come here because of the false attraction of innovations not yet in season, nor because they disregarded all the factors that preceded and accompanied the fact of their invitation to the Congress, but to give a sign—easy for nations sure of their destiny and of their ability to attain it—of that friendly courtesy so gratifying and useful among nations as well as among men. They came here to give a sign of their readiness to discuss in good faith all that is believed to be proposed in goodwill; to give a sign of the affectionate desire to support, along with the United States and other nations of the world, whatever contributes to the peace and well-being of men." "There must be no reprehensible haste either in promoting or contracting among nations any unnecessary commitments beyond the limits of Nature and reality." "The function of the American continent is not to unsettle the world with new factors of rivalry and discord, nor to reestablish the imperialistic system under other names and with other methods wherever republics are becoming corrupt and dying; it is to hold discussions in peace and honesty with those nations which in the hazardous hour of emancipation sent us their soldiers, and in the restless years of formation are keeping their strongboxes open to us." "All nations should meet in friendship as often as possible, to gradually replace the forever-dead system of groups and dynasties with the system of universal growth, regardless of the language of isthmuses and the barriers of oceans." "Every nation's doors should be kept open to the enriching and legitimate freedom of all nations. The hands of every nation should be kept free to develop the country without restrictions and according to its distinctive nature and elements."

When the host rises to his feet, the guests do not insist upon remaining seated at the table. When guests who have come from a great distance, more because of courtesy than appetite, find the host at the door saying that there is nothing to eat, the guests do not push him aside or enter his house by force or shout for him to open the dining room. The guests should explain aloud their reasons for coming, and that it was not out of need or servility, so their host will not consider them to have been carved on one knee like suppliant statues, or that they are puppets who come and go at the whim of the puppeteer. Then they should leave. There is a way of withdrawing that adds stature. A Spanish-American delegate, aware that the Monetary Commission came together for no other purpose than to "achieve what had been recommended," and failing to see that a recommendation automatically includes some discussion and confirmation before being accepted, upheld the patently mindless opinion which went meandering among the delegates that the Monetary Commission had not come, as its promoter the United States believed, to see whether a Pan-American coinage system could or should be created, but to create it now, although the United States itself had realized that it could not be created at this time. And the delegate proposed a minutely detailed plan for American coins which he called the "Columbus Plan," patterned after that of the Latin Union, and in addition a Council of Vigilance "resident in Washington."

The United States had not said that the obstacle to the creation of the inter-American system was the House of Representatives' opposition to voting for the free coinage of silver,[2] but the opposition of the vast world across the sea to

2. The major demand of farmers, who wanted a cheap currency for more ready payment of debts, and of silver miners was for free coinage of silver, meaning that Congress would purchase and coin silver in unlimited quantities. Prior to 1873 Congress had done so under the Coinage Act of 1834, thus providing for a bimetallic standard with an established relationship of 16 to 1 between silver and gold. With the demonetization of 1873, silver was removed from the coinage list, leading to the demand for free silver. As a result of pressure from the farmers and silver kings, Congress passed the Bland-Allison Act of 1878 which required that the government purchase at least two million dollars' worth of silver each month. But since it was purchased at the market price, which was lower than the 16 to 1 ratio demanded by farmers and silver miners, such purchases did not affect the price of silver, and agitation for free coinage of silver continued. This resulted in the Sherman Silver Purchase Act of 1890, which the Republican protectionists supported in exchange for support by silver advocates of the protectionist McKinley Tariff. The Sherman Act provided for almost all the silver minted in the country, but since the government was to purchase it at market prices, the measure continued to frustrate the demands of the silverites, who kept fighting for free coinage of silver at the ratio of 16 to 1.

the acceptance of silver coins in a fixed and equal relation to gold. But a Spanish-American delegate asked: "Would it not be wiser, assuming that the new House of Representatives will vote for the free minting of silver before the year's end, to suspend the conference sessions until, say, January 1, 1892, when this matter will probably have been decided by the U.S. government?" And when, out of respect for the guests, another delegate urged a wise and simple acceptance of the U.S. proposals, except the recommendation of a world congress, a Spanish-American delegate who speaks no Spanish tried to demand and obtain a suspension of the sessions. Who could be interested, even if the Spanish Americans were, in a continuance of the U.S.-sponsored Commission counter to the final opinion of the United States itself? Who, in a largely Spanish-American assembly, provoked opposition to the U.S. proposals? Who, aside from those who make a banner out of the continental policy proposed by the United States, was injured by the fact that a continental coinage system had been declared impossible in the Commission convoked for its study by the United States itself? Why, in a Monetary Commission composed mostly of Spanish Americans, did there arise—and so naturally—the thought of opposing the adjournment of a Commission assembled to discuss a project which the Spanish-American delegates, almost to a man, expressly declared impossible to realize? If they themselves were not benefiting from it, then what interest, in their heart of hearts, availed itself of their excessive good will and put them at its service? Or, according to those familiar with the inner workings of politics, was it that the interest of a political group, or of a fearless and obstinate U.S. politician, by hidden means and private influences roused an assembly of nations against the sober and considered judgment of the U.S. government? Was the assembly of Spanish-American nations going to serve the interests of whoever forced them into confused alliances, dangerous alliances, impossible alliances, scorning the advice of men who—because of their local or partisan interests, or because of international justice—are opening the doors to them so they may be saved from those alliances?

The assembly of delegates pondered, feared, applied pressure, and ran the great risk of doing what ought not to have been done—the risk of leaving undecided, at the whim of a desperate and unscrupulous foreign policy, and through the complex and delicate nature of relations between the United States and many of the Spanish-American nations, an assembly that could, in the hands of a ruthless candidate, yield to the United States more than would be commensurate with the respect and security of Spanish America.

To appear accommodating to the point of weakness would not be the best way of escaping the dangers to which a reputation for weakness is exposed in trading with a competitive nation overflowing with surplus goods. Wisdom does not lie in corroborating a reputation for weakness, but in using the occasion to show oneself energetic without risk. And in this matter of risk, when one chooses the propitious hour and uses it without restraint, the least dangerous course of action is to be energetic. Who builds nations upon serpents? But if there was a battle; if the zeal for progress in the still unformed republics leads their children, because of a singular deflection of reason or a bitter leavening of servility, to greater trust in the efficacy of progress in nations where they were not born than in nations where they were; if a yearning to see their native land grow leads them to the blindness of hungering for methods and things which in other places are due to factors foreign or hostile to their country, which must grow in accord with its own features and their resultant methods; if the natural caution of nations bound to the environs of North America did not consider advisable what is of greater interest to them than to others around them; if local and respectable prudence, or fear, or personal obligation softened men's characters too much for them to keep Spanish-American independence and creation alive—these things were not apparent in the Monetary Commission, for it agreed to adjourn.

La Revista Illustrada (New York), May 1891

Index